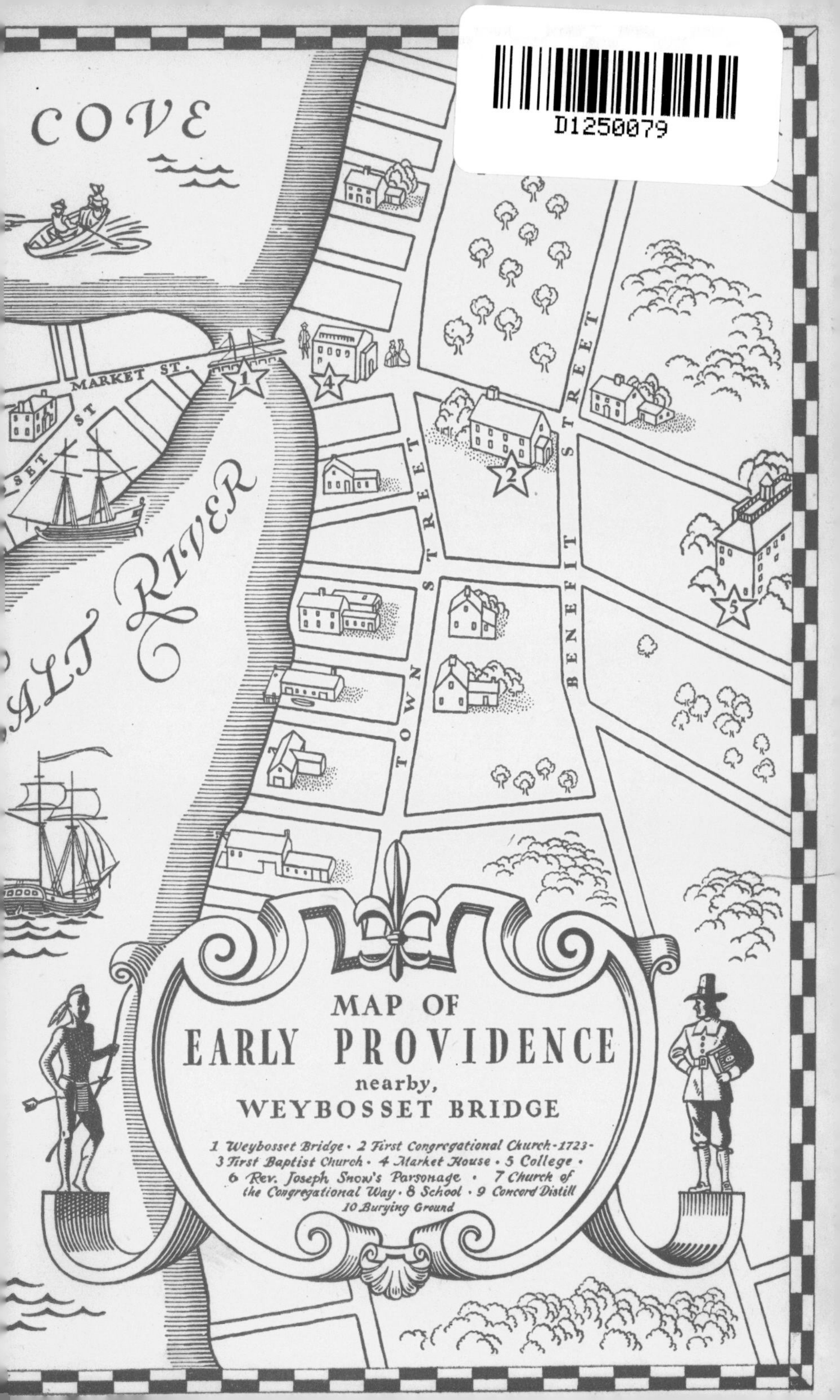
D1250079
COVE
MARKET ST.
ST
SET
SALT RIVER
TOWN STREET
BENEFIT STREET
MAP OF
EARLY PROVIDENCE
nearby,
WEYBOSSET BRIDGE
1 Weybosset Bridge · 2 First Congregational Church-1723-
3 First Baptist Church · 4 Market House · 5 College ·
6 Rev. Joseph Snow's Parsonage · 7 Church of
the Congregational Way · 8 School · 9 Concord Distill
10 Burying Ground

WEYBOSSET BRIDGE

WEYBOSSET BRIDGE

IN PROVIDENCE PLANTATIONS

1700 - 1790

ARTHUR E. WILSON

Being an Account of a Quest for Liberty, with Portraits of Many Saints and Sinners, and a Special Study of the Rev'd Joseph Snow, jun'r

THE PILGRIM PRESS
BOSTON

PRINTED IN THE UNITED STATES OF AMERICA
AMERICAN BOOK-STRATFORD PRESS, INC., NEW YORK

FOREWORD

THE roots of the New World concept of freedom lie deep in the soil of American Protestantism wherever it was a protest movement. Its protest was more often against some form of authoritarian Protestantism than it was against Roman Catholicism.

This book is a chronicle of the religious life of Providence Plantations during the years 1700–1790.

The history of these years up Narragansett Bay relates the conscious and unconscious forming of a pattern of freedom which eventually would become the foundation stone of American democracy. Unique Rhode Island furnishes the smallest and clearest test tube for the study of the forces which ultimately gave birth to the American concept of liberty. Nowhere in the world did men employ greater originality in experimenting with the ideal of liberty than in the smallest of the colonies. The attempt made at the head of the Bay to implement impractical Roger Williams' ideals with a *modus operandi* is one of the most unusual chapters in the religious or secular history of the colonies. Many of their endeavors led up blind alleys and almost missed the avenues of religious, economic, and cultural progress. Others opened great thoroughfares of freedom which the world still strives to make Route 1.

The work has been made a delight by the interest and cooperation of many people. People no longer living who blazed trails in Rhode Island church history were a joy to follow.

Among a score of those who aided me I would particularly mention Miss Anna Learned Greene, historian of Beneficent

Church; Miss Helen Robertson, historian of the First Congregational Church; and Mr. Herbert Chandler Thrasher who has done thorough research in colonial church music. Careful typing of the manuscript with all of its varieties of contemporary spelling has been done by Mrs. Anton Sobocinski and Mrs. Lillian Murphy. Miss Elsie B. Simmons has helped in innumerable ways. My especial appreciation goes to Clarence F. Lamb of Providence who has not only assisted in the preparation of the end papers but has helped me in innumerable ways. He has done much of the genealogical research and has thoroughly reconstructed downtown Providence in its colonial days.

Valuable suggestions and encouragements have been given by professors Benjamin Clough, Israel Kapstein, and Edmund Sears Morgan of Brown University, Mr. William G. Roelker, Director of the Rhode Island Historical Society, and Professor Matthew Spinka of Hartford Theological Seminary and President of the American Society of Church History.

Places of asylum where long and uninterrupted work and writing could be done have been furnished by the Reverend Robert Schacht, Jr., at his summer home in Cumberland, by Hartford Seminary Foundation, and by the Reverend Robert Foster of Gorham, New Hampshire.

Arthur E. Wilson

Providence, Rhode Island

CONTENTS

TO MY FATHER

WHOSE LIVELY INTEREST IN HISTORY

WAS CONTAGIOUS

INTRODUCTION

THERE were rivers to cross for those who would follow Roger Williams into Providence Plantations. It is significant that across the Seekonk, which for a century was the boundary between Plymouth Colony and Providence Plantations, there was no bridge. The air of freedom on the Rhode Island shore was far more stimulating than that of ecclesiastical heaviness over on the opposite bank in Massachusetts. The inhabitants on either side were in no hurry to make communication easy.

But in the center of Providence-town from earliest days there was a bridge across the Providence River at Weybosset Point. Eighteen feet wide in 1670,[1] Weybosset Bridge met the needs of the inhabitants to cross from their homes along the hillside on the eastern bank to their pastures, gardens, wood lots and the clay bank on the west side. For the more adventurous it gave an opportunity to set out dry-shod to Pawtuxet, Meshanticut or even "Connecticut Governmente."

Almost from the start the much appreciated bridge met the stubborn opposition of independent Providence folk to pay for anything out of a common treasury. George Shepard in 1663 gave some of his lands beyond the Seven Mile Line as a contribution to be used for the maintaining of "the Towne Bridge at Waybosset." In 1668 Roger Williams offered to maintain the bridge "with GOD'S help," providing each family furnished one day's work and he be allowed to charge strangers toll. After four years the General Assembly repealed Mr. Williams' grant. Possibly he was prospering too well. In the nineteenth century the bridge was rebuilt by the Providence Washington Insurance Company. At other times the town laid out money upon it and ran lotteries for its support.

It has had placed upon it or beside it everything from a fish market to a whipping post. In 1767 one victim of the latter was sold for one year.

It played a dramatic part in the long and tedious battle to bring hesitant Rhode Island into the constitutional federation of states at the close of the Revolution.

Religion, commerce, culture, and education crossed and recrossed that bridge in whatever stage of repair it and they might be. Because of the river and the early settlements on high ground on the east side, the west side, which became the city's commercial center, developed comparatively late, a fact unique in New England cities.

The greatest significance of Weybosset Bridge was its use to separate and unite the two opposing concepts of freedom being wrought out in the life of the two settlements. On the east side, the original settlement dedicated to freedom and individualism was strung out along the river with community consciousness little evident in physical form or soul desire. On the west side, there developed, a hundred years after Roger Williams' planting, a community which sought freedom and also *unity* and ordered its community affairs more after the pattern of Massachusetts than of Providence Plantations.

These two communities were often in sharp opposition to each other but the bridge led one to influence the other until by a long and often painful process a pattern of Freedom *and* Unity was arrived at which ultimately supplanted both Rhode Island's individualistic brand of freedom and Massachusetts' undemocratic unity through establishment. This truly "lively experiment" became the bulwark of a new nation in a new world.

It was the discovery of these facts which led the author to

undertake to tell the story of the early religious life of these two settlements within the same town as a contribution to an understanding of the slow, painful development of just the right mixture of individual freedom and social unity. The result became our greatest single American heritage.

The task is made simpler by the fact that formal church life did not begin in Providence until 1700. With a complimentary and orienting gesture towards Roger Williams at the start, most of the study falls between 1700 and 1790.

It is impossible to consider the history of the religious life of a city, apart from its economic, cultural, and educational setting. In our exploration we have met people great and small and hope the reader will enjoy their acquaintance as much as has the writer. The vantage point of the survey has been that of Weybosset Hill on which Beneficent Congregational Church has stood for two centuries and where the forces of freedom and unity began to be reconciled. We have tried to do more than shake hands with fellow townsmen and politely bow to kindred institutions of the day. The book explores bypaths which may seem to have little to do with its main thesis, and spends some time on things that are merely interesting and spectacular. The reader is trusted to set them in the humdrum routine of daily life that he may not have an overly high-lighted picture of the times. For everyone who was brought before the church for misconduct, dozens of the saints walked down the street with motives and deeds which would never challenge the watchful eye of the deacons.

CHAPTER ONE

ROGER WILLIAMS—ECCLESIASTICAL ANARCHIST

MASSACHUSETTS, Connecticut, and Rhode Island [1] were founded by men driven by the same religious impulse who were seeking a place where they could experiment with a dynamic idea about God and man. Roger Williams championed the underlying ideals of Plymouth and Massachusetts Bay but established the settlement of Providence Plantations as a living protest to the pattern those ideals had evolved in Salem and Boston.

In that little community echoed the thoughts of men across the centuries of the Christian era who had tried to find an earthly pattern for an eternal idea. A religious community always faces three major indispensables when it goes to work to make its dream a reality: (1) *the teaching of doctrine,* (2) *the perfecting of organization,* and (3) *the bridging of social cleavage.* Christianity had to reckon with these factors the moment Jesus bade his disciples go into the world and preach the gospel.

As long as there were only the Twelve and their Teacher, with a periphery of followers, these three coefficients did not loom large. The disciples did not always understand the elementary doctrines Jesus taught them but they understood his love for them.

In their simple organization they had trouble with their treasurer and sometimes disputed over seniority, but the disagreements were not of the kind which would cause nations to wage war and people to flee across oceans.

Socially, their little band was nearly perfect in its unity. Property measured by the value of a fishing boat caused little or no gulf between a fisherman and a tax collector. The good earth as a bed, and loaves, blessed by God himself, did not separate but united the Twelve.

Immediately after Peter preached such a powerful sermon that he jumped the Church's membership from twelve souls to five thousand, these three problems leaped to the fore. Teachings had to be clear enough so that they could be repeated to and understood by people who never saw the light of Jesus' eyes. The barriers of language and languages would never be wholly surmounted. For teaching and the breaking of bread there had to be a room larger than the one on a certain second floor in Jerusalem, or an outdoor area bigger than a fishing boat on the Sea of Galilee. There had to be leaders and sub-leaders. Some would live in good houses and some would live in no houses; some would know Plato and Aristotle and some would not even know Moses, and if the church were to be Christian each must respect and love the other.

The three problems were born out of man's earthly limitations and his heavenly aspirations. They were the problems of the church in Jerusalem and the one in Rome. They were Luther's problems after his little band became a movement that spread like wildfire in an effort to escape the bungling of these very elements by the mother church. They were John Wesley's problems when he discovered himself with something bigger than a Holy Club on his hands. They were the root of the strange actions of the New England divines when they were joined by those who had not signed the Mayflower Compact.

They should have been also the concern of Roger Williams when his lonely sanctuary along the Moshassuc River began to look like a town. Roger settled them by washing his hands of them, and as a result we have Providence Plantations, with a religious history unlike that of the rest of America—peculiar, faulty, and great. Man's united search for Providence came nearer bogging down in the town bearing that name than anywhere else in New England.

A quick glance at Protestantism's journey from Wittenberg to Providence Plantations shows us that from the beginning, as with every reform movement, the Protestant Reformation did only part of its job.

Lutheranism in Germany and Calvinism in Geneva seemed to repeat the mistakes rather than the successes of the Roman organization. Again the church tied itself to the state; but it surrendered that which kept it supreme over the state, the Roman conception of the sacraments. For the Roman Catholic, man's salvation depended upon the sacraments which the church alone could administer; therefore, the church always was supreme in the issues of life. Calvin denied this doctrine and Luther straddled the issue. Thus in Luther and Calvin the work of reformation was begun, but not carried to its logical conclusion even on the basis of the convictions of its founders.

Giving up the Roman conception of the sacraments necessitated the giving up of the church's identity with the state and the complete liberating of the soul of man for direct intercourse with his Maker. Luther had taught that the prayers of a shoemaker were as readily heard by God as those of a bishop. But the father of the Reformation feared the logic of his own convictions. It remained for the English Separatist to dare the rest of this spiritual adventure.

There arose in England the most peculiar situation in the whole of Reformation history. It reversed the whole experience of the Continent, where ecclesiastical reforms called the tune for political changes. But in England a political break with Rome was made by Henry VIII before the forces of religious reformation were ready; consequently, it took about a century for the Reformation in England to catch up with the organizational split from Rome. It forms an inglorious chapter of Protestant history, marked by bloodshed and political intrigue. On the Continent Protestantism had been a mass movement which, buttressed by its hymns and debates, could not be stopped. In England it was a star-chamber movement, making the task of true Christians that of reforming the Reformation, a slow process, similar to trying to build a house out of two sets of plans.

Into this situation came the Separatists who ultimately would arrive at Plymouth Rock. Gaius Glenn Atkins says that the Separatists "accepted the implications of Luther and Calvin which they themselves refused." Experience would seem to show that a supreme loyalty to a church cannot be built except on the Roman theory of the sacraments. If you throw over that theory then you must go to the other extreme and maintain that a complete approach to God is possible for every child of God without the necessity of intermediary devices. The church then becomes a fellowship in recognition of man's need of togetherness in seeking God and in fulfillment of Christ's gospel of brotherhood. The in-between theories can never reach the vigor of either of the two extremes, Rome and Plymouth Bay. Each of these two recognizes the psychological factors of man's need to know his own significance, his longing to worship and serve God, and his innate desire for social expression.

Separatism was never a "one leader" movement. It did not have a single John Wesley, John Knox, or John Calvin. It had its Robert Browne, its John Robinson, its William Bradford, its William Brewster, its Dr. Samuel Fuller, and many others of almost equal rank. Thus the history of the Pilgrims is the story of congregations, rather than of pulpits, in Scrooby, England, Leyden, Holland, and Plymouth in the new world. This continued be a characteristic of the *New England Way*. Several towns and cities of today were settled by congregations organized elsewhere: Hartford, Windsor, New Haven, Connecticut; Rehoboth, Massachusetts (now Rumford, Rhode Island); Plymouth, New Hampshire, etc. The name Congregational, which was later used, was well chosen.

Had "Separatism" started as a mass movement, it undoubtedly would have succumbed to the temptations of over-organization. But fortunately it began as a tiny movement and so continued until its principles had taken firm root. It would be an interesting but useless discussion to consider whether by the nature of its first principles it remained a small group or whether it developed its principles because it was a small group. The answer would probably be "both and."

Be that as it may, it did not sweep over England as Presbyterianism did over Scotland. One reason was, of course, that it ran along beside the English Puritan movement, a reform which would have seemed quite sufficient to most who wished to see religion purified and revitalized. But Puritanism was not too concerned with the more fundamental changes which the Separatists held were absolutely essential. The leaders of the Separatists or, as they preferred, *True Christians*, were men of high learning, most of them Cambridge graduates; the followers were a fair cross-section of English life, humble and well-born; educated and plain; city and rural.[2]

The chief Separatist principles were:

1. The church is to be "gathered"; a difference from the time-honored principle of the parish. In 1587 Robert Browne had said, "the kingdom of God is not to begin by whole parishes, but rather of the worthiest, were they never so few." [3]

2. Church membership is based not on the sacraments (although their use is to be desired); rather, church membership is a "covenant relationship." Thus the church exists not for in-

dividual salvation, but is a fellowship of believers seeking to help each other in searching after the ways of God "made known or to be made known to us." It is not so much the "navis" of the Middle Ages, the ship which carried the souls of the saved, as it is the shipyard where "the gathered" learn and are encouraged to rig their own craft, that they may sail the roughest seas with Christ as their pilot. Indeed, it was the "soul rigging" of the Pilgrims which gave them courage as a congregation to sail forth in that romantic but frail craft, the *Mayflower*.

3. Each gathered congregation is to be free to administer its own affairs in the light of Christian teaching and to choose its leaders (early called teachers, guards and "releavers," later pastors and teachers) who should "teach them and watch for the salvation of their souls."

It would have been a glorious climax to the story of New England beginnings to say that democracy and Christianity came to full bloom there in the wilderness settlements. Instead of that they "almost did," and then missed fruition by a good deal. The early New Englanders were guilty of mixing some of the "rubbish and misshapen projections of fraudulent device with the fair stones and goodly pillars of the Apostolic edifice." It is too much to ask that man shall ever produce full-grown the perfect pattern for living together and serving God. He must work by trial and error. As the colony grew rapidly the fear for its purity made the radicals become conservatives and put up barriers to preserve that which they had sacrificed so much to achieve. They made church membership a requirement for voting and there was only one church membership recognized. These shores were sacred to the Separatist-Puritan cause. There was room on other shores for those of different minds and ways. Nathaniel Ward wrote, "all Familists, Anabaptists and other enthusiasts shall have free liberty to keepe away from us."

As did Luther a century previously, these early planters of a new Reformation on these shores had a vision of the greatness of the individual soul and conscience and a conviction of its right to freedom. And they, too, failed to leap the hurdle which barred the way for Luther, a fear of the consequences of these their most cherished ideals.

But more than this, as numbers grew and organization became imperative, Massachusetts fell into what we have already called "mistakes" of church organization, as did the earlier Protestants in Europe. The church became a state church or more correctly a church state. As time would go on it would likewise make its doctrines increasingly the *modus operandi* of salvation, forgetting its tenets of the free spirit of man.

Plymouth always stood out as more tolerant, a refuge for the religious outcast, including Roger Williams and the Baptist president of Harvard, Henry Dunster, who was removed from office in 1644. It continued to hold better relations with the Indians than did Massachusetts Bay. But the prestige passed to the Bay colony and to Boston, and the New England Way became filled with the very things which the Pilgrims had risked everything to escape.

Congregationalism almost sold its birthright. But not quite. Restless spirits would not conform to nonconformity any more than to the established church. Thomas Hooker was one of the first to shake the dust of Massachusetts Bay from his feet (more accurately the mud and snow) and set up a free colony on the Connecticut, which he called Hartford. Later, as did the New Haven colony, it too bargained with its birthright.

And here enters Roger Williams, whom the Congregationalists ought to thank more than any one man for saving the Gainsborough-Scrooby-Leyden-Plymouth—"real Christian"—Separatist-Pilgrim conception of the free church. It was left to Roger Williams to see that the logical conclusion to the free, gathered, congregationally governed church was the existence in the same community of other churches of the peoples' choice, none of which should control the civil government except as their members formed a part of the citizenry. This principle, for which the Massachusetts Bay people would have deported Roger had he not fled, actually saved Congregationalism from its own temptations to grandeur and allowed it to reclaim its birthright and develop into a free church, following the Revolution.

It gives Rhode Island Congregationalism something to boast about. Here the churches of colonial vintage were more truly congregational than those of Massachusetts and Connecticut. They were saved from themselves by that "gadfly" (as his enemies called him) who sought to perform a "lively experiment" in freedom, one Mr. Roger Williams.

There seems to be general agreement among present-day historians that Roger Williams came to the settlement as a pure Separatist or Congregationalist without any Baptist intentions. A subject for lively debate is whether he was ever immersed or not. But let us take one thing at a time.

From the moment he came to New England, Roger Williams' chief contention with the churches of Boston and Salem was that they were not wholly separate. His thinking on this theme ultimately evolved into the conclusion that the great principle of the congregationally gathered churches was being threatened in two directions: first, to bring into a covenanted church birthright members by the ordinance of infant baptism was a contradiction of the earliest Separatist principle of a gathered church; second, to require church membership for the exercise of the civil franchise was a denial of freedom. English disenfranchised Separatists had seen only the other side of the problem. But in New England, those who had been denied all participation in Old World government became completely responsible for its total functioning. It is not surprising that they made many errors.

English Congregationalists who had never been turned loose

in a secular pasture were horrified at what they heard of the "goin's on" among the saints abroad. One of them wrote in 1669, "Oh, how it grieves and affects us that New England should persecute! God made none . . . to be lords over faith . . . how do you cast a reproach upon us, that are Congregational in England, and furnish our adversaries with weapons upon us? We blush and are filled with shame and cunfusion of face, when we hear these things." [4]

The "lively experiment" in Providence was to grant full liberty in "religious concernments" not primarily to establish democracy, but to save the church from a membership of unregenerate men who united with it for secular ends. Professor Conrad Henry Moehlman writes:

> Williams boasts that he could have converted all the Indians of New England to an anti-Christian conversion, that is, to observe the Sabbath, to receive a "baptism or washing though it were in rivers (as the first Christians and the Lord Jesus himself did)," to attendance upon stated church meetings, maintenance of priests and forms of prayer, and the whole form of anti-Christian worship in life and death. Precise external conformity to the prescriptions of religion does not constitute conversion.[5]

There are many theories of Roger Williams' relationship to the Baptists. That of Dr. Moehlman seems the best substantiated not only by the few available records but by the whole history of the Separatists and Williams' passion for complete "separatism." The story seems to develop along the following line.

Two years after Roger and Company moved across the Seekonk came Richard Scott and wife to the Williams refuge. She was a sister of Mrs. Ann Hutchinson and seems to have been the one who persuaded Roger that the reformed church might best practice "believer's baptism." Its appeal to Williams would lie in its complete separateness from the "unseparated Separatists" of Massachusetts. Baptism based on experience rather than birth would defend the Providence church from the temptation to become a state church into which people could be born. Thus Roger decided his own infant baptism did not qualify him to be a member of a Separatist church. It must be a conscious, personal, covenanted act. He must be baptized again. He, therefore, in 1639 persuaded Ezekiel Holliman to rebaptize him and then he rebaptized twelve of the Providence venture, most of whom were members of the Salem church. Up to this time they had apparently thought of themselves as "absent members" of the Salem church. As a result of this rebaptism [6] and its consequent denial of the validity of their previous standing in the Christian fellowship, the Salem church wrote their names off the books. Nowhere do we find positive proof that Roger Williams was primarily concerned with the mode of baptism.

It was not until the 1640's that the mode of baptism had much place in current discussion. Even then there were many points of view on the form and proper recipient of baptism. There were the antipedobaptists (opposed to infant baptism), the anabaptists (in favor of rebaptism or "believer's baptism"), the immersionists, etc. To champion one principle did not mean the embracing of the other viewpoints. Charles Chauncy came to the Plymouth church in 1639 and later settled as pastor of the Scituate church. He preached and practiced immersion. Bradford writes, ". . . he holding it ought only to be by diping, and putting ye whole body under water, and that sprinkling was unlawfull. The church yielded that immersion, or dipping, was lawfull but in this could [cold] countrie, not so conveniente." This had nothing to do with antipedobaptism, as we see in John Winthrop's account written in July, 1642, of the situation in Scituate:

Mr. Chancey, of Scituate persevered in his opinion of dipping in baptism, and practised accordingly, first upon two of his own, which being in very cold weather, one of them swooned away. Another, having a child about three years old, feared it would be frightened, (as others had been, and one caught hold of Mr. Chancey, and had near pulled him into the water). She brought her child to Boston, with letters testimonial from Mr. Chancey, and had it baptized there.

The issue of immersion became much more centered in Rehoboth than in Providence. The chief troubler of the waters seems to be Mark Lucar, who had been a member of the Particular Baptist Church of London which began the practice of immersion in 1642. He came to Newport in 1644. The Rehoboth, Massachusetts (now Rumford, Rhode Island) Church, under fiery Samuel Newman, was having trouble with Obadiah Holmes and a minority following over the question of baptism. Roger Williams tells of the meeting in Rehoboth in 1649 and his own doubts about it:

At Seekonk, a great many have lately concurred with Mr. John Clarke and our Providence men about the point of a new Baptism, and the manner by dipping; and Mr. John Clarke hath been there lately (and Mr. Lucar) and hath dipped them. I believe their practice comes nearer the first practice of our great Founder Christ Jesus, than other practices of religion do, and yet I have not satisfaction neither in the authority by which it is done, nor in the manner, nor in the prophecies concerning the rising of Christ's kingdom after the desolations by Rome, etc.

Our earliest Rhode Island documents bear out this general conclusion that Roger came to the refuge on the Moshassuc without benefit of Baptist intentions or enlightenment, but with the determination to establish a truly Separatist community if others should follow him. The first written history of Rhode Island was that of Rev. John Callender, the brilliant liberal minister of the Newport Baptist Church, written in 1736 as a centennial discourse. In a footnote he says there are reasons to suspect that:

Mr. Williams did not form a church of the Anabaptists and that he never join'd with the Baptist church there. Only that he allowed them to be nearest the Scripture rule, and true primitive Practice as to the mode and subject of Baptism.

But ecclesiastical steadfastness was not a characteristic of the one whom Cotton Mather called "the New England Firebrand." Scott wrote, "I walked with him in the Baptist way about three or four months, in which time he broke with the society and declared at large the grounds and reason of it—that their baptism could not be right because it was not administered by an apostle." Richard Scott stuck by until the Quakers came to town in 1656; some time after that he joined them.

Williams was to become a Seeker the year that he went to England for the charter, probably in 1643. It was at this time that the sect was organized there. They believed that there has been no church, sacraments, pastors, or officers since a few years after the apostles. Two or three others in Providence joined with him and "there he continued a year or two 'till two of the three left him," says Scott.[7]

In becoming a Baptist and then a Seeker, Roger Williams was in one sense following a logical course. Increasingly his chief aim of establishing a truly separated church led to a greater passion—to build a community where religion and the clergy could never dominate civil life and where the religious test would never determine citizenship. The church based on full covenant relationship was a first step; adult baptism of believers was a second safeguard, as it discouraged an inherited church. Finally, to have no church at all would completely settle the problem, if problems could be solved by ignoring them.

The Seekers in England were a noble little group and did much to deepen the spiritual side of religion. But for it to be the faith of the founder of a new civic and religious order was disastrous to the first century and a half of Providence Plantations.

Nowhere was a higher price paid for freedom and individualism than in this land of the "lively experiment."

Up to this point Roger had acted as a great religious statesman, but now that element which made his rival in Newport, William Coddington, speak of him as "a mere weathercock; constant only in inconstancy" takes possession. He becomes so interested in the whole history of the rites of the church that he outdistanced the Church of England. He insists that the ordinances must be administered by those in apostolic succession [8] but comes to the conclusion that there has been no true apostolic succession since the first century. The sacraments are invalid without it and the only thing one can do is to await new apostles. Sometimes he may have thought he himself might become just that, but in this respect his better judgment ruled. "The church for Roger Williams [became] visionary speculation not historic reality." [8] Possibly he wanted it that way!

Finally what had started out as a single purpose in Roger's own mind, that of purifying the church and making it truly separatist, became an inner conflict. Instead of harnessing their religious zeal to the erection of meetinghouses and the establishment of Christian schools and cultures, the individualists of the Plantations fell to religious bickering. Chief among the hotheads was Samuel Gorton of Warwick. Governor Winthrop wrote:

> Those of Providence, being all Anabaptists, were divided in judgment; some were only against baptizing of infants; others denied all magistry and churches, etc., of which Gorton who had lately been whipped at Aquiday, as is before mentioned, was their instructor and captain. These being too strong for the other party, provoked them by inquiries, so as they came armed into the field, each against the other, but Mr. Williams pacified them for the present.

Sam was not a Seeker, nor did he quite know what he was. He was charged with being an Antinomian and a Familist. The

Antinomians were a visionary group founded by John Agricola in the Lutheran Church. They opposed scriptural law as a rule of manners or instruction. Believers need not fear their sins as they can do no harm. The Familists arose in Holland in 1555, teaching that the "Family of Love" was now to perfect the teaching of Christ. Their responsibilities did not extend beyond their own religious group.

All of this gave rise to the Rhode Island reputation that "if a man had lost his religion let him go to Rhode Island and he would be sure to find it among the varieties there." Roger listed thirty-eight gods of the Indians and must at times have felt that there were as many for the colonists. He smarts under the saying of his neighbors with which he cannot but concur, "We would be quiet and peaceable enough if it was not for the quarrels and contentions among these holy brethren."

Roger started out as a religious as well as a civil statesman. Perhaps it was the very individualism which he granted his fellows which browbeat him into escaping his religious responsibilities by becoming a Seeker and dwelling in the realm of religious mysticism and escaping into idealistic vagaries.

Providence Plantation's inglorious early history in the realms of education, church architecture, culture, and a trained ministry all sprang from this one phobia, the fear, on the part of Roger Williams and his successors, of again losing their freedom. Perhaps someone, somewhere, had to carry freedom to this extreme if it were to make its indelible mark and become the blessing it subsequently did to the new nation, which patterned its ideas of the separation of state and church on the Rhode Island model.

Just how far this idea of the right of the individual was coupled with a sense of social irresponsibility is shown in the reaction of some on refusing to be taxed for roads or to pay toll for their use. Timothy Dwight, complaining about the Plainfield Pike, writes:

> The people of Providence expended upon this road as we are informed the whole sum permitted by the legislature. The turnpike company then applied to the legislature for leave to expend such an additional sum as would complete the work. The legislature refused. The principal reason for the refusal, as alleged by one of the members, it is said, was the following: that the turnpikes and the establishment of religious worship had their origin in Great Britain: the government of which was a monarchy and the inhabitants slaves; that the people of Massachusetts and Connecticut were obliged by law to support ministers, and pay the fare of turnpikes, and were therefore slaves also; that if they chose to be slaves they undoubtedly had a right to their choice; but that free-born Rhode-Islanders ought never to submit to be priest-ridden nor to pay the privilege of travelling on the highway. This demonstrative reasoning prevailed and the road continued in the state which I have mentioned, until the year 1805. It was then completed and free-born Rhode-Islanders bowed their necks to the slavery of travelling on a good road.

Roger's reminder that in some matters the captain of the ship could and must command the passengers fell on deaf ears when taxes were proposed.

The very nature of the Providence Plantations communities founded in the first century of her life bears testimony to the price of individualism. The New England village green as a center of community life is not to be found. Community life failed to focus; it hardly existed in the religious and cultural sense. Francis Asbury, viewing the Weston, Massachusetts, church, wrote of its "grand steeple, porches, and even stalls for the horses; and it is well if they do not make the Methodists pay to support their pomp. Oh! religion in New England!" Thank God that Rhode Islanders never allowed Methodists to pay for Baptist steeples, but would that there had been a few more steeples scattered through the villages of the Plantations.

It was to be nearly two centuries after the founder came to the banks of the Moshassuc before citizens would be enabled to train the minds of their children in free schools. Not only had the founders opposed tax-supported schools, but each wanted the right to teach his child what he chose and not have a "system" of education thrust upon a pliable mind.

Roger, for all his remarkable intellect, had solved the centuries-old problem of the organization of religious life and the newer problem of education by a do-nothing policy which resulted in ecclesiastical anarchy. For when men deny the need of each other in these concerns they have already paved the way to spiritual and mental darkness. Fortunately the problem was not left entirely with Williams and there were ameliorating elements which brightened it here and there.

Another great price which the colony paid for the withdrawal of Mr. Williams from religious leadership (except in the matters of disputation) was that of a trained ministry. He himself possessed one of the most brilliant minds to come out of Cambridge University (Pembroke College) and into New England. New England was running over with more ministers than it had churches for, and all of them university men. In 1696 Cotton Mather, counting noses, finds ninety-six of the one hundred and four New England churches had Harvard graduates as ministers. But there is no such record in these Plantations. The church at Providence had taken what was left when Roger walked out on her and had resorted almost entirely to lay exhorters. Good men many of them were, but often possessed of more heat than light. This, too, lasted through the seventeenth century and into the first quarter of the eighteenth.

The things that made the rest of New England great, her chaste meetinghouses, her trained and brilliant clergy, her educational system were not to be found here. Plantation folks had to get along on a diet of freedom. Lest we blame the leadership of Roger Williams too much, let us remember another factor, economics. Enough to say now that among the blessings of beneficent Providence good soil was not included. Rocks and poison ivy would hardly prove a boon to a material culture. Trade with a hostile New England was not easy. Some day the sea would be discovered and after that the possibilities of water running downhill. With it they would do more than grind corn. Where individualism had failed, water power would succeed in building churches and schools!

There must have been a tremendous amount of character expressed or latent, for after a pretty dull century and a half there was brought to flower in Providence a great and good society.

Indeed, it shows the lasting power of spiritual things. Here the ideals of religious liberty, individual worth, a high sense of justice (even to the Indians), and Christian tolerance abode without the usual accompanying institutions of church and school. Institutions cannot survive long without high principles, but high principles can survive in people's hearts for a long time without institutions. Cut off by the Seekonk from Massachusetts and orthodoxy, and united by Weybosset Bridge, experimenters in liberty struggled for a hundred years to fulfill the dream which they felt their neighbors had forgotten. They would sacrifice the best things in life itself rather than forswear their allegiance to the freedom of the individual and his soul.

This devotion to liberty produces the strange pattern of a New England settlement with no church building until 1700, no public-school system until the early 1800's, a refusal to be taxed for roads, and a general temperament of negation, that they might be positive in their loyalty to freedom.

More than anywhere else in the colonies Providence Plantations was the crucible in which a community pattern was shaped by the fires of freedom.

Fortunately the experiment had upwards of a century to deepen its roots before the Massachusetts and Old World concepts of unimaginative orderliness moved in, wearing the ecclesiastical armor of Congregationalism and Episcopalianism. Succeeding pages tell the story of the clashes and struggles which finally harmonized the Massachusetts and Providence patterns into what more nearly resembles the American way of freedom than any other colonial endeavor.

CHAPTER TWO

CONGREGATIONALISTS AND EPISCOPALIANS COME TO TOWN

HETERODOXY, poverty, and ecclesiastical anarchy did not make a combination to raise outward monuments to religion in the town called Providence. Unlike much of New England where the meetinghouse followed close on the heels of the first log houses and where the schoolhouse put in an appearance not long after, the settlement of Roger Williams on the Moshassuc raised no churchly timber in its first sixty-four years.

The town had settled down around its one public institution, the grist mill, at Moshassuc Falls, up the river a piece from Roger Williams' spring. Homes were built around it and above it on Stamper's Street. After thirty of the houses were wiped out in King Philip's War in 1676, the community started its southerly journey along Towne (Main) Street towards the navigable part of the river. The fortification of Captain William Field's house below the present site of the courthouse gave impetus to this movement following King Philip's visit and the process gradually continued under the beckoning hand of shipping.

Somewhere along this route of the town's southerly trek the first meetinghouse was erected by the Baptists in 1700. It was built by Parson Tillinghast and was described as a dingy affair resembling "a haycap with a fire-place in the middle and an opening in the roof for the escape of smoke."

The Baptists built their second house in 1726 at the northwest corner of Smith and North Main streets.[1]

John Howland, coming from Newport to work in Benjamin Gladding's barber shop in 1770, as a boy of thirteen, remembered it well. It was forty feet square. At high water the tide flowed nearly up to the west end of the building. Instead of pews there were benches and a narrow stairway went to the gallery.

This house, from the brief descriptions which we have of it, may well have resembled the Elder Ballou Meeting House still in good preservation on Iron Mine Hill off the Wrentham Road, Cumberland, near Woonsocket. Mrs. Downing, in her *Early Homes of Rhode Island,* dates this house about 1740, but describes it as belonging to the previous century in design. "The framework, hewn of sturdy oak logs, shows on the interior beautifully smoothed and chamfered." When one sits on one of the upright benches, the back of which is crowned with a four-inch timber, he realizes why Canon Chase, former rector of St. James' Episcopal Church, Woonsocket, who preached there on one occasion said, "When I noticed that peculiarity as to the seats, I had compassion on my audience and cut my sermon short." But there was no cutting of sermons short in the Baptist house on North Main Street, according to John Howland:

It appears that it never had been the practice to settle an ordained minister over any particular church or society. In this they resembled the Quakers. . . . The elders were generally farmers, and had no salary or any other means of support but their own labor. They officiated in any place where there was a gathering, and the people did not know who was to speak till they saw one begin. They did not approve of singing and never practiced it in public worship. When more than one elder was present and the first had exhausted himself, he would say, "There is time and space left if anyone had further to offer." In that case another and another would offer what he had to say; so there was no set time for closing the meeting. As elder Winsor's home was in Providence, he generally appeared in his place every Sunday, so that this came to be called "elder Winsor's meeting." The house could not contain a large congregation, nor did the number present seem to require a larger house as they were not crowded, though many of them came in from the neighboring towns on horseback with women behind them on pillions.

The Quakers followed close upon the heels of the Baptists. In Newport, Baptists and Quakers were practically contemporaries. In Providence, there was a Quaker meeting well in advance of the coming of the Congregationalists and Episcopalians, although both of these latter groups built meetinghouses prior to the house of the Quakers, erected in 1725–26. Strictly speaking, the house raised at Saylesville in 1703 (near the Arnold House) was located at that time within the boundaries of Providence.

Newport is the oldest Quaker settlement in America. Rufus M. Jones points out that in 1641 "Newport people arranged themselves into two religious groups. One party, with Coddington, Coggeshall, and Nicolas Easton as leaders, formulated views which seem extraordinarily akin to those later held by the Society of Friends; while the other group, led by John Clarke, formed a Baptist Church." [2]

This was even prior to the movement founded in England by George Fox which became the Society of Friends.

What the *Mayflower* is to Congregationalists the *Woodhouse* is to American Quakers. A ship unsafe for ocean travel, she was built by Robert Fowler who said, "We saw the Lord Leading our vessel as it were a man leading a horse by the hand." On June first, 1657, she set sail for America with eleven Friends; five of them disembarked in New Amsterdam and six in Newport.

Here they found the Coddingtons, Eastons, and others who,

though they had not heard the name Quaker, had already organized themselves into an order of very similar religious practice. With the arrival of the *Woodhouse* they quickly adopted the complete teaching of George Fox and his English followers.

George himself arrived in Newport in 1672. Twelve years earlier Mary Dyer of Newport had been hanged as a Quaker on Boston Common, but in Rhode Island, George Fox was to find the "governor, deputy governor and Magistrates were all chosen from among them and the affairs of the colony came under their management."

Quite contrary to the Boston brand of hospitality offered to visiting Quakers, George Fox was entertained in the home of Quaker Governor Easton. Meetings, including a Yearly Meeting of several Friends Societies, were held in Newport, Narragansett, and Providence. "Some at Newport spoke of hiring him as a preacher." When he heard this he said, "It is time for me to be gone; for if their Eye was so much to Me or any of Us, they would not come to [be] their own Teacher. For this thing [of hiring ministers] had spoiled many, by hindring them from improving their own Talents; whereas our Labour, is to bring every one to their own Teacher in Themselves." [3]

George had chosen "the time to be gone" before Roger Williams could enter into debate with him. Roger had tried in Yearly Meeting at Newport in 1671 to engage in disputation, but when "he attempted to speak the Governor's wife started to pray. When she finished he made another attempt, but he was stopt by John Burnett's sudden falling to Prayer and dismissing the Assembly." Then it was that Roger sent a challenge to him to debate on fourteen points. It appears that the friends of George Fox saw to it that he did not receive the message before his departure. Roger felt George had played the part of a sly Br'er Fox in departing. Expecting to meet him, Williams had rowed to Newport (he was upwards of seventy) for the debate. But he went after him with his pen and at least to his own satisfaction "Digged him out of his Burrowes." [4] Freedom to come to Rhode Island with any belief did not mean freedom from disputation, according to the founder of the state. In 1657 the little colony was more than up against it and had it been willing to accede to Massachusetts' and the United Colonies' demands to expel the Quakers,[5] it could have had some help. But this she would not do. In a reply signed by Benedict Arnold,[6] these great words appeared, "We have no law among us whereby to punish any for only declaring by words etc. their mindes and understandings concerning the ways of God." Roger Williams concurred in that sentiment. Quakers and others should have refuge here, but let them look to their arguments for their faith, lest they be torn in shreds.

By the eighteenth century, half of the island of Rhode Island was Quaker and strong meetings were established in Greenwich, Saylesville, Woonsocket, and Providence.

Their house erected on Stamper's Hill in 1725–26 was moved in 1745 to the site now occupied by its successor, which was built in 1844–45. At the time it was moved the hill streets bounding the meetinghouse were Old Gaol Lane and Powder House Lane. Moses Brown or William Wilkinson missed a good bet if they did not take those names as subjects for Quaker exhortation. As for gaols (jails), most Quakers outside of Rhode Island knew them well. Powder House Lane could at any moment touch off a debate on whether the burning of Providence by King Philip had been caused by the pacifist action of the Quaker-controlled colonial government in refusing to raise a military force to meet the threats of the Indians, or whether it had been caused by the military action of the men of Providence "who stayed and went not away," reversing the traditional practice of dealing with the Indians on a peaceful basis. The island of Aquidneck (Rhode Island), directly across the bay from

Philip's Mt. Hope, where Quakerism had its stronghold, had come off untouched and became the refuge for Providence folk who fled before the Indians. Long since the street names have been changed to South Court Street and Meeting Street and there at the foot of a "strait and narrow"—yea, steep—way, the house has continued to shelter those of the Friends' persuasion.

So long had the established church of New England and the established Church of Old England held the Plantations of Providence to be hopeless for organized religion that the significance of the Baptist Meetinghouse of 1700 was not quickly recognized. Already Congregational and Episcopal churches had been established in Newport and Kingstown.

These were far more important towns ecclesiastically than was Providence. They had a degree of respectability and wealth which helped offset in the minds of the orthodox any sympathies entertained for the Providence pattern of freedom of thought and worship.

Newport was the second port of New England and superior to New York in the commerce which passed in and out of its beautiful harbor. It led in the affairs of the state. Roger Williams and Joseph Jenckes were the only governors from the northern part of the colony from 1646 to 1748. Newportians governed the state ninety-four out of one hundred and one years.

In the southern part of the colony was the unique settlement of Kingstown. Its "landed gentry" used the plantation system of farming and lived in comfort. Rev. James MacSparran wrote of the necessity of an intelligent approach to win his Narragansett neighbors to Episcopacy, saying that the "posterity of the old Puritans here, are a sagacious and prying people."

Thus a quarter of a century ahead of their endeavors in the Plantations the two establishments organized churches in Newport and Kingstown. The first Congregationalist in Newport was undoubtedly the Reverend John Clarke who did not become antipedobaptist until four years after he settled upon the island.

There then followed several decades of Quaker and Baptist ascendency, until in 1695 Nathaniel Clap came to Newport as an unordained Congregational minister. There was a meeting-house erected in 1696. Mr. Clap preached without ordination and the church remained informally organized until 1720. Present at the ordination were parsons Samuel Danforth, Joseph Belcher, Peter Thacher, and John Danforth, whom we shall meet in a few pages writing an historic epistle to the people of Providence Plantations.

Nathaniel Clapp preached his own ordination sermon. He was a lovable, headstrong parson who would spend his life in Newport. His refusal to accept an assistant resulted in a split in the church which was healed a century later, but which allowed Newport to have in the 1770's, as contemporary pastors, two of the colonies' greatest divines, Samuel Hopkins and Ezra Styles. The former founded a school of theology, the latter became president of Yale College and was a diarist.

A Church of England group was organized in 1698. James Honyman became rector in 1704 and served until 1750. Under his able leadership, Trinity became one of the strongest of old England's establishments in New England.[6]

While Newport and Kingstown had been considered proper towns for the establishments, Providence Plantations had to be approached more adroitly. The first Congregational services since the founding days in Providence were probably held under the leadership of Rev. Thomas Greenwood of the Rehoboth (Rumford) Church. This was prior to 1720. Greenwood was near enough the ferry at the Seekonk crossing to know how to bring a little of the New England Way into the Plantations without giving offense. It gave other reverend ministers in Connecticut and Massachusetts courage to make occasional sorties among Providence Baptists and Quakers. On October 27, 1721, an exchange of letters begins. These have been preserved in Staples Annals of 1832. The New England Way makes bold to bid for a permanent home in the Plantations. The following are portions of the first letter addressed to some of the first citizens of Providence by three Massachusetts Congregationalists, rank outsiders, who had perhaps discussed the matter at Mr. Clap's ordination service in Newport the year before. It was couched in phrases intended to woo a place in Roger Williams' home town for the spiritual descendants of those who had banished him. It sounded sincerely humble, repentant, and brotherly.

To the honorable Joseph Jenckes, Esq., late Deputy-Governor, William Hopkins, Esq., Major Joseph Wilson, Esq., Joseph Whipple, Esq., Col. Richard Waterman, Esq., Arthur Fenner, Esq., —— Wilkinson, Esq., Philip Tillinghast, Esq., Capt. Nicholas Powers, Esq., Thomas Harris, Esq., Capt. William Harris, Esq., Andrew Harris, Esq., —— Brown, Esq., Jonathan Burton, Esq., Jonathan Spreague, Jun. Esq., and to the other eminent men in the town of Providence. Pardon our ignorance if of any of your Christian names, or if your proper order be mistaken.

Honorable Gentlemen—

With what peace and love, societies of different modes of worship have generally entertained one another in your government, we cannot think of without admiration. And we suppose, under God, 'tis owing to the choice liberty granted to protestants of all persuasions in the Royal Charter graciously given you; and to the wise and prudent conduct of the gentlemen that have been improved as governors and justices in your colony. And the Rev. Mr. Greenwood, before his decease at Rehoboth, was much affected with the wisdom and excellent temper and great candour of such of yourselves as he had the honor to wait upon, and with those worthy and obliging expressions of kind respects he met with when he discoursed about his desire to make an experiment, whether the preaching of our ministers in Providence might not be acceptable; and whether some, who do not greatly incline to frequent any pious meeting in the place, on the first day of the week, might not be drawn to give their presence to hear our ministers, and so might be won over, by the influence of Heaven, into serious godliness; and although God has taken that dear brother of ours from his work in this world, yet it has pleased the Lord to incline some reverend ministers in Connecticut and some of ours to preach among you; and we are beholden to the mercy of Heaven for the freedom and safety they have enjoyed under the wise and good government of the place, and that they met with kind respect, and with numbers that gave a kind reception to their ministrations among you. These things we acknowledge with all thankfulness.

If it should come to pass that a small meetinghouse should be built in your town to entertain such as are willing to hear our ministers, we should account it a great favor if you all, gentlemen, or any of you, would please to build pews therein; in which you and they as often as you see fit, may give your and their presence and holy attention. And we hope and pray that ancient matters, that had acrimony in them, may be buried in oblivion; and that grace, and peace, and holiness, and glory, may dwell in every part of New-England; and that the several provinces and colonies in it may love one another with a pure heart fervently. So recommending you all, and your ladies and children, and neighbors and people to the blessing of Heaven, and humbly asking your prayers to the Divine Throne for us, we take leave and subscribe ourselves your servants,

PETER THACHER,
JOHN DANFORTH,
JOSEPH BELCHER.

Peter Thacher was the seventy-year-old minister at Milton, John Danforth had been minister at Dorchester nearly forty years, and Joseph Belcher was the minister at Dedham, a daring one hundred per cent Massachusetts overture to her neighbor who had revolted eighty-five years before.

They must have wished they had not included as the last name of the addressees "Jonathan Spreague Jun. Esq." as one of the "eminent men in the town of Providence." He seems to have been one of the many Baptist preachers or elders of that day, although he is not counted in the succession at the First Baptist Church. He begged to answer the letter, depriving the Massachusetts friends from a more polite answer by Joseph Jenckes, but giving posterity a view of the feelings which on the part of many still existed towards the established Congregationalists. And who will rise to say that, with some reservations, they did not deserve it? Here are excerpts from Jonathan who has no misconceptions about any of the three gentlemen being a friend David. His arrows are not shot in the air but aimed with the hope of a mortal victory.

To John Danforth, Peter Thacher, and Joseph Belcher, Committee of the Presbyterian Ministry.

Sirs— We, the inhabitants of the town of Providence, received yours, bearing date October 27, 1721, which was read publicly, in the hearing of the people, and we judge it uncivil to return you no answer. But finding the matter to be of religious concernment, we counted it our duty to ask counsel of God, lest we should be beguiled as Israel was by the Gibeonites.

And in the first place, we take notice of the honorable titles you give to many of us. Your view, as we take it, is to insinuate yourselves into our affections, and to induce us to favor your request. But, we find flatteries in matters of religion to be of dangerous consequence; witness the Hivites, who said, "We are your servants, and have heard of the fame of the God of Israel." In this way did Joash set up idolatry after the death of Jehoida.

We see that flattery in matters of worship has been, and now is, a cloak to blind men and lead them out of the way; and serves for nothing but to advance pride and vain glory. Shall we praise you for this? We praise you not. Next. You salute all as saints in the faith and order of the gospel, wishing all of us blessings for the time present and to all eternity. It is not the language of Canaan but of Babel to salute men of all characters as in the faith of the gospel.

This is the voice of false prophets, which daub with untempered mortar, sewing pillows under every arm-hole, and crying Peace! peace! when there is no peace. Is this your way to enlighten the dark corners of the world? Surely this is darkness itself.

This is but a preface to make room for your request, which is, "That we would be pleased, according to our power, to countenance, protect, and encourage your ministers in their coming and preaching in this town of Providence." To which we answer:– We admire at your request! or that you should imagine or surmise that we should consent to either; inasmuch as we know, that (to witness for God) your ministers, for the most part, were never set up by God, but have consecrated themselves, and have changed his ordinances; and for their greediness after filthy lucre, some you have put to death; others you have banished upon pain of death; others you barbarously scourged; others you have imprisoned and seized upon their estates.

And at this very present you are rending towns in pieces ruining the people with innumerable charges, which make them decline your ministry, and fly for refuge some to the Church of England and others to dissenters of all denominations, and you, like wolves, pursue; and whenever you find them within your reach, you seize upon their estates. And all this is done to make room for your pretended ministers to live in idleness, pride, and fullness of bread. Shall we contenace such ministers for Christ's ministers? Nay, verily these are not the marks of Christ's ministry; but are a papal spot that is abhorred by all pious protestants.

And since you wrote this letter the constable of Attleborough has been taking away the estates of our dear friends and pious dissenters to maintain the minister. The like has been done in the town of Mendon.

Christ bids us beware of such as come to us in sheep's clothing, but inwardly are ravening wolves; and your clothing is so scanty that all may see your shame.

And since you admire the love and peace we do enjoy, we pray you to use the same methods and write after our copy. And for the future never let us hear of your pillaging conscientious dissenters to maintain your own ministers.

And we count it our duty to pray for you, that God will open your eyes and cause you to see how far you have erred from the way of peace; and that God will give you godly sorrow for the same, and such repentance as is never to be repented of; and that you may find mercy and favor of our Lord Jesus Christ at his appearing. And so hoping, as you tender the everlasting welfare of your souls and the good of your people, you will embrace our advice; and not suffer passion so to rule as to cause you to hate reproof, lest you draw down vengeance on yourselves and on the land. We, your friends of the town of Providence, bid you farewell. Subscribed for, and in their behalf, by your ancient friend and servant for Jesus' sake,

JONATHAN SPREAGUE.

This letter brings even a *Mayflower* Congregationalist to his feet to cheer. In it truth is exaggerated, but seventy-three-year-old Jonathan hurled at Massachusetts everything Rhode Island had thought about her for more years than Jonathan Spreague had lived. In this letter we get a glimpse of how Rhode Island had managed with untrained lay leaders; they knew their Bible, they knew their own religious and civil convictions, and if Jonathan and a few others are typical, they knew how to hurl the king's English with tremendous clarity and goodly aim.

Jonathan Spreague had made his first public appearance in 1687 when he was fined for refusing to take an oath as a juryman. Here was a Six Principle Baptist adding a good Quaker principle to make seven. This interacting of the tenets of one religious group on another is an interesting feature of Providence church life which we shall see develop down through the years. Jonathan became quite a man about town, serving as a deputy, a justice of the peace, a speaker of the House of Deputies, and clerk of the Assembly. He was an exhorter, but not ordained.

Fortunately the sins of Massachusetts were not quite as glaring as Jonathan Spreague's letter would lead one to believe. In 1691 liberty of conscience had been granted, but still taxes for church support continued. Plymouth Bay Colony had even earlier passed an ordinance (1641) "That no injunction shall be put on any church or church member, as to doctrine, worship or discipline, whether for substance or circumstance, beside the command of the Bible." In 1727 the Episcopalians were allowed to use taxes from their communicants to support their own churches. In 1739 the town of Rehoboth voted a salary for the Baptist minister. Her nearness to the Providence Plantations chastened her Massachusetts pride!

A significant event for better fellowship had occurred in 1718. Rev. John Callender of Newport (Rhode Island's first historian) had an uncle Elisha, who was to succeed his brother and John's father as the minister of the First Baptist Church in Boston. Cotton Mather accepted the invitation to preach the ordination sermon! He chose for his subject "Good Men United" and said:

> . . . if the brethren in whose house we are now convened met with anything too unbrotherly, they now with satisfaction hear us expressing our dislike of everything which looked like persecution in the days that have passed over us. . . . Cursed the anger for it is fierce and the wrath for it is cruel; good for nothing but only to make divisions in Jacob and dispersions in Israel.

Insincerity was never a characteristic of the New England Way, but a weather eye was sometimes turned towards the correct timing of religious matters. It was perhaps more than a coincidence that shortly afterwards Harvard received its largest gift up to that time from Mr. Hollis, an English Baptist. Cotton Mather had done a good job for Harvard College as well as Christian fellowship by his sermon in the Boston church.

There were those who would conscientiously refuse to pay taxes because part of them would support the established church. There would be others who would be glad of a pious excuse for their failure to meet the deadline. Such failures, minus pious excuses, still persist in Attleborough, Mendon, and way stations.

Such were the convictions of Jonathan Spreague that had there been a good intolerant Massachusetts law lying around the freedom-loving colony of Rhode Island, he would have invoked it for freedom's sake, exactly as Massachusetts folks had done. But Roger Williams had foreseen such outbursts of intolerance and guarded well against them in the charter he had secured in 1643.

The only weapon left was frightening the intruders with the pen and the related threat of social ostracism once they arrived. But they did not scare, and Providence folks seem to have acted very decently, once the Congregationalists called Jonathan's bluff and began a small invasion of the territory.

Let us introduce some of the more important actors in the drama. We have already mentioned "Mr. Greenwood of Rehoboth." The ancient Rehoboth (Rumford) church had two pairs of fathers and sons who served it as ministers. Samuel and Noah Newman covered the years 1643–78 and Thomas and John Greenwood 1693–1757. It was the elder Greenwood who before his death in 1720 had crossed on the ferry at the narrows of the Seekonk [8] (Red Bridge), then made his way between the Marsh and Cat Swamp to Dexter's Lane (Olney Street) and hence down Towne Street to someone's house to hold a Congregational service. It was probably the home of Dr. John Hoyle, chief lay promoter of Congregationalism in Providence, or it may have been at Daniel Abbott's at the foot of Rosemary Lane (later Presbyterian Lane, later College Hill). Abbott would soon become benefactor as well as promoter of Congregationalism.

Thomas Greenwood was a graduate of Harvard and was probably the first college graduate to exhort in town since the voice of Roger Williams had been stilled. His son John was to have a hand in helping shape affairs in forthcoming Congregational struggles.

John Hoyle, "Practitioner of Physicke," was a busy man about town whom it is hard for posterity to judge. It was he who interested the three distinguished Massachusetts divines in the missionary territory of Providence and urged them to write the letter. He asked not only for their words of encouragement and a guiding ecclesiastical hand, but for cash on the line to build that "small meeting house" mentioned in the historic letter.

His application to keep an inn had been refused by the town

council a few years before, but was subsequently granted. He was something of a realtor and at least in the year 1722 did considerable traveling in the interests of religion. People must have been well and hearty in those days for this doctor had considerable spare time.

A goodly amount of cash was collected in "currant New England" money and taken out of Massachusetts and brought in the doctor's jeans to Providence. On June 1, 1722, he bought from Zachariah Mathewson "one and a quarter acres and sixteen poles of land" at the triangle of the "two Great Country Roades" made by the "Roade to Connecticut Government" and the "Roade to Pawtuxet" (now Weybosset and Broad streets) within a stone's throw of the future site of Beneficent Church. On the second of July—one month later—he sells an acre of the upper part of the lot for a Congregational meetinghouse, horse sheds, minister's dwelling and "buring" place. The front "quarter acre, sixteen poles" he keeps for himself. The sale price is twenty-four pounds of good Massachusetts Congregational money. We do not know what he gave Zachariah Mathewson, but our guess is it was less than twenty-four pounds.

The land is deeded to the minister and a deacon from each of four churches in the neighboring Congregational colonies: Rehoboth and Taunton, Massachusetts; Hartford and Windham, Connecticut.[9]

The deed was signed by John Hoyle; Deborah, his wife, made her mark. Richard Waterman, Towne Clerke and Justice of the Peace, recorded it. Waterman's future house lot would border on the west side of the new church lot.

The tidy acre was doomed to that uncertainty of circumstance which attended the fortunes of its previous owner once removed, Zachariah Mathewson. His father, James, had made a deathbed will and had left "to Zachariah and ye child unborne, if son, my house and land—but if it be a daughter then it all remaines to my son Zachariah." Unfortunately for "Zach" it was a boy and dividing up with his brother may have led Zachariah to the necessity of obtaining cash by selling the land to Dr. Hoyle.

From the point of view of giving the new venture a proper blessing the trustees were well chosen. Deacon Samuel Newman bore the name of the founder of the New England Way in Rehoboth. His illustrious forebear had more than the fathering of the Newman church to his credit. He had compiled a Bible concordance, in monumental fashion. With him was John Greenwood, son and successor to Thomas who had preached the first Congregational sermons in Providence. Rev. Timothy Woodbridge had been filling the shoes of famous Thomas Hooker of First Church, Hartford, since 1685; Samuel Whiting was the first minister at Windham, Connecticut, a community which would loom large in Providence Congregational developments. Samuel Danforth of the Taunton church was brother of John of Dorchester, one of the *three who wrote the letter*. Their father had been a colleague of Rev. John Eliot of Indian fame at Roxbury.

None of the three who wrote the letter were made trustees. A factor here would be the greater convenience of Taunton and Rehoboth than Dorchester, Milton, and Dedham. Windham and Hartford may well have been added to make sure this was a church of the New England Way, not just Massachusetts style ecclesiasticism.

It is of equal interest to note the churches not included. There were Congregational churches at Newport and Kingstown before the turn of the century. But these would be excluded as beyond the pale of New England. The church at Bristol, then in Massachusetts, might well have been invited but their new twenty-five-year-old minister, Nathaniel Cotton, would have been considered too inexperienced for great missionary responsibilities. But he was soon to have quite a finger in the Providence venture.

The meetinghouse was commenced but before the roof was entirely over it a great stir was being made. Those interested were accusing the trustees and Dr. Hoyle of building the church out in the country accessible to no one. Young Nathaniel Cotton, of Bristol, rowed across the bay and said things the way a Cotton would say them. The upshot was that the timbers already in place were taken down, a new piece of land at the top of Rosemary Lane on Benefit Street was purchased from Daniel Abbott, and the meetinghouse erected in the center of population.

Poor Dr. Hoyle! His dream for which he had labored vanished or at least was rudely transplanted. It seems to have been the end of the doctor's religious enterprise except to give consent that the acre of land be used for a "buring" ground, *sans* meetinghouse, *sans* minister's dwelling, *sans* horse sheds!

We shall never know how pure the motives of this first Congregational layman of Providence were. Probably they were mixed, like those of many others before and since.[10]

When the doctor died in 1766 he left an estate of nearly three thousand pounds. He had not done badly with his practice of Physicke, his inn-keeping, and his real-estate developments. Miss Kimball makes a happy suggestion in his defense: "His acre of land at the junction of two highways may well have seemed worth the price (twenty-four pounds). When the society finally obtained from Daniel Abbot a rear lot on the side hill above the Towne Street it cost them thirty pounds." Locating in a new section may also have seemed best to the doctor because of the wrath of Jonathan Spreague and others. Also to be on the "Greate Roade to the Connecticut Government" was a strategic place, if there were to be any influx of population from Congregational Connecticut.

We do not find a similar opposition to the coming of the Church of England to Providence. It was once removed from the wrath of the town's founders who had fled from the establishment of New England, whose founders in turn had crossed the wintry ocean to escape the establishment of Old England.

Episcopal churches established along with Congregational churches had gained a strong foothold in Newport and Narragansett some years before Providence was considered as a favorable mission.

While Rhode Island Episcopacy was to feel the barbs of New England opposition, yet she had a greater problem to face, that of remote control from across the Atlantic. History owes a great debt to this attempt to order the affairs of American parishes from the See of London, for it resulted in voluminous correspondence between the local rectors and the Society for the Propagation of the Gospel in Foreign Parts or the bishop himself. "The History of the Narragansett Church" by Wilkins Updike contains much of the Rhode Island correspondence.

There were three chief actors in the Rhode Island scene. The ablest was Rev. James Honyman, rector of Trinity, Newport, 1704–50. The other two were Rev. James MacSparran, D.D., rector of St. Paul's Church, Narragansett, 1721–57, and Rev. John Usher, rector of St. Michael's, Bristol, 1723–75.

In spite of the handicap of seeking to fashion the closely knit garment of the English church out of the loose fabric of wilderness and colonial mores, these three men all established strong colonial churches.

By the time the English Church was entering Rhode Island, precedent had already "centered religious control of England's North American colonies in the Bishop of London." One of the great bishops of London was Edmund Gibson, who served from 1723–48, the period in which the Rhode Island churches expanded. The Society for the Propagation of the Gospel in Foreign Parts was organized in 1701.

The lack of a resident bishop was the major problem of American Episcopacy. Even Edmund Gibson, "tho' a verry inquisitive and penetrating Prelate, sat several years in yt *See* wth no other knowledge of ye civil state of New England than yt it was all under ye jurisdiction of y Govr. of ye Massachusetts whose residence is in Boston." MacSparran remonstrates with Edmund's successor, "But, my Lord, New-England contains diverse colonys, of different constitutions." He points out that while the Governor of Massachusetts is Crown-appointed that the one in Rhode Island is chosen by "ye Freemen."

Near the beginning of Edmund's lordship, MacSparran had remonstrated with him for allowing disturbances in the Boston church, for "Boston, my Lord, is a large and populous place and the Mistress of North America; Disturbances therefore in ye Church there must be of very prejudicial consequence to us in ye country parishes." MacSparran is sure that dealing with the internal dissension in the Boston church will "give no future encouragement . . . to any to put ye Dissenters on a level with, much less above ye church of England here." [11]

Candidates for the priesthood had to travel across the ocean to be ordained. In a petition addressed in 1725 to the Society in which the rectors of Providence, Narragansett, and Newport joined with others in urging the appointment of a bishop for the colonies, it is pointed out that it would win over "useful ministers whom the hazards of the seas & sickness & the charges of travel discourage from the Service of the Church, & tempt them to inlist themselves as members or Ministers of Dissenting Congregations."

The weather on dry land also proved difficult for the faint of heart. William Guy of Narragansett wrote in 1718:

"The only season of the year I can best be spared from the Church of Narragansett there being in this Country two or three months at least wherein the Congregation can't meet together publicly to hear the Word of God by reason of the extream cold and snow in the winter." [12]

The lack of any local appraisal of the fitness of a candidate for the priesthood led to frequent ordinations of unqualified men. Providence suffered from such early leadership. One of its first rectors became absent-minded about his possession of a wife and was ready to take another when he was reminded of the fact in the nick of time. Sometimes a little ignorance about a candidate's past worked for good, as in the case of Dr. MacSparran, whose Bristol reputation was of such a nature that the ecclesiastical council of elders and messengers of the county association advised the Congregational Church of Bristol not to ordain him. Whatever the truth in the serious charges against him, James seems to have thoroughly reformed and lives in history as one of the most interesting clerical figures of Rhode Island.

The Rhode Island churches seemed to take leadership in the demands for a bishop.[13]

Some encouragement was received, for Honyman writes in November, 1725:

> By the last ships from London we had some pleasant intimations of two Bishops being appointed for America, which has (in a manner) given new life to our people and it would be of a sad consideration to have their expectations frustrated.

In the same letter he tells of further campaigns against the Church of England by the *Independent Whig*. It "is extremely admired by all sorts of Dissenters, and in a particular manner by the Quakers."

Actually when these letters were written, the first American Bishop, Samuel Seabury, would not be born for four years. His mother and Mrs. MacSparran were cousins. It would be nearly sixty years after Honyman heard the "pleasant intimations" before the defenses of the Puritans were sufficiently lowered to make it feasible for the establishment of Old England to have a bishop in New England.

Indeed the early opposition was to more than a bishop. It was to the sending into Massachusetts and Connecticut of missionaries by the Society for the Propagation of the Gospel. In 1734 the Hampshire County (Massachusetts) association of ministers, with William Williams as moderator and Jonathan Edwards as scribe, addressed a petition to the Bishop of London. Its well-chosen phrases would indicate that the man who was in another decade to be recognized as America's greatest theologian had composed it. After due humility in address is displayed, the petition desires to acquaint his Lordship with the state of religion in Massachusetts and Connecticut that "you may be sensible that the sending of Missionarys hither does not answer the good & noble professed Design of the Royal Charter of the Society for the Propagating the Gospel in foreign parts, nor, as we suppose, of many of the generous Don^{rs} to that Society, and that they are neither necessary nor profitable, but as to many instances, rather injurious to the Intrests of the Kingdom of Christ & ye good of his Maj^{tys} Subjects in these parts." [14]

There follows a most enlightening statement of the practice of the New England church. It is orthodox, "consenting to & receiving all ye Doctrinal Articles of the Established Church of England" and yet independent "nor dare we call any man upon the Earth our Father or Master."

"It is o^{r} Civil Constitution, that every town in the Province shall be provided with a learned & orthodox Minister . . . We take care that the doors of our Churches be opened to all persons of competent knowledge in the Doctrines of the Christian Religion & who are of a regular conversation."

There then follows a complete condemnation of the methods of the missionaries as they disturb this well-ordered Zion:

4. The Missionarys that come among us shew a very uncharitable & unchristian spirit, partic^{ly} insinuating that our Ministry is no Ministry, not having had Episcopal Ordination, and that so all our

administrations are null & invalid, and that our Churches are no Churches of Christ, and that o^{r} people are to be looked on as strangers to ye Commonwealth of Israel—— A Tenet or Principle which came from Rome, and which in years past has bin disclaimed in England, & is stil by all ye other Reformed Churches in Europe; as also by their endeavours to render ye Governm^{t}. of o^{r} Churches insignificant, by receiving into their Communion & protection, such as lye open to or are under censure in them for immoral behaviour

5. Which things tend to breed disorder & confusion in our Churches, by cherishing a small number of disaffected persons in several places to the ill example of a whole town, produces, wranglings, strifes, ill names, needless disputations, instead of Godly Edifying, and tends to lead men to place Religion rather in some external observations & ceremonies than in love to God & our neighbor & in a life of Faith Repentance & Holiness——

6. We cannot but look upon it as a great Injustice, it having bin often openly declared to the world that o^{r} Fathers left their Native Land & at a vast expense purchased & subdued a wilderness, that they might in a place of their own serve God according to their consciences in peace, without giving offence to the then governing Powers, a liberty which we account dearer than any temporal interest whatever, which some Missionarys have endeavoured to wrest from us, partly by setting themselves to lay blocks in the way of our having Synods convened for the reforming such evils as have a threatning aspect upon us.

And we have reason to fear that ye prospect of a better Salary than what o^{r} Ministers generally have, (which is not, unless in some great^{r}. towns, forty pounds sterl! per annum, as o^{r} Bills are now sunk) has bin ye great inducement to some of o^{r} young men to go over to receive Orders – tho' we would not take upon us to judge mens' hearts.

But heartily wish that yr Lordship & the Honble Society might not be misled, in those weighty affairs, and that ye Missionarys might have the worthy visions of carrying the Gospel among the miserable Heathen who have not known the way of Life or to such parts of his Maj^{tys} Dominions where Ignorance & Errour have prevailed and have no provision made for them.

Relying on y^{r} Lordships candour & assuring you that we have not any personal views nor interest that has moved us thus to address you, but from a real desire that ye Donations from ye Honble Society in their sever^{l} Missions may not be misapplied & from a sincere regard to the peace & prosperity of o^{r} Churches.

We are
Yr Lordships
most humble Servants
William Williams Mod^{r}.
In the name of the Associated Ministers
of the County of Hampshire

Jonathan Edwards Scribe
Hatfield. Septr. 1734.

While we do not find internal opposition to the coming of Episcopal churches to Rhode Island, the churches themselves were conscious of the waging of pamphleteer war against them elsewhere in New England. MacSparran writes in 1749, "I am sure it behooves us, to be greatly on our guard, among an Enemy, yt so closely watch our steps; and are ready to enter at every opening. That published by Nehemiah Hobart [had the] assistance of the ablest hands among the Independent Teachers . . . As it is hazardous provoking of Hornets . . . I am confirmed in this opinion yt the Church gains most by easy & soft Measures."

But Rhode Island, with its law against taxing for ministerial support and its tradition for unsalaried laymen-parsons, dealt a financial problem to both establishments.

Dr. MacSparran's temporal affairs were further plagued by a long litigation over the church lands of Narragansett. Some three hundred acres had been given "many years ago to ye Minister." To which establishment did they belong, Congregational or Episcopalian? After thirty years in and out of the courts, the petition of James MacSparran to the effect that he was the minister to receive them was denied. In 1752 he writes, "The Dissenters were so elevated at their success that the earliest advice I had of the fate of my cause, was from the publick news papers printed at Boston."

In Providence it was the enterprise of the Congregationalists which spurred the Episcopalians to cultivate this stronghold of Baptist-Quaker interests. They had an able layman at hand, Gabriel Bernon, French Huguenot, who had made his way from Boston to Newport and thence to Providence. Here he became an enterprising and prosperous merchant and a leading churchman. With the help of his friends, James Honyman, Rector of Trinity, Newport, and Dr. MacSparran of the Narragansett church and the Society for the Propagation of the Gospel in Foreign Parts, King's Church was begun in 1722.

It would become the first "steeple-house" in town and was described as "neat and pretty." The drawings of it bear this statement out. The present St. John's replaced this first house in 1810 on the same site. For the Society for the Propagation of the Gospel in Foreign Parts it was the true beginning of religion in Providence. Dr. Humfries of the Society wrote:

> The people were negligent of all religion until about the year 1722; the very best were such as called themselves Baptists or Quakers, but it was feared many were Gortoneans or Deists.

The doctor was not informed that religion in Providence had expressed itself in debate rather than carpentry. Had the leaders of the two establishments recognized this underlying quality of the religious life of Providence, they would have approached the situation with more understanding and come off with fewer burnt fingers.

King's Church would not have been built as soon had the feeling of competition between the established church of New England and the established church of Old England not been strong.

On September 25, 1721, James Honyman wrote from Newport to Gabriel Bernon:

> I am very sensible the Presbyterians are very forward and earnest

in their applications and endeavours of having their worship established among the people of your town;

The following June, just as Dr. Hoyle was arranging the land deal, Gabriel sounded his trumpet of warning to James Honyman:

The gentlemen, Minister and Presbytery of the government of Boston and Connecticut are very busy to promote and advance their cause, and preferred to build their meeting in our said town. If they are for the glory of God in Heaven, peace in earth, good will amongst men, they should agree with the Church of England or give a good reason for their separation from the Church of England as the Church of England gives for their separation from Popery.[15]

The Congregational overture of the three ministers aroused Bernon to see possibilities that its addressees and others would become stanch Episcopalians. On September 21, 1722, he writes James Honyman:

It is necessary to consider with all wisdom, that we have in our town, learned men that make their application to read the Holy Scriptures and are very well able to give an account of their faith, for instance;
Mr. Jink, our Lieutenant Governor, by his answer to William Wilkinson, the greatest preacher among the Quakers, and Mr. Samuel Wilkinson the old man, deserves dignity for his erudition in divine and civil law, historical narrative, natural and politic; and you may see by the letters of Messrs. Jonathan Spreague, Richard Waterman, Harris and several gentlemen, by their answers to Messrs. John Danforth, Peter Tacher, Joseph Belcher ministers commissioned of the Association of Presbyterian Ministry, gentlemen of New England.[16]

November 7, 1722, a petition was addressed to the Lord Bishop of London for a missionary to Providence. But it was not signed by any of those whom Gabriel had seen as good prospects for the Church of England. The picture which the petition draws of religion in Providence in 1722 is accurate except in the intimation that it gives that people are particularly aroused over the various and diverse ordering of religious concernments. It had been the normal atmosphere for nearly a century.

Providence in the Colony of Rhode Island America
Novr. 7th 1722

We are may it please your Lordship, a very considerable number of people in this Town, but as sheep without a shepherd, hearing different voices of Lo here, and Lo there, and in constant danger of being deluged in the floods of Schisms and Heresies, nay of Atheism and Deism, that everywhere exceedingly prevail; and we being very sensible that our Souls and their Salvation, are of the last consequences unto us, we are extreamly willing to put them under the conduct of a faithful Guide, who may instruct and build us up in the most Holy Faith of the Established Church of England: and therefore most earnestly beseech your Lordship to commission for us a Gentleman of piety and learning, who under the Divine Influence will be capable of doing very great services for the Interests of Religion which at present are very much mistaken, lie languishing, or neglected amongst us, and on our part we promise him the kindest reception in our power, and our utmost endeavours to make his life comfortable, and his Ministry successfull. It is indeed a most sad truth, that we are not able to support a Minister according to the dignity of his character, and therefore we earnestly intreat your Lordship to become a charitable Intercessor for us with the Honble Society for the propagation of the Gospel in Foreign Parts, that we may be made the objects of their compassion, by adopting our Minister as their Missionary, and assisting him in his First Services for our Infant Church.

A footnote endorsing the petition is made by James Honyman:

My Lord,

Nothing can be more sincere and just than this peoples representation of their unhappy condition without a Minister, and it is humbly hoped and earnestly desired by all that wish well the Church in these parts, that your Lordship will be pleased to express your compassionate concern for their pitiable circumstances by sending them a Missionary as soon as may be.

I am my Lord
Your Lordships most dutiful
Servant JAMES HONYMAN [17]

Twenty-seven names are signed and the last one is "Danll Abbot." Daniel apparently felt that varieties of religion were good for a town. He would sponsor at least three different churches.

By April of 1724 things have gone too far to keep the Congregationalists out and there is nothing left to do but to hope they will not prosper. Gabriel writes to the "home office" in London:

The gentlemen Presbyterian ministers are very busy and urgent to come into our town of Providence to preach; they come often, from Massachusetts and Connecticut governments, to solicit us to be our ministers and they have sent us several letters; they did raise a meeting house the other side of our river, to their charge and cost,—that they have pulled down to build a big and greater, on our side of our river that is not finished, so they preach in any house where they can, and, for all that, they get but little ground.[18]

This last letter would indicate that the two religious groups had come off about even in honors. The Congregationalists had apparently organized a little earlier. But the Church of England had its building begun late in 1722 and a pastor settled in 1723.[19]

The traditional date for the Congregational meetinghouse at the head of Presbyterian Lane is 1723, but its completion seems to have bogged down and it was not used until after April, 1724. Its sponsors must have been tempted to wish they had built on the doctor's lot across the "Greate Bridge." They missed his money-raising activities.

History seemed to want to make sure that the experiment in

Freedom had its roots deep down before it should be exposed to the storms of opposition from the older organized forms of religion and society. Almost a century was given it in Providence, with hardly any outside interference. But now the issue was joined between three forces: Plantations individualism, the New England Way, and the Church of England. Each would modify the other, sometimes after the manner of yeast, other times as hammer and anvil. Nearly another century would be needed to work out the synthesis and to produce at the head of Narragansett Bay a community which embodied the fruits of the Lively Experiment.

CHAPTER THREE

A HARVARD SHEPHERD FOR PROVIDENCE SHEEP

A NEW set of godfathers was chosen for the Congregationalists' second building venture at the top of Presbyterian Lane. There was only one holdover from the trustees of "Dr. Hoyle's" church. This was good John Greenwood of "Rehobeth" who could be counted on to help, no matter where the physical church should wander. Mr. Baxter of Medfield was the freshman on the list. The most important name was that of Nathaniel Cotton, of Bristol (then in Massachusetts) who could not longer be overlooked, youth or no youth. He had led the revolt against Dr. Hoyle's purchase and now with that money sunk in a "buring ground" he came forth and furnished the thirty pounds for Daniel Abbott's lot. These three parsons with their oldest deacon successors were designated as "feeoffees." The deacons are not named. Samuel Newman was probably the senior deacon at Rehoboth, which would retain the blessing of that ancient name. The new location had once been the site of Chad Brown's burial place, the first minister of the Baptists. The antiquity of a founding father's last resting place might serve to give prestige to late-starting Congregationalism in Providence.

Later, as this little group which became the founders of the First Congregational Church looked back on their beginnings in the New England Way, they would remember 1720 as the year when they first felt themselves to be an united congregation.

For eight years thereafter they continued to meet without formal organization or a permanently settled pastor. After Thomas Greenwood's death, Nathaniel Cotton, John Greenwood, and others met with them to lead them in worship and to instruct them in the Congregational persuasion. Before the meetinghouse was finished in 1724 they met at houses, often in "Cap. Abbot's Chamber" at the foot of the hill.

A happy and hopeful interlude came in 1727, when Parson Samuel Moody of York, Maine, tarried with them awhile. He had visited the little company several times. March 7, 1725, he baptized Elnathan Brown, Margaret Bagly, and Mary Calender. Samuel Moody was "so well approved of by the people in general that the Society afterwards sent a messenger to York to treat with him and his people upon the affair of his removal to Providence. But his people could not be persuaded to part with him and he thought he could not be justified in breaking away from them; at the same time they consented that he might go and preach with them at providence three months, which he did to very great acceptance." These three months were in the summer of 1727, when he baptized nearly a score of Hunters, Smiths, Laurances, Hopkins, Churches, and Potters. Most of these were children, a few adults.

It was indeed a labor of love to leave the breezes of York in the summer time, but the traveling would be better. He had served the York church for twenty-nine years when the Providence messenger came to fetch him away. For many parishes and ministers it would have seemed like the messenger of the Lord and a true intervention of Providence, but not for York and its parson. York would not be York without Samuel Moody, his able mind, his love for the people, and his delightful eccentricities.

Once he tried to imitate his son-in-law, Mr. Emerson, the minister of Malden, by writing out an elegant sermon instead of preaching in a "scattering manner." Halfway through the written discourse he became weary and stopped, saying to the congregation, who had been enthusiastic over his son-in-law's preaching, "Emerson must be Emerson, and Moody must be Moody. I feel as if I had my head in a bag. You can call Moody a rambling preacher, and it is true enough; but his preaching will do to catch up rambling sinners—you are all runaways from the Lord."

But frequently after a sermon he did commit himself to paper to the extent that we know the subject of his best sermons which he would have trotted out for his Providence sojourn. They were: *The vain youth summoned to appear at Christ's bar; The doleful state of the damned; Judas the Traitor hung up in chains to give warning to professors; A summary account of the life and death of Joseph Quasson, an Indian; A sermon on the way to get out of debt and the way to keep out of debt.*

Perhaps it was on the basis of the last sermon that the messenger of the little company in its "infant state" struggling to make a go of church finances was dispatched to Maine.

Mr. Moody had a way with those who slept in church on a hot summer's day. One time he stopped and called, "Fire, Fire, Fire." One man, waking out of a particularly sound sleep, asked in the utmost consternation, "Where is the fire?" "In hell, for sleepy sinners," came the answer.

During all his long ministry at York he refused a stated salary, depending upon voluntary gifts and offerings, many of which would come in the nick of time and seemed divinely sent.[1] In this respect he would have appealed to Providence Congregationalists, whose first century of existence was marked by many problems in meeting the parson's salary.

Mr. Moody loved the little company at the head of the Narragansett and they him. He would visit them several times through the years ahead. His last visit was in 1739. York might seem to be a more exciting life to him for there they carried muskets to church, never forgetting the Indian attack of 1690, which wiped out the town and in which the minister was shot dead. After the great decision was made to stay in York, he could sit back and enjoy Maine coast breezes and Maine clam chowder. For Maine people there is only one way to honor the lowly clam when he inhabits a chowder. Samuel was horrified at the unorthodoxy and nonconformity of Rhode Island chowder habits.

With Mr. Moody's refusal, the church in 1728 called as its first minister Josiah Cotton, younger brother of Nathaniel, the minister at Bristol and a trustee of the church property. They were great-grandsons of John Cotton, Boston's first minister, who had failed to welcome Roger Williams as an assistant.

Josiah had graduated from Harvard in 1722 and would thus become the first college graduate to preach as a settled minister in Providence, since Roger Williams had washed his hands of preaching ninety years before. In 1723 Josiah had gone to Rehoboth to keep school at forty-five pounds a year.[2] Here he would meet another trustee of the Providence church property, John Greenwood. That he was a youth of great promise for the ministry would not seem too evident, as he was within reach for six years before Daniel Abbott and Jabez Bowen were instructed to "repair to (Josiah Cotton) and acquaint him with the vote and pray his answer." This was on May 15, 1728, and Josiah said, "Yes," on August 29, 1728. One wonders how much the energetic guiding of the flock by brother Nathaniel may have figured in the call of Josiah.

On October 23, 1728, a great day arrived which would crown the efforts of the last eight years. The church was "gathered and constituted" and its first minister ordained. Twenty-three Congregational churches were invited to be present with pastor and messengers; eighteen came. Josiah Cotton tells the details: "We sent to twenty-three Churches: viz To the Seven United

Churches in Boston, and to two In ys Colony (both at Newport), to one In Coneticut and to thirteen In the Massachusetts Bay: eighteen of which were on the spot, assisting in the Ordination, With their Reverend Elders and Messengers, and of the Band-Men there were supposed to be near forty, Besides many Candidates for the Ministry etc. The like to which as to Ministers and Churches for ye Numbers and possibly too for ye populace, this North America never saw." We cannot discover what the Band-Men were, unless they were other ministers not of the council and so called for their clerical dress with the white bands at the collar.

The *Boston Weekly News Letter* estimated the attendance at a thousand people. Why the crowd? Such occasions always drew goodly numbers, but this one in Providence was of especial significance. At last the New England Way was to be firmly established with church and teacher in Providence Plantations. Field says, "The quiet introduction of Congregationalism into Kingston and Newport might be considered an illustration of the truth that 'the Kingdom of God cometh not with observation.' But the advent of the order in Providence was to a large degree a demonstration." There must have been humble rejoicing on the part of the visitors, some muffled grumbling from Jonathan Spreague and his friends, but externally the whole affair passed off in great good spirit. The *News Letter* itself from its safe perch in Boston struck the only recorded smug note:

The Elders and Messengers were very civilly treated and were entertained not only by those of our own persuasion but of every denomination also and it is to be hoped that prejudice and enmity will cease among you and Religion and good neighborhood prevail and flourish.[3]

It is to be hoped that Providence citizens paid as little attention to Boston news as they do today and that they did not see this "foreign missionary" attitude in print. The wish, however, was realized, for from this date the right of intruding Congregationalists to be among those present was never raised by those whose grandsires had crossed the Seekonk to escape the forebears of Josiah Cotton. One of Rhode Island's proudest boasts is found in Edward Field's history: ". . . from Rhode Island no protesting colony ever went forth. In her the spirit of ecclesiastical revolt attained its equilibrium." But we should add to the quotation the word "eventually."[4]

Josiah Cotton gives the details of his ordination, written when he was still excited or a little tired from the great event:

My Eldest Brother John Cotton Began the meeting with Prayer: (I might have first said yt before we went to meeting the Reverend Baxter did in Cap. Abbot's Chamber open the Council by Prayer: Thirteen Churches with yr Elders and Messengers being actually present, at which time the Reverend Baxter (being our Moderator) was unanimously Chosen to give me the Charge, and the Reverend White to give me the Right hand of Fellowship, and severall others to lay on hands, &c.) Then The Reverend Appleton preached from 6: Isaiah: 8: After Sermon was over, the Reverend Prince Embodied Our church; we each of us Pastor and Church mutually renewing of our Call and Answer to and accepting of each Other: yn the Reverend Baxter (after yr appearing no one to bar our proceedings) gave me the Charge, And the Reverend White the Right hand of Fellowship: Those that imposed the hands of the Presbytery were The Reverend Baxter, Eells, White, Prince, Cotton, And Appleton: The Reverend Eells concluded with prayer. (I might have said (in its place) that the Reverend Baxter did pray both before and after his charge to me.) Then I appointed the last part of the 118 Psalm to be sung and to itt I added the Gloria Patri extempore. And then we concluded all by my pronouncing the Divine Blessing: And all the Council resorted to the house and great chamber of Cap Daniel Abbott: Where they had prepared for them a very Sumptuous Dinner, And I served the Table, &c.

The Reverend Baxter[5] of Medfield was one of the trustees.

The Reverend Prince was Thomas Prince, the colleague minister of Old South, Boston, more famous as a historian of the New England church scene. Subsequently he would have much to do with the Great Awakening, which would split in twain this church which he was this day embodying. We do not know whether my "Eldest Brother John Cotton" was the John Cotton who was minister at Newton at this time or another John Cotton who was minister at Halifax a decade later. There was also a Ward Cotton, minister at Hampton, N. H. He may have been a brother, as in one place Josiah speaks of "my frater W. C." The one flaw in the great day was brother Nathaniel's absence. He may well have been unable to come, for he died the following year at the age of thirty-two.

The sermon by Rev. Nathaniel Appleton, D.D. was published. Dr. Appleton was the minister of the Cambridge church. At this ordination Increase Mather and Cotton Mather had taken part. He and Increase Mather were the only ones in one hundred and thirty years to receive a Doctor of Divinity degree from Harvard. He served that institution for sixty-one years as a Fellow.

The sumptuous dinner at Cap Abbott's was by no means the least feature of the day. From his "distil-house" on the parade he would be able to bring reviving refreshment for any so minded. The large company would have to be entertained overnight. Homes of many besides the adherents of the new church would open their doors to this distinguished company of Elders, Messengers [6] and Band-Men.

With the excitement over, Josiah Cotton still felt its lasting impression and wrote:

And oh That I may ever more keep itt in the Imaginations of the Thoughts of my heart The awfulness the weight and the Moment of this most Arduous Work In which I'm engaged; and Particularly of the most solemn and tremendous charge that has now been laid upon me and I wish to God that I may so preach Christ to others as not to prove a cast-away myself but may save both you and me. Amen.

Not only had Josiah been ordained but the church had been formally constituted by nine males. They were: Cornelius Salisbury; Nathaniel Blague; William Randall; Joseph Bagley; Timothy Carpenter; Joseph Barstow; John Church; Thomas Pollok; and John Taylor.

Of these nine none figure largely in the history of either the mother or daughter churches. The first deacons were Joseph Bagley and Timothy Carpenter.

There followed a dozen years of reasonable peace and tranquillity and some prosperity in the life of the little church. A great many children were baptized. Here both the newly arrived Episcopalians and Congregationalists would do a rather flourishing business because there would have been many in the colony without antipedobaptist traditions, who were forced to neglect this rite.

Josiah kept accounts of the communion offering and expenses: September, 1729, "Our Disbursement this day 4S. and the Contribution was 9/9." A year later the net profit was better. "Disbursement was 4/8 and our contribution was 14/2." A collection under four dollars would make the tithingman a misnomer for even a poverty-stricken congregation, and not all the worshipers on the hill were poor.

A little charitable endeavor is recorded in 1732:

2 April 1732
We had in our Little Flock a Contribution for Mr. Cole of Swanzey, who had his house burnt down with fire and we gathered for him Three pounds, four shillings.

9 April 1732
We had another for Mr. Luther of the same town and under the same circumstance, and gathered Two pounds, Six and six pence.

N.G. These two were the first and only gatherings that were ever in our assembly and possibly the first in the Town and County of Providence, if not in the Colony of Rhode Island and Providence Plantations; Oh Mirum sane!

Here begins that philanthropic note which is one of the great heritages of Providence churches and people. They have always responded well to the needs of those in distress. Possibly Josiah wished they would do as well by their servant, the pastor.

The next Sabbath after Mr. Cotton's settlement it was decided that the Old Testament should be read at the forenoon service and "in the afternoon out of the New Testament." A typical service conducted by a Harvard trained parson at this time has been described from a Boston church:

After the deacons had taken their places beneath the high pulpit, the minister in his black gown and white bands, accompanied by his wife and children, walked majestically up the aisle. Then was heard the clatter of many feet as the minister's entrance was the signal for the men and boys to enter (the females already having taken their seats).

The tithingman took his place among the boys in the gallery, his long pole in hand, the Sexton tiptoed to the pulpit stairs. Then the Parson rose and read two lines of a Psalm and the deacon stepped forward and repeated them. The precentor set the tune and the people sang. Then followed the long prayer, the expounding of the scripture and the preaching of the sermon. The benediction having been said, there was a moment's pause, then the minister descended from the pulpit, took his wife by the arm, and followed by his children, proceeded down the aisle, the people respectfully bowing.[7]

The Providence church in its official acts seems to have modeled itself upon the New England Way as generally practiced. On November 9, 1729,

Phineas Fisk desire of owning the Covenant in order to the Baptism of his child was propounded and accordingly November 30 John the son of Phineas and Mary Fisk was Baptized.

This was in accord with the principle of the halfway covenant. It had a particular usage in Massachusetts in giving voting rights in church and civic affairs to those who would not come into the stricter communion of the church. It also gave them the right of having their children baptized. This latter application of the halfway covenant was used in the Providence church. The possession of one believing parent was sufficient, as in the case of "Mercy, the Daughter of Elisha and Mercy Hopkins of Providence was baptized on its Mother's account . . . Deacon Joseph Bagley held up the Babe."

The little church was happily without caste save that of doctrine. January, 1730, "was propunded to Baptism, Elizabeth, the Servant child of Margaret Betty (whose Father was a negro and Mother a White woman)." Indians and Negroes frequently appeared on the list of those "propunded." On the occasion of admitting the "negro, woman-servant of Colonel Jabez Bowen, and Hanna Newfield, a free Indian woman," Josiah preached from Acts 10, 34-5, "God is no respecter of persons but in every nation he that feareth him and worketh righteousness is accepted of him."

Problems of discipline arose early in the life of the church. Elizabeth Anthony, alias Jack, an Indian woman, had stood propounded a fortnight before being taken into the church, but it was not quite long enough, for she strayed from the path and returned to her cups.

Occasionally Josiah Cotton preached and baptized in other communities, Newport, Rehoboth, Scituate, and as far afield as Arrowsic on "Keenabeck River" in the province of Maine.

And so the early years of the first Congregational church in Providence were spent as the years of most churches are spent, trying to make the wicked reform, urging the good to remain good and to grow in grace, mending the roof, interpreting the word of God, choosing wisely and not so wisely the leaders of the church, and attempting to manage without money and without price. It was the first Congregational church in New England which tried to do all the things a church should, without benefit of taxation and the prestige of an ecclesiastical establishment. As with all ministers Josiah was sometimes up and sometimes down, alternating between great hope and discouragement. But in his worst moments of discouragement he did not anticipate the rough sailing which was immediately ahead.

CHAPTER FOUR

PRESBYTERIAN LANE AND THE NEW ENGLAND WAY

For a few pages, let us leave Josiah Cotton and his flock to the peace which was theirs for the first dozen years in the meeting-house at the head of Presbyterian Lane and try to answer the question which must have already confused us. Why did they call it "Presbyterian Lane" when at its head stood a Congregational church? Why as late as 1836 were the Congregational churches on the West Side in Providence still commonly called Presbyterian churches? The "Congregational or Presbetarian way" appears in the Dr. Hoyle deed and the two names are frequently used interchangeably.

A surface fact which explains some of the confusion for us is that denominationalism as we know it today did not then exist. There were no high-powered executives in metropolitan office buildings to remind their constituencies that it was important to be a certain kind of Christian. In the United States today one might say he was a liberal, a progressive, or a conservative without thinking in terms of a particular political party, or even remembering that in England and at other times in the United States these connoted definite party allegiance. So for those not too close to the Old World founders of Presbyterianism and Congregationalism, these religious handles were unassociated with strict historical interpretation.

In the letter to the Bishop of London from Jonathan Edwards

quoted earlier, there is the assumption that the New England church is as much the Church of England as that over which the bishop presides.

But behind the names there was deep historical significance which, in popular use, was forgotten by the New England populace, because in coming to America the situations and debates which gave rise to their use were circumvented for nearly a century. In England there were many reform groups in the sixteenth century. The largest body was the Puritans who wished for the reform of the existing church structure along the lines of the Scottish Church. The more extreme reformers were the Separatists who saw no reform adequate because the fundamental structure of the church was false, being inclusive rather than *gathered,* and governed by a hierarchy rather than the congregation.

Of great importance was a middle group which has received particular study by Perry Miller in his Ph.D. thesis at the University of Chicago.[1]

Dr. Miller points out that some of the strongest Puritan-Presbyterians became convinced of the fundamental soundness of the Congregational principles of Separatism. Some were converted, as for example Henry James, as they nagged the Separatists who were imprisoned in the Clink. Searching the New Testament for ammunition to be used against the Separatists, James became convinced that the first-century church was Congregationally organized. Others in the group of converts were Robert Parker, William Bradshaw, Paul Baynes and Dr. William Ames. In Presbyterianism, Bradshaw saw "a terrible Popedome and Primacie." All but Dr. Ames had completed their earthly work before the *Mayflower* set sail. Ames died in 1633.

This group was convinced of the rightness of the two chief tenets of Separatist Congregationalism: the restriction of membership to the proved elect and the autonomy of the particular congregation. But being practical churchmen they did not want to wait forever or to submit to persecution before these ideas should be accepted. They tried to find ways to make them fit into a reform of the established church or to coexist beside the established church without resorting to Separatism and the condemnation of the Church of England.

Dr. Miller tells the story of the various devices these non-Separatist Congregationalists tried to employ to make their position logical. The Separatists had held that a church could "not be a true church wherein the elect communicated with the reprobate, ergo, the Church of England was a false church."

This problem had been met by the Presbyterians by distinguishing between "true substance" and "accidents." The Church of England was true in its substance but supported accidents. The accidents were false but not mortal. Dr. Ames held that the non-compulsory and non-prayer book services of the established church recognized the theories of Congregationalism and paid tribute "to its fundamental nature of a true church—congregationally organized."

Again, the insistence on a covenant relationship was met by saying that those who worshiped of their free will belonged to the covenant while those there by constraint did not.

The congregation's right to choose its own minister and leaders was answered by "Mr. Facing-both-ways" in saying that a bishop could nominate, but what made a minister a true minister was his acceptance by the congregation. Polite things were also said about the magistrates: their power was derived from God even when abused.

The great object of all this was to secure recognition from the Crown, as in the petition addressed to King James in 1610. It was felt by this group of non-Separatist Congregationalists that acceptance of the Church of England as a true church with some faults was a small price to pay for recognition as a part of the establishment; it seemed far better than persecution.

Even John Robinson was somewhat persuaded by this expediency as leaders of the movement journeyed to Leyden to convince him of its reasonableness. He wrote, "I did through my vehement desire of peace and weakness withal, remit and lose my former resolution and did to speak the truth, forget some of my former grounds."

King James, who had been a Presbyterian in Scotland and from whom the English Puritans hoped for so much, was unpersuaded and wrote in answer to the petition which expressed Puritan loyalty to his person and respect for his right to oversee the churches, "Quhy then do ye not obey the Kinges lawes that are already maide, quhome ye grawnte to be your supreme magistrate?"

In the reign of Charles, Cotton tells us "that the Separatists were more favored by the authorities than Puritans." Roger Williams, who remained an unreconstructed Separatist, as we have already seen, explained this when he said, "it is a principle in nature to prefer a professed enemy before a pretended friend."

Finally for these non-Separatist Congregationalists, America seemed to offer the solution for their tangled logic of expediency. "Here they could keep the magistrates in line and they could call any church they established part of the Church of England, they could choose their own magistrates and enforce obedience to it."

It is little wonder therefore that outside of Separatist Plymouth, the people of the New England Way were not just sure whether they were Presbyterians or Congregationalists or just a new-world edition of the Church of England.

With no opposing pattern for comparison some of the differences which troubled ecclesiastical life in England for a time disappeared. The problem of the *gathered* versus the parish or community-wide church was settled by the fact that for a few years the *gathered* were the community. Immigration had changed this idealistic setup by the time Roger Williams appeared.

Congregationally governed churches were a "natural" in the wilderness for they were too few in number to require a bishop or to form a powerful Presbyterian synod. The Presbyterian offices of ruling elder and the teaching elder remained in use in the Congregational churches for well over a century, without any thought of following a particular pattern. The councils for ordination and consultation were frequently called synods. Few were as diligent as Roger Williams in ecclesiastical consistency. The few Presbyterian and Anglican marks on the Salem church caused Roger Williams to withdraw; he held it was not a completely separated church. It took as inconsistent an apostle as Roger to be this consistent.

Later in England Independency was to come again into its own, "When the yoke of rigid Presbyterianism seemed falling on England about 1644, Independency sprang into national importance as the system which by contrast with the bonds of episcopacy or of the presbytery was the natural religious home for men of free spirit." [2]

We are indebted to another Ph.D. thesis, that of Paul T. McClurkin, for the clearest picture of what happened as these Old World conflicting ideas came to be worked out on this side of the Atlantic.[3] He makes a particularly helpful contribution in his study of the American background in which these terms, Presbyterian and Congregational, were intertwined.

For the uninitiated the three distinguishing marks of Presbyterianism are the session, the presbytery, and the synod. Each of these is a delegated body having considerable *standing* authority. The session is within the local church, the presbytery is made up of churches within an area, the synod includes several presbyteries.

Dr. McClurkin quotes the Congregational historian, Henry

Dexter, as saying that Massachusetts' Separatism became a "Congregationalized Presbyterianism or a Presbyterianized Congregationalism."

In Newburyport the ministers, Parker and Noyes, attempted to give complete Presbyterian inner government to their church in 1635. It was in part a result of this that the Cambridge Platform was drawn up in 1637 and the Ministerial Convention was held in 1643, which gave recognition to the *council* as an instrument for aiding churches in important matters such as ordination and installation. The important point is that the council was not established as a continuing body but was called intermittently in time of need by the local church.

Early in her establishment Massachusetts almost went Presbyterian. The disenfranchised non-church members caused a remonstrance to be sent to England which, if it had been granted, would have given her Scotland's Presbyterian polity which regarded all as members of the parish, and this in turn would have given everyone the right to vote in town meeting. Cromwell's coming to power in 1647 brought an end to the remonstrance.

Connecticut church government and internal organization was a close duplicate of Massachusetts until the eighteenth century. Then both states attempted to establish the "consociation" form of government which much more approximated Presbyterianism than did the council. People were divided in both places, but in each case the issue was arbitrarily settled by the legislature. In Massachusetts the law-making body was uninterested in the church at that time and turned it down; but in Connecticut the governor was Gurdon Saltonstall, who was a parson. He pushed the matter and the legislature ordered the churches to draw up a new platform. This was done by twelve ministers and four laymen, meeting at Saybrook in 1708.

Back in England the Congregationalists and Presbyterians had come very close together in 1691, adopting as their common ground of Calvinistic faith a slight modification of the Westminster Catechism; at the same time they drew up "Heads of Agreement" on the matter of church government. Against this salubrious background the Saybrook convention adopted the Confession of 1680 (also a slight modification of the Westminster Confession), the heads of the Agreement of 1691, and fifteen new articles, the most important effect of which was to establish "consociations" with considerable power over the affairs of the local church.

As were the presbyteries, the consociations were *standing* councils, composed of a minister and layman from each church. They would handle affairs in the local church which were too much for the congregation, such as cases of extreme discipline. The ministers of the consociation became the licensing body for new ministers. Rhode Island, which much later organized a consociation, still follows this practice in licensing ministers. The more general Congregational practice is to leave this to the association of clergy and laymen.

But even under the Saybrook Platform New England remained New England and the various parts of Connecticut followed their own inclinations. The New Haven Consociation remained pretty much the old council. The Fairfield Consociation became a fully empowered church court.

As both a cause and result of the Saybrook Platform, a close association grew up between Connecticut churches and the Presbyterian groups in the middle colonies, particularly New York and Philadelphia. As early as 1766 and until the Revolution, the two groups joined in annual conventions. One strong uniting motive was to prevent the appointment of an American resident bishop for the Episcopal churches.

Nathan Strong, minister of the First Church in Hartford, called the association of churches in the north of Hartford the

"North Presbytery" and in 1805 the General Association in Connecticut speaks of the "Presbyterian *Church* in Connecticut." Congregationalists were sticklers for the term *churches* as opposed to *church*. In 1799 the Hartford group boasts that all but twelve of the churches in Connecticut are Presbyterian. Dr. McClurkin points out that this was overenthusiasm, as none of the churches seemed to have had the inner organization of the session.

In 1801 there was drawn up the since much debated "Plan of Union" by which the Connecticut churches and the Presbyterian synods would work together in the mission fields west of the Hudson, each giving ministerial standing to ministers of the other body in their respective conferences. Church historians on both sides seem to agree that the more loosely organized Congregationalists lost their shirts as a result of the bargain; perhaps the Kingdom profited. The practical effect was to leave New England in the nineteenth century predominantly Congregational and the states immediately south and west predominantly Presbyterian.

By the middle of the nineteenth century the power of the consociation waned in Connecticut. It was attacked especially by the New Light movement which, peculiarly enough, was fired in Windham County and elsewhere by Presbyterian evangelists from the middle colonies. New England independency reasserted itself. Even Fairfield Consociation renounced its power as a court. The Cambridge and Saybrook platforms were gradually forgotten. Still later (middle of the nineteenth century) Congregationalism in New England began to feel a self-consciousness under the dynamic leadership of Leonard Bacon of New Haven and Henry Dexter of Boston. They brought unity out of its overloose organization.

In both Connecticut and Massachusetts there had been at the other extreme independent churches which would come into neither councils nor consociations. There were likewise a handful of genuine Scotch-Irish Presbyterian churches established in both colonies.

In 1802 Timothy Dwight of Yale, counting steeples, says that in Worcester County, Massachusetts, there are "two Presbyterian churches in the proper sense and fifty-four Congregational or Presbyterian churches in the New England sense." Dwight quotes an English traveler (Volney) as saying of Marlborough, "The inhabitants are nearly all congregationalists. This denomination of Christians practise a form of worship that easily reconciles the Presbyterian and Episcopalian to meet in one church. It is in some sort a relaxed Presbyterian service."

James Wilson, minister of Beneficent Church in Providence, wrote in 1835 at the age of seventy-five, "Strongly attached to the order in which I still hold a Standing, having frequently acted in their Ecclesiastical Councils, and still oftener in their Associations—[I have been] ever opposed to Consociations, as destructive of the rights of the Churches."

As a result Beneficent Church was the last church in the state to join the Rhode Island Consociation, nearly twenty years after the death of Wilson.[4]

As far as Providence Plantations is concerned there was never any conscious attempt to introduce Presbyterian government into the churches of the New England Way. The strongest battles for Congregationalism were waged against dominating personalities rather than church polity.

Different names seem popular at different times. James MacSparran in 1751 writes of the "Independents or Presbyterians as they now chose to call themselves." The name did not matter much in that period. Doctrines and personalities loomed large. Denominational handles would have small significance in the eighteenth and early nineteenth centuries. In contemporary manuscripts the two words were seldom honored by capitalizing. This was true of all denominational labels which would one day loom too large.

For all practical purposes when the word "presbyterian" appears in eighteenth-century Plantations history it means "congregational."

CHAPTER FIVE

RETURN OF THE NATIVE'S GRANDCHILDREN

FEW men have added more to a town's history by the simple expedient of walking out for two generations than did the son of one of its founders. John Field II upped stakes and pulled out of Roger Williams' settlement the year after King Philip's disastrous visit in 1676. His father, John I,[1] had settled in Providence the same year Roger Williams planted the colony. He is the third signer of the agreement of the "second comers" to submit to orders for the public good "only in civil things." His name appears in all the early agreements and changes in town and colonial government.

In the King Philip's War which burned Providence in 1676, John Field I and his son John were probably among the large majority who accepted the hospitality of Newport and Portsmouth. Only twenty-eight out of a probable two hundred men "stayed and went not away" in an endeavor to defend the town. Zachariah Field, brother of John II, was among these.

The future of the decimated town must have looked dubious to those who straggled back from the island Aquidneck. Thirty houses had been burned. After forty years Roger's Planting seemed at last the flop Bay Colony folks had predicted. Many, finding Newport all that her residents had boasted, had no intention of returning to the poverty of the settlement on the Moshassuc.

John II had married Elizabeth Everenden. They were scarcely twenty and with their future before them may well have asked the question which has always separated the philosophy of the pioneer from the village dweller: "Why repeat our father's struggle when two days' journey away there are settled and safe lands with school and church?" To be sure in Bridgewater you breathed the less free air of Massachusetts, but sometimes it seemed as if Roger Williams' freedom did not add up to much in the way of crops or culture. John's father had not been able to sign his name; John planned better things for his and Elizabeth's children.[2]

With the Fields once settled in Bridgewater there was eagerness for news from the Plantations. John's father, John, and brother, Zachariah, died in the early nineties. Zachariah left a family of five sons. John deeded over his share of their father's land to the widow, Sarah, in trust for the boys. Zachariah before his death had a taxable estate of one horse, two oxen, two cows, four heifers, thirty sheep, one hog, eight acres in fence, eight acres of homeland, of which one was orchard, two worn out and two in planting, and four of meadow. This, with the father's bequest and brother's gift, left a good heritage for his widow and five sons. But Sarah was a poor manager; the property started melting away. She was soon relieved of the trusteeship, which was given to John Thornton, who managed things well not only for the five boys, but, as we shall see, for Zachariah's grandchildren and his generous brother's great-grandchildren. John II was shrewd as well as generous and did not break all ties with the Plantations, retaining title to considerable land out in the wilderness across Weybosset Bridge and down towards Cowpen Point.

John III became known as Captain John Field and was one of Bridgewater's leading citizens. He married Elizabeth Ames, daughter of John Ames, and in turn they had John IV and an Elizabeth.

Over in West Bridgewater there was an ambitious young man by the name of Joseph Snow. He was the son of Joseph and grandson of William Snow who in 1635, at the age of eleven, had come from England with his master, Richard Derby, and landed in Plymouth. In 1638 he was assigned to another master, Edward Doleia (Doten ?). After his seven years' apprenticeship he lived for a while in Duxbury and then became one of the first settlers in West Bridgewater. He married "Rebeckak" Brown, daughter of Peter who came in the *Mayflower*. Among their eight children was Joseph. There would continue to be a succession of Joseph Snows for nearly two centuries. Joseph's wife's name was Hopestill and she probably was a granddaughter of John and Priscilla Alden. Joseph and Hopestill were the parents of the Joseph who now enters the picture. He was born September 7, 1690.

Joseph Snow II was interested in all that was going on, town government and the churches and ministers. He wandered around the countryside and sometimes went over to East Bridgewater. He was well into the twenties and still unmarried when one day over in East Bridgewater he discovered that John Field's daughter, Elizabeth, had grown up and was a beautiful girl. They were married and before Elizabeth's seventeenth birthday she had become the mother of the third Joseph Snow. We shall speak of her husband as Joseph Snow and their son as Joseph Snow, Jr.

The new town of Easton was a set-off of land that had been part of Norton in 1725. Here Joseph and Elizabeth moved with their family. Joseph liked to pioneer, to buy and sell land, to incorporate new towns, to take an active part in church life, and to watch his family increase. He became one of the first selectmen of the new town. Father and mother-in-law, John and Elizabeth Field, were good sorts and helped their daughter and family with sound advice on land and children.

The Easton church was just across the road from the Snow's

homestead with its thirty-three acres of land and goodly barns. Every two years a new baby was taken to the church for Parson Matthew Short to christen. After Joseph, Jr., there were John, Elizabeth, Susanna, Sarah, Daniel, and James. Later there would be Mary and Lydia. The minister had a son who bore his name, Matthew Short. He and the Snow children played together. Sometimes they played wedding and Matthew would be the groom and Susanna the bride, with Joseph, Jr., the minister.

Matthew Short had become minister in 1723. In 1731 at the age of forty-four he died. His widow remarried and Matthew, Jr., bought her right of dower. Mr. Short was followed in the pastorate of the church by Joseph Belcher, nephew of Rev. Joseph Belcher of Dedham, one of the three "who wrote the letter."

The meetinghouse on the eastern edge of the new town was poorly located for the people in the center and on the West Side, but was very favorable for the Snows and their neighbors. West Side folks kept agitating for a new meetinghouse centrally located and finally the town appointed a committee on which was Joseph Snow and with him a hundred per cent group of East Siders. They solemnly reported that if a new meetinghouse were to be built the best location was on its present site. Later the Snows would have an opposite point of view in another east-side, west-side controversy.

On Thanksgiving and other days during the winter, journeys would be made by Joseph and Elizabeth over to Father and Mother Fields. It was always a delight to go there; Joseph liked his father and mother-in-law. Increasingly they spoke in a nostalgic tone of another land, Providence Plantations. They were unlike most of their neighbors in that they had their ancestry in another colony rather than in England. John Field would say with a faraway look in his eye, "Guess Father made a mistake when he walked out on the Plantations; things are happening there, population has tripled in the last thirty years"; and with some underlying scorn for land-bound Bridgewater he would say, "You can sail a vessel from anywhere right up to your front door in Providence." Then Elizabeth would remind John that his father, John, had left Providence because of its churchlessness and its lack of schools. But John would point out that now his cousins John and Zachariah II were reporting that there were three churches and there was talk of schools.

But Joseph Snow had even more information. In all probability he had accompanied his minister, Matthew Short, to the ordination of Josiah Cotton in 1728. Never had he forgotten that great day. It was a worthy ambition to transfer his deaconing from the unhappy Easton church to Josiah Cotton's church, which had had the greatest ordination in North America!

What started out as winter-evening chatter ended with John Field and his wife, Elizabeth, and not long after their daughter Elizabeth Snow and her husband Joseph and children, moving to Providence.

The captain and his family established themselves in their home at the northeast corner of what is now Chestnut and Friendship streets. Their barn was at the southeast corner across the street. By 1732 the Snows had joined them. Joseph sold his thirty-three acres in Easton to the church as a parsonage for the new minister, Joseph Belcher.

In Providence much of the Field holdings lay to the south of the Roade to Pawtuxet (Broad Street). Believing that the town was going to need more room, Father-in-law John urged Joseph Snow to buy neighboring tracts of land with the money he had received from the sale of his Easton property. In April of 1732, Joseph bought from James Arnold "three acres and fifteen poles." This land lies just west of the site of Beneficent Church.

Joseph Snow had a blacksmith shop in Easton. With new houses being built in Providence, it looked as if he might sell newcomers their home sites and then hire out to make the hinges and hardware for their houses. His seventeen-year-old son, Joseph, Jr., was already turning his hand to the "joiner's trade" and would be able to enter into the general scheme of the Snow-Field venture.

Little did Josiah Cotton and his flock dream that a Plantations-shaking chapter of religious history would result from the return of the Fields' grandchildren from Bridgewater and Easton to Providence. This chapter, in which Captain John Field's son-in-law and grandson (the two Joseph Snows) would be chief actors, would change not only the religious but the physical pattern of the community.

Things were going well in the fourth year of Josiah's pastorate and under the date of July 16, 1732, he records:

At a church meeting were voted the 4 following things.

1. The reception of Joseph Snow and Elizabeth, his wife, and him to the office of Deacon.
2. That Deacon Bagley and Eleazer Gibbs with myself, their unworthy Pastor, should be a standing Comitee to dispose Mr. Baxter's 4 practicall pieces.
3. That we would in a short time sing in our church Tate and Brady's Version of the Psalms.
4. That those Bretheren and Sisters that are constantly comuning with us be requested to gett letters of recomondation from their respective Churches whether nearer or farther off.

The second item refers to a gift from London of the works of "the venerable Mr. Richard Baxter" to the church and himself. Books were of enough importance to appoint a whole "comitee" to circulate four volumes. On that day Josiah would have been particularly pleased with the church and himself. They had followed his recommendation on Tate and Brady. He loved the church music and could pitch the Gloria "extempore." Valuable books had been acquired and two new members, real Congregationalists from Massachusetts. Such was their reputation in their letter of dismissal from the Easton church that Mr. Snow was immediately elected deacon.

With the return of the Fields to Providence after an absence of a generation, relationships with their Providence cousins were quickly re-established. The great-grandchildren of John, who had moved away, found the grandchildren of Zachariah, who had "stayed and went not away," good companions. Eventually Elizabeth Snow, daughter of Joseph and Elizabeth, would marry her second cousin once removed, another Captain John Field, on January 12, 1736. Her brother, Joseph, Jr., followed the same scheme and married Captain John's sister, Sarah Field, on November 1, 1737. The young captain died at St. Eustatius in the West Indies two years after his marriage and did not live to see his son, who was christened John by Josiah Cotton. He had served as the captain of the ill-fated ship *Rainbow* owned by James and Obadiah Brown. Obadiah wrote of the *Rainbow* to James, "You have all ways had misfortin in this vessel which maeks me afraid but . . . If I should never venter nothing, I should never have nothing." Elizabeth Snow Field, his widow, might have wished the "venter" of one husband had not been as readily made. The young captain left an estate of 818½ gallons of molasses, 434 gallons of rum, 4 Pistols of Gold and a quarter interest in the sloop *Merigold.*[3]

Thus bread cast upon the water did return for the Bridgewater Fields. It was Joseph Snow Junior's great-grandfather, John Field II, who had given his brother Zachariah's children a part of the original John Field lands when he moved to Bridgewater. Under John Thornton's able administration, much of the property came back to John's great-grandchildren, Elizabeth Snow and Joseph, Jr., by their marriage to Zachariah Field's grandchildren.

Josiah Cotton baptized yet another John Field who was destined to play a major part in Providence church life. His baptism is recorded by Josiah Cotton: "29 April 1733 I baptized Mary the daughter of Deacon Joseph and Elizabeth Snow and also John the son of the Widow Mary Field of Bridgewater which is the grandson of Capt. John Field and his wife Elizabeth of Providence." This John Field became the well-known Deacon John Field of the West Side. His deceased father was a brother of Elizabeth Field Snow, making him and Joseph Snow, Jr., first cousins. Three of Deacon John's daughters would marry Joseph Bowler, Daniel Proud, and Bennett Wheeler.

Even Josiah Cotton must have had difficulty not only in sorting out the many John Fields and progeny but in keeping straight all of the names and faces of the family of his new deacon, Joseph Snow. In addition to seventeen-year-old Joseph, Jr., there were nine others: John, Elizabeth, Susanna, Sarah, Daniel, James, Hannah, Mary and Lydia. Five years later Joseph Junior's marriage to Sarah Field made another Sarah Snow, and many of their children would be named for uncles and aunts on the Field and Snow sides. There would be John, Elizabeth, Susanna, Lydia, Abigail (for their maternal grandmother Field), and of course, another Joseph.

Joseph, Jr., and his bride, Sarah, joined the church in May, 1738. Apparently from the age of seventeen to twenty-three he let his father, Deacon Snow, carry on the family's religious traditions. Their eldest son, John, was baptized March 9, 1740, but not by Josiah Cotton. It was during the "quarter of year when I was detained by reason of Broken Bones etc. Oh! lord Christ." Josiah baptized Lydia and many daughters of Joseph, Sr., and Elizabeth; and for Joseph, Jr., and Sarah he baptized Sarah, Joseph, and a second Joseph named for the older baby who died.

Back in Easton things were lonely for Matthew Short, Jr., whose father had been the Snow's minister and neighbor. Matthew's father had died, his mother moved away, and his boyhood friends in the Snow family had left town. He could not forget Susanna Snow, the deacon's daughter. Her curls and dancing eyes stayed in his mind and increased his loneliness. After nine years he came to Providence in 1741 and married nineteen-year-old Susanna, uniting the son of Easton's former minister and the daughter of her former deacon. Matthew purchased a lot of land on the West Side next his father-in-law's homestead for the goodly price of forty pounds. Here he opened his shop for the manufacture of nails. But the romance so happily consummated had not long to run an earthly course. Susanna died in 1743, probably in childbirth.

The growth of the town in this period is reflected in the records of Josiah's church, written in his own hand. It was the custom in most of the early churches for the minister to serve as clerk. In the Hoyle deed parsons are referred to as "clerk" rather than minister. The older usage of the word is the basis of "clerical." Josiah Cotton had a curious way of keeping the records, writing at first one end of the book and then the other, and numbering the pages from both ends without regard to chronological order. These records were almost lost to posterity by the well-intentioned copying of only the more savory parts into another book. It was done in the 1770's, probably by good Deacon Green, in a beautiful hand on fine watermarked rag paper.

There seems to have been every intent to destroy Josiah's records of the troublesome years, but fortunately they are still in the possession of the First Congregational Church, with only pages one and two at the front and pages one to six at the other end of the book missing, thus saving us from the kindly censorship of Deacon Green. At the same time he enriched us by his fine historical account of the years preceding and following Josiah Cotton's records.

Among the names which Josiah was recording along with the Snows and Fields were John Paine, received into full communion July 6, 1740, Solomon Searle, and Barzillai Richmond, May 3, 1741.

Samuel Tift "of Scituate in this County" who on January 1, 1743, was baptized by total immersion at widow Randall's, "being the first person I ever so baptized, having the consent of the whole Church herein, and then and there preached from 14 Acts 22." The Baptists had not been in business a hundred years for naught.

It was at Joseph Snow, Junior's, where the church meeting was held which voted to immerse Sam Tift of Scituate.

Josiah was gathering unto himself an increasing flock and some of his new members were able and enthusiastic supporters, determined to see the church flourish.

Already some of the older members of the congregation were becoming "sot" in their ways and the newer ones were for waking them up. There was the matter of the one hundred acres of land promised the parson which after fourteen years he still did not possess, so " 'twas voted that Deacon Snow and Brother Metcalf be a committee of our church to wait upon the Honorable Comitee called the Grand of our Society: Viz. Governor Abbott, Judge Gibbs, Col. Bowen and Mr. Antram, in consequence of one paragraph in my call, viz., the peoples proposing to give me 100 acres of Land without the 7 mile line and to forward the affair with all convenient dispatch and make return thereof to this Church."

If there were difficult but exciting tasks to perform these newer members were ready for them. That Indian member was at it again and so "Solomon Searle, William Compton and Joseph Snow, Jr., were voted a Comitee to treat with Elizabeth Anthony, alias Jack, for again falling into the like sin, Viz: Drunkenness."

The chief excitement and saddest chapter in these early years centered around the wife of Timothy Carpenter, the first deacon. She, too, had the tippling habit. Nothing much had been done about it until the newer members took hold of the disgraceful matter:

Then the Church voted and sent a second Admonition to Deborah and a first to Timothy Carpenter by Solomon Searle and John Paine, which tho on the Sabbath delivered to them, was directly flung out into the highway, the woman saying to the above said Bretheren could not Cotton or the Church find out other Devils to bring the Letter, etc.

A year and a half later Deacon Bagley and Deacon Snow were chosen as emissaries in the same matter and as a result of their reception the following is noted:

An excommunication was exhibited against Deborah, the wife of Deacon Timothy Carpenter, after her dreadful usage of the Deacons when they acquainted her with our resolution, etc. Oh!

This is the first use of Josiah's "Oh!" at the end of unhappy accounts he had to relate. He will use it many times in the next few eventful years when he may be tempted to agree with Deborah that some of these are Josiah's devils.

This downfall of the senior deacon would serve to bring the junior deacon Joseph Snow, his son, and the other newer members of the church into increasing prominence and activity. There was a certain informality about religious services in those days which these newer people seemed to help promote. Meetings were frequently held in homes, sometimes to transact the business of the church, other times to hear Mr. Cotton or a visiting minister speak. Joseph Snow, Jr., often entertained. It may have been while Josiah was laid up for three months with his broken bones that the number of these meetings increased. The absent parson began to feel that too much rein was being taken by the laity and the doctrines preached were not of the best.

Josiah Cotton tried to prevent the increasing number of traveling preachers, "itinerants," from interfering with the life of his flock. Had he been as good a student of human nature as of theology he would have known that something was in the wind. An upsurge of feeling was covering America. It would take many forms, do much good, and a lot of damage. It would awaken men's souls and bring out in them their best and sometimes their worst qualities. It would be led in New England by Jonathan Edwards, the first great creative mind (Englishmen claimed) we had produced. It would be fanned in Providence by the greatest preacher of his day and one of the greatest of all time, George Whitefield. It would be further inspired by a man who had as many enemies as friends, Gilbert Tennent. It would cause an unhappy split in the church family on the hill; it would settle a new part of the city and give Dr. Hoyle's vision fulfillment. It would bring a new synthesis out of the struggle between Massachusetts orthodoxy and desire for unity with Providence Plantations individualistic liberty.

CHAPTER SIX

AWAKENINGS AND AWAKENERS

IT HAD all started up in Calvin Coolidge's town—Northampton on the Connecticut—and its earliest apostle was Jonathan Edwards. In retrospect it came to be known as the "Great Awakening." If it had not started in the Connecticut Valley it would have begun somewhere else, and had not Jonathan Edwards and the other great names of the 1740's been its leaders there would have been other leaders. It was one of those things which are bound to happen; the stage was set for it. The brave religious impulse of the preceding century had spent itself, the meager life and culture it had produced along the fringe of the coast was already changing. New frontiers were opening; population was on the increase. Men who had been too busy to think much in the battle with the wilderness were insisting that some be taken from the sea and soil to attend school and college. A moving population could not be held in check by the moral strait jacket of the previous century and immorality was on the rampage. The Rehoboth church records of this period are a series of trials for fornication and lesser sins. People needed a moral tonic, a purge of the soul, a new morality born of heart conviction rather than tradition. On the frontiers they also needed consolation in their loneliness and for the frequent loss of children and young wives. Life in the older communities needed to be more exciting than the four volumes of Baxter carefully circulated by Josiah Cotton's committee could make it. People craved without knowing it for something deeper and more satisfying than the meager existence of securing rooftree and provender.

Excesses were bound to come and, as in every fresh venture in religious affairs, its leaders could have been wiser, but they could have been very much less worthy.

Theologically, the situation rather than the men who so valiantly championed it made the doctrine. It was a rigorous doctrine of sin and salvation, it stressed God's anger more than His love; it scared men out of their sins into repentance. Because it failed to provide spiritual techniques for a new life except within the shelter of the church, it resulted in excesses of emotion and vindictive feelings. It operated on men's souls without hospitalization and the shock was terrific. That there was opposition to it helped both sides feel they were champions of the Lord. As Dr. Hall of the First Church, Providence, would say a hundred years later, "Multitudes were seriously, soberly, and solemnly out of their wits."

It gave birth to many new churches and lent an impetus to religion which would not spend itself until the Revolution. The Methodists would help ameliorate its theological harshness, but the new and more rigid Calvinism would last among the Congregational churches until Unitarianism would split the New England Way and by Horace Bushnell, the great Hartford pastor of the next century, would introduce the doctrine of Christian nurture.

The name of Jonathan Edwards became known across the seas. For British theologians it was the greatest name in America and did more to convince Britains that Americans were ceasing to be barbarians than anything else. His was a mind to be reckoned with. Going to Northampton as his maternal grandfather's assistant, he became pastor of the church [1] in 1729 at the age of twenty-six years. The preaching which so awakened New England began with a series of sermons in 1734; but by 1737 the revival which started in his own church was sweeping through the Connecticut Valley. Soon it had reached into all New England, with the possible exception of Providence Plantations, where we find no reference to a visit by Edwards. Providence would have its awakening in its own special way, but it could not avoid the onrush of the force engendered by the whirlwinds coming out of Northampton.

Edwards was dismissed from the Northampton church in 1750 as a result of his refusal to observe the halfway covenant. He insisted that those who would have the privileges of the church must be fully converted. A future Newport minister, Samuel Hopkins, then pastor and founder of the Great Barrington Church, was asked to serve the Indian mission and church at Stockbridge, but feeling himself unqualified recommended his friend Edwards, who by then was up against it financially.[2] Possessed of a wife and ten children it was not easy to lose a reliable stipend; some would have more willingly given up their convictions. In 1758 he was called to be the President of Princeton, succeeding his son-in-law, Aaron Burr (father of the duelist). After serving the college only a few months, he died from an inoculation for smallpox which he had requested.

In 1743 there was published "Some thoughts concerning the present revival of religion in New England and the way in which it ought to be acknowledged and promoted, humbly offered to the public in a treatise on that subject, in five parts by Jonathan Edwards, A. M. 1743." This book shows that Edwards himself cautioned against the extremes to which the revival could and did go. He stands fast for the fundamentals of the revival but is temperate in all his admonitions. Other treatises which Edwards wrote on the subject were: *Narrative of Surprising Conversions*, and *Distinguishing Marks of a Work of the Spirit of God*. His most famous work is his sermon *Sinners in the Hands of an Angry God*. As a youth he had been brilliant as a naturalist and wrote a remarkable original treatise on the spider. He makes good use of the spider in his descriptions of the sinners of Northampton.

Of more direct influence in Rhode Island was George Whitefield. A member of John Wesley's Holy Club at Oxford, he was urged to come to America by Charles Wesley. In the opinion of Professor William Warren Sweet he was "perhaps the greatest revivalist of all the Christian centuries." A great friend of the Wesleys, he was not a Methodist, but maintained his connection with the Church of England "without a denominational hair in his head." [3] During the Great Awakening he traveled all over America, crossing the Atlantic thirteen times. The contributions he received he used for an orphanage he had established in Savannah, Georgia. They were generous from both sides of the Atlantic. Whitefield was a friend of Benjamin Franklin, who printed his sermons. There is no record that Ben was overly influenced religiously by the friendship. Both Harvard and Yale closed their doors against him, but he had a hand in founding New Jersey College (Princeton) and Dartmouth. In the latter case he brought Samuel Occam, a graduate of Eleazar Wheelock's Indian college, in touch with Lord Dartmouth. His earthly journey ended at Newburyport, Massachusetts, in 1770. He was entombed beneath the pulpit in the Presbyterian church there, where at least up to within a few years his bones have been left pretty much to rattle around.

On his first tour of New England in 1741 he lands at Newport, stops at Bristol, but passes by Providence. He arrives in Newport on Sunday, September 14, 1741. After a flattering description of the harbor, he records his impression of the inhabitants of Newport in his journal: "Rhode Island seems to be a place where much good may be done. They are a very plain People for the generality; though I observed there were some foolish virgins at Church, covered all over with the Pride of Life. I find they are sadly divided amongst themselves as to outer things . . . The established church [4] is in excellent order as to Externals but many of the Head-Members I soon found were exceeding great Bigots . . . Nor is there less bigotry among those of other Communions. All I fear place the Kingdom of God too much in Meats and Drinks and have an ill name for running of Goods. One day when I said in my sermon, 'What will become of you who cheat the King of his taxes' the whole congregation seemed surprized and looked on one another."

Whitefield is delighted with old Mr. Clap, the minister of the Congregational Church. He writes in his journal,

(I met) Mr. Clap an aged dissenting minister but the most venerable man I ever saw in my life. He looked like a good old Puritan and gave me an Idea of what stamp those men were who first settled New England. His Countenance was very heavenly; he rejoiced much in spirit at the Sight of me, and prayed most affectionately for a blessing on my coming to Rhode Island. I could not but think that I was sitting with one of the patriarchs. He is full of days, a bachelor, and has been a minister of a congregation in Rhode Island upwards of forty years. Old Mr. Clap abounds in good works, gives all away and is wonderfully tender of little children.

Mr. Clap had begun work in Newport as early as 1695 although the church was not organized under him until 1720. Dean Berkeley confirms George Whitefield's opinion with, "Before I saw Father Clap, I thought the Bishop of Rome had the gravest aspect of any man I ever saw; but really the minister of Newport has the most venerable appearance."

He also encounters Mr. Honyman, the rector of Trinity: "Asked Mr. H-n, Church of England, to use his church; he asked what extraordinary call I had to preach on week days . . . (Saying) it was disorderly." Whitefield replied, "Be instant in season and out of season."

The governor, Samuel Cranston, pleased Mr. Whitefield not so much because he was a "very plain man" as that he "had a very plain house." He was a Seventh Day Baptist.

With probably an evangelist's love of numbers, Whitefield estimates that there were three thousand at Trinity to hear him preach. On Friday he felt a little low, but preached with much "Flame, Clearness and Power." Once inside Trinity its communicants rejoiced in the fact and "seemed very fearful lest I should preach in Mr. Clap's meeting house and gloried much in my bringing the good old Man to Church."

When he left Newport for Bristol, Mr. Clap gave him something for his orphans. Mr. Clap died in 1745, aged seventy-seven.

An adverse account of this trip to New England was written by Timothy Cutler, Boston rector, to the Bishop of London. He had previously written him "at your Lordship's commands" concerning the "Northampton Enthusiasts."

Now under date of December 5, 1740, he writes:

The general expectations of Mr. *Whitefield* were much raised by the large Enconium of the Dissenters bestowed on him. Dr. *Colman* and Mr. *Cooper* stile him the *Wonder of the Age,* and that Panegyrie I presume to lay before your Lordship. The Dissenters invited him here, and accordingly was he lodged in Town at Dr. *Colman's* Brother's.

His first landing in *New England* was at *Rhode Island,* Sept. 14. From thence, after a few days, he rode to *Bristol,* where, in the Rev^{d}. Mr Uther's absence, he was by the Church Wardens invited into ye Chh, but refused from a preingagement by the Dissenters there in whose Meeting-House he prayed *extempore,* and preached; the Superior Court then sitting, and adjourning to attend him.

In Boston Dr. Cutler describes his first visit:

Between 3 and 4. o'clock after he left us, he was in Dr *Colman's* pulpit, in his gown (which he constantly wore in Town) before a large audience of Teachers and people, praying *extempore,* and preaching, commending the faith and purity of this country, the designs and lives of our Forefathers who settled it; and this was a topic he never forgat upon all Public Occasions. He also reproved the people for their slack attendance on ye weekly Dissenting Lectures, assigned it to the late fashonable preaching among us. He also reproached the Church universally for her corruption in ye Faith, and Deviation from her Articles, faulted the Scholars at *Cambridge* for reading the most celebrated writers of our Church, and recommended to them, *Willard's Body of Divinity, Shepard's Sound Believer,* and *Stoddard's Safety of appearing in the Righteousness of Christ.* . . . He preached in this town and many of the towns adjacent, in Conventicles, Commons and open Places, where he was always throng'd, and seldom by less than 20,000. Before his departure he made one excursion of 60 miles, preaching all the way, going and coming. He always minded us of the Orphan House at Georgia, and obtain'd a collection in one place and another of above £3000 this currency.

While he was here the face of things was quite altered, little business went forward, people were always flocking him, and he was the subject of all our talk, and to speak against him was neither credible nor scarce safe. Governor & Council and all Authority, Teachers of people tryed to excell in showing respect to him. Nor do I know when things will subside into that safe condition they were in before he came. The variance he has caused remains in too great a degree.

From Boston Whitefield went to Northampton; he writes delightfully of Jonathan Edwards and his wife, Sarah:

Felt wonderful satisfaction in being at the house of Mr. Edwards, he is a son himself and hath also a daughter of Abraham for his wife, a sweeter couple I have not yet seen. Their children were dressed not in silks or satins, but plain as become the children of those who in all things ought to be examples of Christian simplicity. She is a woman adorned with a meek and quiet spirit. She talked feelingly and solidly of the things of God and seemed to be such a help for her husband that she caused me to renew those prayers which for some months I have put up to God that he would be pleased to send me a daughter of Abraham to be my wife. I find upon many accounts it is my duty to marry. Lord, I desire to have no choice of my own, Thou knowest my circumstances. Thou knowest my only desire to marry is for Thee. Thou didst choose a Rebecca for Isaac, choose one for me to be a helpmeet for me in carrying on that great work which is my charge. Forgive, Lord, let my cry come unto Thee.

One would not judge by this that he had heard of Mr. Edwards' reputation over that of other New England divines. This may be accounted for by the growth of an Edwards legend in subsequent years, but undoubtedly was influenced by his preoccupation with his own unhappy lack of a helpmeet. Edwards' wife, Sarah Pierpont, was the great-granddaughter of Thomas Hooker, founder of Hartford. Everything we can find indicates that George saw her through uncolored glasses.

Rev. Mr. Smith of Charlestown, Rhode Island, wrote of Whitefield's visit: "He is the Wonder of the Age and no one Man more employs the Pens and fills up the Conversation of People. None more admired and applauded by some, contemned and reproached by others."

Whitefield was a commanding figure in the pulpit, good to look at as well as to hear, in his flowing Geneva gown with white bands and gathered white cuffs. His large white wig set off to excellent advantage his fine face. Prince describes him in the pulpit:

As to Mr. Whitefield's Preaching . . . It was, in the Manner, moving, earnest, winning, melting: But the mechanical Influence of this, according to the usual Operations of mechanical Powers, in two or three Days expired, with many in two or three Hours; and I believe with the most as soon as the Sound was over, or they got out of the House, or in the first Conversation they fell into.

Dr. Chauncey of the First Church, Boston, one of his strongest critics, accused him of preaching with a smile on his countenance, which Whitefield suggests is a good way to preach. Perhaps it was Dr. Chauncey's influence in the pulpit of Josiah Cotton's great-grandfather, John Cotton, which led Josiah to oppose the movement.

Thomas Prince of Old South, in writing Mr. Whitefield, tells him that the movement is performing amazing works in "Taunton, Middleboro, Bridgewater, Abington, York, Ipswich, Rowley, Cape Ann, Kittery, Berwick, Portsmouth. At Portsmouth before the day was over the Spirit of God came down and seized them at once by scores and hundreds and every one in the large congregation clearly saw and owned it was a work of God. And in three days' time it was computed there were a thousand in that town in deep distress about their souls and crying out for bitterness of anguish, 'What shall we do to be saved?' "

Whitefield seemed courageous in all of his decisions. He eventually desires to turn the Savannah orphanage into Bethesda College and sends the proposed charter to the Archbishop of Canterbury for approval which it does not receive. But George goes to bat with his Grace on the disputed points. He urges against tying it to the church, as has been done in New York (King's College, now Columbia). The one in Pennsylvania (University of Pennsylvania) is much more prosperous because it has no such attachment. He has also omitted from the charter the reading of prayers twice daily.

Whitefield writes to the inhabitants of Maryland, Virginia, North and South Carolina, concerning their Negroes. He points out that they treat their horses and their dogs better than they treat their Negroes and that when this two years last past he had been in a remarkable manner contending with the people of South Carolina, their houses had been depopulated with the smallpox and fever, their own slaves had risen up in arms against them. "These judgments undoubtedly were sent abroad not only that the inhabitants of that, but of other provinces should learn righteousness, and unless you all repent, you all must in like manner expect to perish."

He is even willing to do doctrinal battle with his good friend

John Wesley in answer to John's Arminian sermon on "Free Grace." As with Edwards, Whitefield opposed the Arminian doctrine that man is capable of availing himself of certain means which would render his salvation more likely. Edwards said that God does what he likes with men. Whitefield, in his letter to Wesley writes, "You have propagated the doctrine of Universal Redemption rather than Election." He knows that this "letter will lose me many friends."

Among the "herd of heretics" which he lists in his *Vindication and Consumation of the Remarkable Work of God in New England* there are: Arminians, Socinians, Pelagians, Arians, Latitudinarians, Moralists and formal Professors. In a second group: Blasphemers, Swearers, Drunkards, Unchaste, Liars, Sabbath-breakers, Dishonest, Proud, Covetous, Sensual.

How we wish that his diary gave an account of a visit to Providence. Would he have found all of them here? Josiah Cotton could have pointed out some whom he would classify in the second group. Dr. MacSparran, along with the Church of England in America as a whole, was unawakened by the awakeners. Writing in 1749 he hopes the dissensions will redound to the glory of his church and give support to his claim to the three hundred acres of ministerial lands. He shows his complete misunderstanding of Whitefield by calling him a Methodist.

Ever since Mr Whitefield first propagated *Methodism,* (called here *Ye New Light,*) thro' New England, those enthusiastick fires have been breaking out, lo and again, to ye almost utter confusion of the Sectarys of all sorts; but with some advantage to our churches. Our present attention is taken up, with this false Fire's breaking out among the Antipedobaptists in ye places under my care; And as their extravagancys are very extraordinary and uncommon, I am not without hopes the Church will gain by the Confusion: And I will do my best among the soberest of them, to reduce them by this handle.[5]

The extent to which rumor was used to discredit Whitefield is nowhere better illustrated than by MacSparran writing in all seriousness to the Bishop of London:

Whoever is acquainted but with English History, can be no stranger to the stratagems of ROME; and how eagerly She embraces every opportunity of mixing her Missionarys in Masquerade, with all our Discontents and Enthusiasms, and I make no doubt, my Lord, but She is making Her markets among us, even by Methodism. I have good assurance, yt one of Mr Whitefield's Attendants, (or Armour Bearer, as he and another was called,) when he took his tour thro' New England, was *then,* and *now,* a *Jesuit* residing lately at *MARTINERO.*—If a discovery and full proof of this, will, in your Lordship's opinion, be of service, to either the Church, or Government of England; and you require it of me, I can, if God lengthens out the person's life to that time, get the same authentically proved by the gentleman who knew, and conversed at *MARTINERO* with said *Jesuit,* upon Whitefield's scheme; and who, when he was with Whitefield at Rhode Island, lodged at ye Informant's house.—It might be dangerous for me to be named in this matter; but nothing shall fright me from getting full information, upon the least signification of your Lordship's pleasure.

Two events in 1742 would have diverted men's minds and pens, even in Charleston, from George Whitefield and the Awakening. The royal commissioners came to Providence in that year and decided to allow Rhode Island's claims to land three miles eastward of the Bay, awarding to the state the towns of Little Compton, Tiverton, Bristol, Warren, and Barrington. There was great agitation against it and it was not confirmed by the King in Council until May 28, 1746. Over in John Greenwood's parish in Rehoboth there was something more immediate than the state of one's soul; it was the state of one's soil. August 23, 1742, was appointed as a day of fasting for rain. That very night there was "some rain, some Wednesday and much rain (Wednesday) night."

But a man was about to appear on the Providence horizon who

would take all minds back to their soul concerns. He was Gilbert Tennent, who had wrought in the middle states what Edwards had wrought in New England, and what Presbyterian, Baptist, and Methodist leaders would bring to pass in the South. George Whitefield worked with all three of these groups.

Of all of the "awakeners" Gilbert Tennent had the most violent opponents and proponents. It is hard for us to judge him on the basis of the conflicting evidence. He was an able leader; of that there can be no doubt. The direction of his leadership was certainly not always wise.

Gilbert Tennent was the oldest of four famous brothers, all Presbyterian ministers and sons of an equally famous father. Born in Ireland they played a major rôle in shaping the destinies of Presbyterianism in Pennsylvania, New Jersey, and New York.

Gilbert was the oldest and most illustrious of the four brothers. William, who succeeded his brother John as the pastor of what came to be known as the Old Tennent Church in Tennent, New Jersey, was renowned for his famous trance. Pronounced dead at the age of twenty-six, his family and friends gathered for the funeral, only to have his close friend and physician bring him back to life. He was a stranger to the world, having to learn to speak and read all over again. He described his experience in heaven as being like the words of St. Paul, "I heard and saw things unutterable." He lived to the age of seventy-two.

William Tennent, Sr., the father, established the famous Log College in Buck's County near Philadelphia for the training of ministers, which for over a generation gave colonial Presbyterianism its principal leadership and was a forerunner of Princeton.

Gilbert Tennent was the one more than any other responsible for the schism in the Congregational flock in Providence. By his preaching Joseph Snow, Jr., was "converted" and became the leader of the new church.

He likewise caused a split in his own New York-Philadelphia

Presbyterian Synod.[6] It was his "New Side" Synod which formed New Jersey College (Princeton) in 1746, a venture in which the majority of the founding fathers were Yale men! He served as one of its most active trustees and from it there poured a stream of zealous evangelists into the "New Side" Synod who took Gilbert Tennent as their saint and model. Sweet says of the split, "Instead of scattering God's enemies it divided his servants."

In 1749 he repented his mistakes in causing the split and published *Irenicum Ecclesiasticum*. This reunited the two synods.

Thomas Prince (pastor of the Old South, Boston, and who constituted the First Church, Providence) is the one who carefully and sympathetically checked on the work of Edwards, Whitefield, and Tennent in New England. We have a thorough account of what took place at Middleborough where Peter Thacher was the minister. He was the son of Peter Thacher, one of the three "who wrote the letter."

Mar. 30, 1741—We are thankful to God and you who sent him (Tennent) into this sleepy, secure and dead Part of the Vineyard . . . Tennent observed he hardly ever but once in his Life perceived such a Flatness of Spirit, such a Straitness as tho the Spirit was withdrawn etc.

But by the time Gilbert left, the Spirit of Middleborough was no longer flat.

Sometimes it took more than the powers of Gilbert Tennent to shake a community loose. Westerly, Rhode Island, was trying the heart of its minister, Rev. Mr. Parks, who had been sent in May, 1733, by the

Honourable and Reverend the Commissioners for the Indian Affairs, to preach the Gospel to the Indians and such of the English as would attend.

At my Arrival I found a comfortable Appearance of Humanity and Courtesy among the People: But a Spirit of Profaneness and Irreligion awfully prevailing . . .

I ministred among the People for Several Years; but all in vain: There appeared no Impressions of Religion and Virtue upon their Minds. But the more I laboured and contracted an Acquaintance, the more I saw of their Iniquity abounding; which was very discouraging; that I could by no Means prevail upon them to be better, but that they rather grew worse.

So Mr. Parks continued for nearly a decade, winning neither white nor red men to the gospel. And then:

And it pleased God in his Providence to bring the Revd. Mr. Gilbert Tennent this Way, both going and coming in his Travel through *New-England.* Going he preached a Sermon to a Number of the People from Math. 11.28. And coming back, to a Number more, from Gen. 3.9. which last more especially roused up the People, and filled some with great Wrath: and it raised the prejudices of People the more against me, for concurring in the same Testimony; but all served to keep their Consciences something more awake. Now my Hearers became very slack about coming to Meeting: seldom above Ten, Twenty, or Thirty Souls appeared at the public Assembly; sometimes not so many: and if the Weather was so as they could have any Excuse, many Times none at all. Yet Conscience was stirring.

But a breach had been opened and subsequent preaching by Rev. Mr. James Davenport in Stonington produced results which surprised Mr. Parks.

He preach'd a plain and awakening Sermon, from John 5.40. I heard nothing extraordinary, but the wholsome Truths of the Gospel, and expected no extraordinary Effect, when to my Surprize their was a Cry all over the Meeting-House. I went about and inquired of one and another the Meaning of their Out-cry: And when I came to understand the inward and secret Spring thereof, viz. A deep Conviction of Sin; I could not but say, "This is the LORD'S Doing and it is marvellous in our Eyes." Several of our People were pricked to the Heart; who heard him give another additional Testimony to the Truth, and saw the wonderful Effects of it. And several attended his Ministry longer there, and returned deeply wounded.

A subsequent meeting in Stonington in January, 1742, under Rev. Mr. Fish and a sermon in Westerly by Mr. Eells of Stonington also brought results.

And there was some-what of the Power of God visible among the People; some crying out under a sense of their sinful and undone Condition.

God began then to work more powerfully: several were pricked to the Heart: Two hopefully received Light and Comfort that Day:

A year later great results among the Indians came:

When upon the Lord's Day, a Number of Christian Indians from Stonington came to visit the Indians here:

I attempted to preach from 2 Cor. 6.2. but was unable to continue my Discourse by Reason of the Outcry. I therefore gave it up: And as I had Opportunity offered a Word of Exhortation, as the Lord enabled me. I spent the Evening until late with them.

Religious indifference was common not only among the Indians but in multitudes of communities and was particularly noticeable in the smaller settlements.

Before we leave good-hearted Mr. Parks of Westerly, it is interesting to note that he was not too greatly swayed by the extreme Calvinism of the revival. Of his religious concern for himself and the "secret imagery of my own Heart" he writes:

And tho' I had been somewhat indoctrinated in Gospel-Truths, and had a Work of Conviction so far graciously carried on in me, that I could by no Means embrace the Arminian Principles at large; yet something I had secretly imagining, that there was something in Men to begin with, and that Gospel Grace came to make perfect:

The fact that in the image of God man is made has seldom

been put more simply or beautifully: "there was something in Men to begin with." Sometimes the revivalists forgot this.

Providence is omitted from Prince's account of Gilbert Tennent's travels. It was in all likelihood because Josiah Cotton, whom Prince had helped ordain, either refused to be a reporter or reported the doin's in such an unfavorable light that they did not find a place in Prince's *Christian History*. But we are fortunate in having an account of his first visit in the letters of John Checkley, then rector of King's Church in Providence.

John Checkley is one of the most colorful figures who ever hit town. He had kept an apothecary and bookshop in Boston under the name of "Dr. J. Checkley." He became Episcopacy's greatest lay champion in the city of the Puritans. He got himself tried and fined for the publication of *The Short and Easy Method with the Deists: To which is added, A Discourse Concerning Episcopacy; In Defence of Christianity, and the Church of England, against the Deists and the Dissenters.* It was a compilation of many things against the Deists, most of them from the works of Rev. Charles Leslie of England, the rights in which Checkley purchased. It was sold "by John Checkley, at the Sign of the Crown and Blue Gate, over against the West-End of the Town-House in Boston, 1723."

In it Checkley had gathered all the ammunition he could find to hurl back at Increase and Cotton Mather and others who had taken cracks at the Book of Common Prayer and the rites and order of the Church of England. No holds were barred. A council of Boston divines summoned him to court and before the jury on July 14, 1724, such choice passages as this were read:

And now I (meaning the Author) apply myself with a Christian Concern to our misled Dissenters (meaning among others the sd. Ministers & their Congregations) & let them see & Consider that when they receive (what they call) the Sacraments of Baptism & the Lords Supper in their Congregations, they receive no Sacraments, Nor are their children baptized any more than if a Midwife had done it, nay that it had been less guiltily done by her in Case of necessity than by the others (meaning the sd. Ministers) in the ordinary way, whose Ministrations are not only void & null (if they have not a lawfull Authority) but are sacralegious, & like the Offerings of Korah, and Rebellion against the Lord.

Before the court they were called "false, wicked and Scandalous words." His defense was long and eloquent. The jury found him guilty of most of the indictments, if the book "be a false and scandalous Libel." Taken before the Supreme Court, he was ordered to pay a "fine of Fifty Pounds" to the king whose church he had valiantly defended. He continued to leave no stone unturned to discredit the New England Way, even writing to England to check up on Cotton Mather to see if he were a Royal Society Fellow as Mather signs himself in the *Christian Philosopher*. It was as if one had questioned the titles of the Pope!

John Checkley called himself a virtuoso. He writes to a friend in Connecticut asking for some Indian stone instruments to add to his collection, saying:

Nothing comes amiss to a Virtuoso; and more than that, besides the vain & empty Pleasure (as some call it) of ranging them in their several Orders, accompanied with the various Species, of Butterflies here, Shells there, Rattles, Skins & Teeth of Rattlesnakes in that Drawer, and on this Shelf dried Toads, Beetles & Pismires &c; beyond all this, I say, I have a further Use for them (fit Instruments for an airy Architect you'll say!) in building my Castles in the Air.

He gave as well as received in his hobbies. To a friend in England he sent two dozen acorns of the "best and fairest white oak in the country" and tells him of the other American trees, the chestnut, black, gray, and red oaks.

With his much learning he had wit and humor, so much so as a college youth that Cotton Mather warned his nephew, Thomas Walter, who enjoyed Checkley's company, "to be aware of that man." Checkley enjoyed life to the full and his one severity seems to have been his great seriousness for the English Church. One can see him marching up to King's Chapel on Tremont Street, keeping all the church days while the majority of the populace knew nothing of their existence. They smiled, not always indulgently, at a man in his Sunday best on Ash Wednesday or Maundy Thursday. The rectors themselves would not exceed John Checkley, bookseller, in punctiliousness. On Christmas day his joy was dissipated by the ignorance of those about him who were hardly aware that the "popish day" came and went. Of them he wrote a friend:

> I mourn, I mourn for those unhappy Wretches (tho' otherwise my Friends) who crucifie afresh, and add new Tortures to their suffering Lord. Unhappy Men! who think to merit Heaven by Acts of Disobedience, and vainly flatter themselves, that they shall gain the Favour of the eternal Father, by doing (what He has expressly forbidden) Despight to the eternal Son.
>
> Is it not amazing, that Men shou'd glory in their reviling of those who religiously observe it, and (which is worse) take pains to make all Mankind detest & abhor it. This is what I call doing Despight to the Son of God; and 'tis this which has now overwhelm'd me with grief.
>
> Flow then my Tears,
> For Tears flow nobly shed for lost Mankind.

Another day he celebrated quite alone was January 30, which he resolved to keep as a fast day "forever" in memory of the "innocent and sacred blood of the Royal martyr." This must have gone over big in Puritan Boston. While Checkley closed his shop in honor of Charles, Boston's "wretched men react the horrid crime and revile and laugh at us even while we are praying for them."

Twice he applied for holy orders, but was not accepted until 1738, at which time he was appointed missionary to Providence.

Here he stayed until his death in 1759. The freedom of Providence and the influence of the groups stronger than the Church of England mellowed him over the years until we find him along with Josiah Cotton immersing candidates for baptism!

His estate at his death was inventoried at thirty-six hundred pounds, including four hundred and fifty unsold copies of the *Easy Way* which had cost him so much trouble, plus fifty pounds' fine. John was not the first author who got stuck with his publication. In his front study, perhaps reposing beside the butterflies and dried toads, he had a hundred and sixteen glass bottles, valued at twelve pounds.

All this in spite of letters which to the Venerable Society sounded as if he were on the point of bankruptcy. He was still a good businessman and in 1749 got the town of Rehoboth to vote forty pounds a year to his support, probably the first New England town to give tax support to three denominations, for in 1739 she had voted to pay the salary of the Baptist elder. A very adequate law for the Episcopalians was passed in Massachusetts in 1742, directing that tax money of Episcopalians be turned over to the minister of their church. But this was different from an appropriation from the town treasury. Rehoboth's acceptance of her neighbor's principles of religious liberty without benefit of their laws against tax-supported parsons made her glad to leave Massachusetts and come under the shelter of Rhode Island law.

John Checkley takes credit for the 1742 law, and fear or respect of his ability as an agitator may have led Rehoboth to comply quickly with his request. He writes:

One of my parishioners living in Barrington (then Massachusetts) being imprisoned for not paying to the Dissenters, gave Occasion to my applying to his Excellency Gov. Shirley, under whose influence I have procured a general and perpetual Law in Favour of the Church people inhabiting the Massachusetts Bay. I say, I procured it, for it was contrary to the Expectation of the Clergie in general.

But I rode Night & Day, and was 7 Times down at Boston, and what with visiting the Man in Prison & making Interest with the Members of the General Court, I rode above a thousand miles; which was very expensive to me and put me in great straits.

When Gilbert Tennent came to town, Checkley acted more wisely than Josiah Cotton, but it produced a reprimand from the Venerable Society for the Propagation of the Gospel in Foreign Parts, to which he replies:

But it is a Grief to me that I should do any Thing to give Offence. I do therefore most humbly beseech the Venerable Society to put a favourable construction upon my conduct respecting Mr. Gilbert Tennent. The Fact is this, viz. The Town of Providence was in an Uproar, and many of them almost distracted, running after Mr. Tennent, who prayed and then discoursed to the people, morning, noon and night. Had I sate still I should have lost many of my People. I therefore went and publickly invited Mr. Tennent and his numerous Followers to come to Divine Service and preach a Sermon to them. They did accordingly come, a very numerous Assembly, hundreds of whom were never in a Church before, from whom, after Divine Service, I had a Collection of Mony which effectually mended our Church windows broken by the Hail, which we were not able to mend. I have reason to think that my Sermon was of Service to many of them, they tarrying in the Church and seemed very desirous to hear more.

Mr. Tennent told them that in the afternoon he would say something to them in the same place. I did not contradict it. For, the truth is, I had a great Desire to see what they would be at; that I might be the better able to oppose them.

Those who went out returned in the afternoon, and Mr. Tennent made use of every petition in the Lord's prayer, and then paraphrased it for his prayer, and after that, made a short Discourse to the people, who then departed quietly. Mr. Tennent the next morning went out of Town, and I performed Divine Service and preached that day and the day after to great Assemblies, many of his Followers frequenting the Church, and I doubt not but in Time (by God's Blessing) to give a good Account of some of them. While the said

Tennent was in Town I had a great Deal of private conversation with him, which I hope did him good; for he hath since publickly in print renounced many pernicious tenets.

All that hath been amiss in my conduct respecting this matter, I heartily beg pardon for, and as I never permitted any before; so I never will permit him or any other again. God knows my Heart, I am far from encouraging Enthusiastick Teachers, but in the Hurry of that Distraction, I did not know how otherwise to appease the people.

And this Good comes of it however, that Numbers of the Dissenters come to me for Advice, and I have many Opportunities of reclaiming them from their Errors, who will now converse more freely with me than they would before.

I am satisfied no Minister in the Country hath opposed their mad proceedings more than I have done, and by God's Grace I will continue to oppose them, and will strive to the utmost of my power to promote true, Catholick Christianity, as it is professed and practised in the Church of England.

This letter seems to be in reply to one sent to him under date of February 9, 1741, but as Checkley's letter was written October 1, 1742, it may be that the society's letter was written in 1741 "old style," which would be 1742. It would seem that Tennent was there sometime in 1742.

Others have commented on his eye to getting the windows mended by inducing a large and enthusiastic congregation inside the doors. The windows had been broken in 1739–40 by a severe hailstorm. It was time they were being repaired! At least, much maligned Gilbert Tennent had that to his credit. But John soon writes of other happy results. In October, 1743, he gloats to Dr. Bancroft, who had administered the reprimand:

I have received several to the Communion who were Followers of Mr. Tennent, but are now steady and regular Communicants, and of unblemished Lives. Two have been reconciled to the Church upon their Death Beds, in the Midst of their Dissenting Friends, who heard their Discourse, and were Witnesses of their devout Behaviour, during the Celebration of the Sacrament.

On the day Gilbert Tennent preached in King's Church you can be assured that the Snows, Junior and Senior, were there, also the Richmonds and the Paines. Sam Tift would drive in from Scituate; Solomon Searle would come and William Compton and his wife would walk way over from their house in the country across the bridge. Mrs. Compton had recently brought her letter from Old South Church, Boston, to Josiah's meetinghouse. Pretty much the whole town would come. Josiah Cotton would sit dourly at home, perhaps reading the fourth volume of Baxter, or rubbing his poorly mended bones, which ached when it rained.

Gilbert Tennent's kindest friends would say of him:

The good old Puritan Spirit that has for a Series of years been asleep seemed to revive and blaze forth in him with a genuine lustre . . . As he knew the composition and make of the human Heart so he knew how to speak to it . . . His very appearance in the Pulpit filled the minds of his Hearers with a kind of religious Awe . . . The Thunder and mighty Vociferations of Mt. Sinai seemed to roar from the sacred Desk, when he announced the Wrath of God . . . he was no less warm in proclaiming that in Christ all are made alive.[7]

His published sermons read well and seem not extravagant. As Mr. Parks said of Mr. Davenport in Stonington, we are surprised that people became excited.

But stirred they did become. Whitefield found on returning to Philadelphia, after a former visit, "so many under soul sickness that even G. Tennant's feet were blistered with walking from place to place to see them." [8]

Much is said by historians of the "excesses" of these days. These in a large part seemed to have come after this period of the three great leaders (Edwards, Whitefield, and Tennent) had passed and lesser lights tried to stir the emotions without the intelligence of their leaders. Mr. Prince says of Boston:

> I don't remember any crying out, or falling down, or fainting, either under Mr. Whitefield's or Mr. Tennent's Ministry all the while they were here; tho' many, both Women and Men, both those who had been vicious, and those who had been moral, yea, some Religious and Learned, as well as Unlearned, were in great Concern of Soul.

Admittedly "frost-bitten Boston" [9] was not the place where excesses would be apt to occur.

Jonathan Edwards was not even dramatic in the pulpit. He was:

> A Preacher of a low and moderate Voice, a natural Way of Delivery; and without any Agitation of Body, or any Thing else in the Manner to excite Attention; except his habitual and great Solemnity, looking and speaking as in the Presence of God, and with a weighty Sense of the Matter delivered.

But the greatest excitement was among the ministers themselves. The revival split them into two camps. Harvard, against whose professors Whitefield had written and spoken, turned all its guns against the awakeners. Pamphlets and books in large numbers were written and their arguments hurled back and forth. A classic was the one written in answer to Rev. William Hobby, of Reading. He had modestly written *A Defense of the Itinerancy and the Conduct of the Reverend Mr. Whitefield.* In answer to it this irreverent title was chosen, *A Twig of Birch for Billy's Breech, a letter to the Rev. Hobby of Reading a gentle and necessary correction for publishing A defence etc.* Its author signs himself "J. C." No, it is not Josiah Cotton, but rather John Cleveland.

Finally a conference of ministers was called together in Boston to try to arrive at some means of healing the increasing divisions. It was held on the day after Commencement, July 7, 1743;

To consider whether they are not called to give an open conjunct Testimony to an Event so surprizing and gracious; as well as against those Errors in Doctrine and Disorders in Practice, which thro' the permitted Agency of Satan have attended it, and in any Measure blemished it's Glory and hindred its Advancement: And also to consult the most likely Methods to be taken, to guard People against such Delusions & Mistakes as in such a Season they are in Danger of falling into, and that this blessed Work may continue and flourish among us.

Ninety ministers came, including Josiah Cotton, attracted by a happy combination of Commencement at his alma mater and some light on his perplexing problem. The awakening was generally approved. With situations like the one in Providence in mind it was resolved:

That Laymen do not invade the Ministerial Office, and under a Pretence of Exhorting set up Preaching; which is very contrary to Gospel Order, and tends to introduce Errors and Confusion into the Church. . . . That Ministers do not invade the Province of others, and in ordinary Cases preach in another's Parish without his Knowledge, and against his Consent, Nor encourage raw and indiscreet young Candidates, in rushing into particular Places, and preaching publickly or privately, as some have done to the no small Disrepute and Damage of the Work in Places where it once promis'd to flourish . . . That People beware of entertaining Prejudices against their own Pastors, and don't run into unscriptural Separations . . . we would most earnestly warn all Sorts of Persons not to despise these Out-pourings of the Spirit, lest a holy GOD be provoked to with-hold them, and instead thereof to pour out upon this People the Vials of his Wrath, in temporal Judgments and spiritual Plagues; and would call upon every one to improve this remarkable Season of Grace, and put in for a Share of the heavenly Blessings so liberally dispensed.

Sixty-eight ministers signed it, among them some of our old friends: Thomas Prince, John Cotton, Samuel Moody of York and his brilliant son-in-law, John Emerson of Topsfield (the one who read his sermons), Ward Cotton, and Josiah Cotton. Some signed with protest that the article against intrusion of outside and uninvited ministers had not been made strong enough. Three signed with special qualifying phrases after their names. Thomas Prince wrote his agreement "To the Substance"; Joseph Sewall "To the substance, Scope and End"; and Josiah Cotton, who had not found too much help for his particular problems, wrote "To the general Scope and Tendency." Most ministers were listed as from *the church of* Plymouth, Dunstable, Concord, Charleston. Josiah, down in Baptist Rhode Island, was from *a church in Providence.*

Absent were the names of Dr. Chauncey of the First Church, Boston, the reverend professors of Harvard College, and some twenty others who had been well inoculated by commencement and the Harvard tradition, the day before.

It was the same sort of problems which made the Presbyterian split in New York-Philadelphia. The Old Side demanded that the authority of the synod be respected, high academic requirements for ministerial candidates and no inter-presbytery preaching without permission. The New Side emphasized the rights of the presbytery (the local governing bodies), requirement of special religious experience for ministers, and the practice of preaching anywhere the spirit moved. "Uncharitableness and self-righteousness were the exercised prerogatives of both sides."

But in spite of the Boston Conference, pamphleteering continued. Rhode Island's only clerical native son entered the lists, Samuel Niles, minister of Braintree. He was born at Block Island, May 1, 1674, and had many distinctions to his credit; one of these is that he was the only Rhode Islander to attend Harvard in its first three-quarters of a century.

Only one boy fr R. I. (Block Island) so far as we know, attended college in the entire 17th cent'y. (Entered at age 21 and allowed to graduate in three years) on the plea of his age and his petition to the effect that a grt part of his life "hath been spent in a land of darknesse prophanenesse Sabbath breaking and Atheisme." [10]

He returned to Rhode Island and from 1702–10 was minister (unordained) at Kingstown. He would be part of the long dispute between the Congregationalists and Episcopalians concerning the "Ministerial Lands." His three marriages give him a claim to our record if nothing else would. His first wife was Elizabeth, the daughter of Rev. Peter Thacher, "who wrote the letter." His second wife was Ann, a daughter of Hon. Nathaniel Coddington of Newport, and the marriage was performed by Governor Cranston in 1716. His third wife was Elizabeth Adams Whiting, the widow of Samuel Whiting, minister of Windham, Connecticut, who was one of the godfathers of the Hoyle church venture and first minister of Windham. Elizabeth's daughter was the wife of President Thomas Clap of Yale. Samuel Niles not only married often, but well.

In 1711 he was ordained as the minister of Braintree and in 1745 entered the controversy on the side of Harvard and Dr. Chauncey. A possible knowledge of "goin's on" in Providence might have influenced him. But a greater influence would be his stepson-in-law, President Thomas Clap of Yale, who vehemently opposed the whole movement. His treatise is entitled, *Tristitiae Ecclesiarum or A Brief and Sorrowful Account of the Present State of the Churches in New England by Samuel Niles —A mournful spectator and sharer in the present calamities and Pastor of a Church of Christ in Braintree, Boston N. E. 1745.* It gives us the other side of the picture and furnishes us with names of some of the minor actors in addition to Whitefield and Tennent.[11]

Samuel Niles goes on to say that their harmony "has been the distinguishing Glory of the New England Churches" which, while somewhat nostalgic, had a reasonable amount of truth in it. Particularly valuable is his enumeration of those criticisms which the wisest made of the whole movement:

> We find by sorrowful experience that wise and good men have fallen into very different ways of thinking, speaking and acting in matters of religion and pursuing my purpose, therefore, it may be proper to inquire in the grounds of our present difference. If I have a true idea of things our present controversy is not about fundamental points of religion. All agree on the doctrine of original sin and the necessity of new birth etc. . . . What is it then that they oppose? In the first place they oppose so much itinerant preaching . . . Again they oppose public exhorters . . . Moreover they oppose not the regular conduct of those who appear to have brought on a genuine evangelical manner, but that unlimited liberty which many have given themselves to judge the extent of faith of others . . . they oppose dreams, visions, revelations, bodily appearance of Christ to the natural sight of the eye.

Here, as in the Boston Conference, the finger is placed on that which would continue to disturb the churches, the preaching or exhorting of irresponsible, poorly trained, and untrained ministers and laymen quite outside the churches. It would plague the church at Providence for some time to come. On the other hand, men like Josiah Cotton and Samuel Niles were at fault that they did not do more to direct the movement and use it to repair some damaged souls as well as broken window panes. Thomas Prince rightly said, "The greatest errors and disorders were in those Places where the ministers opposed the work and thereby lost much of their Respect and Influence."

The American Revolution may well have been born in the period of the Great Awakening. Leonard Kramer writes, "The great Awakeners . . . aside from their religious results were responsible for a political progressivism sharply contrasting with the conservatism of the movements opponents." He quotes

Mason in his *Great Awakeners in the Middle Colonies* as saying it gave emphasis to individual rights, democracy, inter-communion co-operation, opposed establishment, and advocated the separation of church and state.

Gilbert Tennent's Rhode Island sojourn could not fail to have advanced the cause of democracy in his mind. Here he had preached in an Episcopal church and was probably unaware that its rector had received a reprimand. In Providence he had seen many brands of religion existing side by side, unmolested by state, synod, or bishop. Later he was to settle down as pastor in Philadelphia. "Cosmopolitan Philadelphia, with its free-thinking, ingenious printer-journalist Benjamin Franklin and its pious, commercially successful, politically ascendant Quakers, was to polish Tennent's religious edges and to sharpen his politics." [12]

There was a noticeable difference between the respect for constituted authority in the established churches and in the churches of the Awakening. The latter were the inheritors of John Knox who in his "Second Blast" had made these points:

1. Neither birth nor blood allows a person to be king over Christian people.
2. No idolator—one expert in transgressing God's precepts—ought to be set forth as the head of a government.
3. No oath or promise can bind a people to obedience and the support of tyrants against God and his known truth.
4. If people have foolishly and ignorantly chosen such a ruler a tyrant and an idolator the people can with justice depose and punish him.[13]

On the other hand, the Bishop of London had written in 1723 to James MacSparran with complete ignorance of Rhode Island political patterns:

The less Assistance you have from the Spiritual Power to restrain Vice and Immorality, the greater Need there is to engage and secure the Assistance of the Temporal Power in that pious and important Work. And the best Way to secure that, both in Influences from hence, and in seasonable Interpositions there, is to make yourselves Examples, in the first place, of Duty and Loyalty to our most gracious Sovereign King George, and then of a respectful and decent Behaviour towards the Governour who is sent by him; to whose Favour and Protection I have in the most earnest manner recommended the Concerns of the Church and Clergy. And you will do well to avoid, as much as may be, all Concern in Civil Affairs; making it your Choice to confine your self to your proper Business as a Minister of the Gospel, which is the surest way both to avoid Offence and to gain Respect.

With the Great Awakening, minds which had been occupied with the business of safety, food, and shelter were kindled. The spirit of freedom again flared up. Congregations as well as ministers would assert their right to speak and act and lead. The lessons which laymen learned in the administering of the affairs of the church gave them an experience valuable for political freedom as well as furnishing them with the philosophy of that freedom.

Some of this spirit soon broke forth in eagerness to share with the mother country in her new war against France, fanned by the presence of French privateers on the New England coast and a destruction of many of the fisheries. Rhode Island privateers were fitted out and twenty prizes were brought into Newport in 1745. The same year the expedition against Louisburg was undertaken, Rhode Island raising an one-hundred-and-fifty-man regiment and ninety men to man the sloop *Tartar*. The fall of Louisburg in June brought great joy, not merely in its victory for England but the recognition it gave to the prowess of the colonies.

Gilbert Tennent preached a sermon entitled *The Necessity of Praising God for Mercies received . . . occasioned by the Success of the late Expedition.*

Rhode Island's native son, Samuel Niles, burst into poetry on the event. He had been more awakened than his protests against Whitefield and Tennent disclosed. Some of the verses of the much longer poem are:

My Pen and Skill fall exquisitely short
To give the World an adequate Report
Of what high work was done, in wondrous wise
By Providence both on the Land and Seas.
In this great Action which I here relate
'Gainst Cape-Breton, and of the Frenches fate.

Venerable Moody, white with age
Habits himself in hostile Equipage
With Sword of War
But on the Spirit more
Firmly relying, leaves his Native Shore
His Skill in arms to prove as he had twice before

And soldiers all, who for your countries Good
Laid down your lives, your Limbs and dearest blood
Give Thanks to God, devote yourselves to Christ
Your Captian Genial, who did you assist
On Papal Ruines to Erect Christ's Throne

The venerable Moody was Samuel Moody of York, Maine, who had baptized the first members of the Congregational Church in Providence. He was seventy at the time of the expedition and preached the first Protestant sermon in the Catholic church of the captured Cape Breton.

Having been awakened, men's minds would not doze again until after 1776.

The more immediate effect in Providence was on Joseph Snow, Jr., who up to now had let his deacon-father do most of the church work. But so enthused was the younger Snow over Gilbert Tennent that he drove to Newport to fetch the great preacher a second time to Providence. Much of the town's subsequent history began with that ride.

CHAPTER SEVEN

THE FLOCK DIVIDED

By the latter part of 1742 storm signals were flying atop the meetinghouse of Josiah Cotton. The thing against which the wiser among both the friends and foes of the Awakening had warned was happening. In the train of Whitefield and Tennent, exhorters were pouring into town and the saints who had had sufficient arousing for one decade were being whipped into a frenzy of which they themselves would be ashamed after sobering off. The exhorters for the most part seemed to be folks of greater lung than brain power. Some of them resembled Red Jacket, the famous chief of the Iroquois, who had gained his office by eloquence. He had neither birth nor exploits. There was nothing dignified in his appearance or character. He intoxicated himself whenever he could get ardent spirits and was on this account regarded with contempt by his nation, yet they said "he is necessary to us on account of his eloquence." Comparing the physical intoxication of Red Jacket to the spiritual intoxication of the exhorters is not too bad a description of some of them. Morally they seem to have been above reproach; many of them are to be admired for their sincerity and devotion.

The New Lights in New England were a product of the Great Awakening, much as was the "New Side" synod of the Presbyterians in New York and Philadelphia. The idea of a Separates movement in New England may have been suggested by Gilbert Tennent, although we do not find evidence that he urged it.

Its real impetus came from the local exhorters who followed in the trail of the mighty men whose voices had awakened the colonies. Ultimately it became the founding stone of many new Baptist churches but at first it was a split within the New England Way. Its main strength was in Connecticut where the Saybrook Platform gave much less flexibility to the life of the local church than was found at this time even in Massachusetts. Two Congregational churches stand side by side on the New Haven green as a result of the New Light movement. Its center, however, lay in Windham County, and it was from there that the movement spread into Providence.

That a movement born in part out of the shortcomings of a state church should flower in the Plantations seems an anachronism. But here was a vehicle of expression for that constantly sought synthesis between freedom and essential organization. Too much freedom and poverty had sent the Fields from Providence to Bridgewater, and too little freedom and adventure had sent them back again, accompanied by the Snows. It is of note that it was these comparative newcomers from Massachusetts who would oppose the Harvard orthodoxy and ecclesiasticism in Providence.

They had caught something of the Providence heritage and yet were not ready to swap the values of a social dynamic for its extreme individualism. Rather they would, without thinking it out too far in advance, try again to bring the good of both points of view together. To this end they became devotees of the New Lights or Separates or New Measures, as the followers of the exhorters were variously called.

For the story of the effect of these men on the flock of Josiah Cotton we are fortunate to have his own handwritten records. An early editor took these blow-by-blow accounts and summarized them in the beginning of the record book of the First Church referred to in Chapters I and V. The book has a beautiful paper of English manufacture watermarked with the knight and lion and "Pro Patria." The charitable spirit of the editor told the story, omitting its more violent parts. The original loose pages of Josiah's account were found only recently by Miss Helen Robertson, First Church historian, and have been copied. They were apparently torn from a book as the editor (probably Deacon James Green) finished with them. A peculiarity is that the record was kept at both ends of the book.

The first of these exhorters to appear on the Providence scene seems to have been "a certain Lion of Plainfield." On a "Fryday night" he had preached "at the house of Deacon Joseph Snow." Josiah Cotton brought up the matter at a church meeting and "every particular member present did discountenance this same rash speaking of said Lion except the person at whose house he held his meeting."

The "said Lion" had come out of a theological lion country, Plainfield, in Windham County, Connecticut. Here practically every town of the section had a strong New Light or Separate movement. In many cases it was far stronger than the established church, particularly in Plainfield. Unlike the movement in Providence it was possessed of a large number of native exhorters. It also had the added incentive of opposing an established church. Several were jailed for refusing to pay their taxes for the support of what had been their own church. In this they were prophetic, although this phase of their movement would not be victorious for decades, and in the meantime their own organization would in nearly every instance slip out of existence.

Prior to this October appearance of the Lion of Plainfield, Josiah Cotton notes:

Some months before in our town the said Lion and Mr. D. Whipple preached in the Friends Meeting here, which was attended with great disorder and caused a formal Church meeting at the request of Deacon Joseph Bagley who was displeased with the management of our Sisters, Sarah and Ann Ames. But with the favor of our Good God was happily treated and so Satan is now twice defeated in his attacks upon our Dear Flock for their disipation and confusion. Oh let us praise the Lord.

The boldest of the exhorters seems to have been one John Murray or Mrs. John Murray, who "dishonourably obtained the key of the meeting house this aft. & as we judge for the purpose of your preaching in it this evening. We thot it our duty agreeable to the trust imposed in us to inform you that such a proceeding will be very disagreeable to the greater part of the society."

James MacSparran of Narragansett, writing to the Bishop of London on October 18th, 1742, says:

God has (contrary to the purposes of Whitefield, and those who envited him into New England) overruled the enthusiasm of yt man, to the almost utter overthrow of the Dissenters cause here. They are so broken into Divisions and Parties, yt I think, they cannot be healed or united, without returning into the unity of the Church. Nothing like them, since the French Prophets, has appeared, and they run riot with Religion to yt degree, yt 'twere too tedious to trouble your Lordship with a detail of their distracted doings; I cannot omit however giving an instance or two; They are said seldom to pray for the King, when they do, they pray for his Conversion; wch, wt a tendency it may have to make him vile in the eys of the people, and w[t] the consequence of yt may be, I leave to yr Lordships greater penetration. One of them lately after his extempore prayer, instead of giving out the psalm to be sung, as the preacher generally does by saying, let us sing to the praise and glory of God, such a psalm, and such a verse; began thus, *let us sing to the praise and glory of the Rev[d]. Doctor Watts.* The Precentor fearing this would give offence to the people, mentioned to him his mistake; but he repeated it; and then the Precentor not being able to bear the blasphemy, gave out the psalm himself, and the people sang it; when that Exercise was over, the Pulpiteer not bearing to be so baffled, said the third time, *let us sing to the praise and glory* *of the Rev^{d}. Dr Watts* such and such a hymn of Dr Watts's, and added yt he *would sing to said Watts praise and glory in spight of Men and Devils.*

I hope God will give grace to the clergy of our Church here to behave with such a steddiness, as I thank God they generally do, yt we shall reap advantage by these confusions, and many souls be saved by taking sanctuary in the Church;"

By January of 1743, Satan (according to Josiah's definition) was again on the loose. A meeting was called to enquire into

the conduct of several members there present with regard to their asking or permitting one Mr. Denison,[1] a Layman and perfect stranger (to them, tho not to me) and Mrs. Samuel Aldridge, a Quaker preacher, (who has preached at Brother Joseph Snow, Jr's house before, viz. on the Sabbath, at which time also Silas Carpenter and other Quaker preachers did preach) to preach amongst them without and against my Leave.

This church meeting began by singing the 133d Psalm, "Deacon Snow (Joseph Snow, Sr.) setting this tune and singing this." But by the time of the closing Psalm:

I could not get Deacon Snow to tune the Psalm tho several of our members with myself importuned him, nay, I took him by the hand and entreated him, telling him the ill Consequence of parting so, etc., yet I was allone and he replyed he could not or 'twas against his conscience to sing with us, and sat down and was dumb whilst we sang praises. I think tho' Brother Benjamin Cary tuned it and sang with us, yet as I remember, Deacon Snow sat down both in singing and in the time of prayer.

The Psalm which went untuned by Joseph Snow, Sr., was the fifty-first, and he may well have had a reason for refusing to sing, "For I acknowledge my transgressions and my sin is ever before me." A fault of the established church everywhere is that it gives a priestly power to its leader which the Congregational way had denied. Harvard-trained Josiah Cotton could not escape this natural tyranny of our lords the brethren which Massachusetts had unwittingly substituted for the tyranny of our lords the bishops. All through the controversy he takes the father-bad-boy attitude which would have even failed to ameliorate the attitudes of less stubborn men than old Joseph Snow.

During the meeting Benjamin Cary (who seems to be the most extreme of the dissenting party) asks, "Will Mr. Cotton hinder us from going to the Kingdom of Heaven?" This gave Cotton a chance to repeat other charges which Brother Cary had aired against the minister, among which were, "I was an opposer of the work of God's Holy Spirit, a preacher of Cursed Damnable Good Works alias Doctrines." As all this is recorded by Josiah Cotton himself it is little wonder that here he uses increasingly the characteristic "Oh! etc." It was indeed enough to make a minister swear or appeal to high heaven for judgment and justice.

As this was one of the rare occasions when the opposing parties and Josiah met together it was undoubtedly the meeting described by Joseph Snow, Jr.:

> When [Josiah Cotton] was offended with a perticuler Brother [probably Benjamin Cary] he did not folow the Rule of the gospel with him; that is he caled the church together and complained of him before he lett that Brother know that he was ofended with him; and that repetedly; again when Mr. Cotten had offended any he denied them the priviledg of following him with the Rule of the gospel for when sum of the Brethren ware offended with him went and told it to him alone; he not hearing them took the opertunity to tel it to him before one or two of the Brethren, and when they saw that he gave no satisfaction they would fain have told it to the Church . . . and Mr. Cotten would not alow of it . . . when the Brethren pleaded with Mr. Cotten that they might have a hearing Mr. Cotten would stamp on the flore; and command silence; saying that the holy ghost hade made him moderater, and he would magnify his office.

In a meeting when the aggrieved brethren attempted to state their grievances, "Mr. Cotten in a dreadful heat of spirit said, 'I dismis this meting in the name of the holy ghost,' and went away: the church being much surprized fell silent a little while and then arose and went away."

It was following this unfortunate meeting of stubborn tempers that the Separates began calling meetings of the church, choosing their own moderator and "clark," claiming to be the true church. An early action was to request that a council be called. On April 11, 1743, a polite and charitable answer to the request is written by Mr. Cotton:

That matters of Difference and Difficulty in Church are *not* proper to be laid before a Council, till all due methods have been taken for healing and removal, but prove ineffectual, which methods have not been taken by yourselves who thus sue for a Council.

He asks that a bill of particulars against his conduct and doctrine be prepared and signed by the dissenters. But even Josiah feels the need of prayer and advice for he says:

We the abovesaid Church of Christ have now unanimously voted to set apart Wednesday the 20th of this month as a day of fasting and Prayer to humble ourselves before God on the account of our Divisions and to ask the help of the Reverend Weld and Crocker and pray you to joyn hand and heart with us herein. After which we propose to ask your Advice what steps to take in order to win happy Accomodation. In the meantime, we rest your Bretheren in Christ.

The Fast Day was several times postponed because of the inability to secure outside ministers to come and preach. The events of this spring are in part unknown, being recorded among the loose pages of Josiah Cotton's records which are now missing. It may have been too bitter a story for even the unknown editor to save, or there may have been a momentary stay in the increasing fire of dissent, charge, and countercharge. But by September things were in a most proper stew.

In the meantime Josiah had met one of the charges against him that he had not proceeded according to Matthew 18:15 when he had complaints to make against a brother: first go himself; then take witnesses; then bring it to the church. He sought out Brother Benjamin Cary and said things vis-a-vis, which we suspect Benjamin well deserved to hear. Next he took on Deacon Snow himself and reprimanded him for "runing to Attleborough" and for "spreading among all my Church . . . (as he saith) a parcell of sermons (and I think lyes) with a direct view to discrediting my ministry and farther his unjustly detaining the key of the meeting house two days and preventing a worthy minister as well as myself from going into my Desk and persisting in it till our Comitee the third day were forced to break in and buy a new lock and so usher us into my Pulpit, etc."

At last the long awaited Fast Day arrived. But it was two fastings instead of one. At the meetinghouse Josiah Cotton's party met and at Joseph Snow's the Separates. It resulted not in a doubly contrite heart, but one fast cancelled the other, and left spirits sad but unrepentant. Several ministers, one after another, had been invited, but all failed to come except good Mr. Greenwood from Rehoboth who had never forsaken the unhappy church in its troubles. "Mr. E. Polk (coming in providentially the preceding eve with his Wife) preached at one service and Mr. Greenwood at the other." At Joseph Snow's house "One Mr. Britt there preaching, as he had done several preceeding Sabbaths." The September fourteenth Fast Day had been preceded by a church meeting at which both parties were present, the Separates in the majority. Here the two parties clashed, head on, over the choice of moderator: should it be Josiah Cotton or Deacon Snow? The argument grew warm with Josiah, "by virtue of my authority from God's word and the Church's platform"

(Cambridge Platform), demanding silence. Josiah adjourned the meeting "on which he (Joseph, Sr.) declared they were not dismissed nor disolved for that he had as much right as any person to do the same and desired them (if not ordered) to tary, which that party of Christians did tho' we drew off."

The Fast Day was long and best remembered for what was found posted in the church. As Josiah Cotton, Mr. Polk, and Mr. Greenwood entered the house:

> We the ministers saw a notification placed in the Deacon's seat signed by Deacon Snow and others informing of a Church meeting intended on the morrow, to choose at his Son's house one or more to head, moderate and lead this Church, etc. which was immediately pulled down as suposing 'twould divert the minds of Christians that day from the sermons, etc. they should then hear.

The notice apparently had been well fastened with pins for today it reposes in the archives of the First Church with the four corners torn from it where Josiah, in his chagrin at being so humiliated before his brother ministers, yanked it down.

One of the declarations of congregational freedom made in the "notice" was to the effect that "tho the powr of office is rested in the Elder or Elders of a Church yet the powr of previlidg is rested with the Brethren in Common so that they have right to Call the Church together in Extrodinary cases without the Elder or Elders."

More exhorters were arriving weekly as the affair grew warmer. The Paine brothers, Elisha and Solomon, of Canterbury and Plainfield, had visited the rump sessions of the church. These were two of the ablest of the exhorters, and they came from Windham County where the New Light movement had most prospered. They had learned much in their unhappy contacts with the established church. Elisha Paine was a lawyer and may have been the one who gave Joseph Snow, Jr., such a good understanding of ecclesiastical law, so that he often came off legally on top in his struggles with Josiah Cotton.

Another aspect of the fall of 1743 was the increasing boldness of those who decried "damnable good works" and insisted on inner conversion. Every time the church has fallen into ways of stolid and Pharisaical ecclesiasticism, this doctrine of justification by faith has been revived. Jesus insisted on inner purity rather than outward conformity; Luther's battle cry was justification by faith; George Fox had championed the inner light. The New England Way needed shaking loose and the old and good doctrine of the soul stirred from within still had potency. The reform made its greatest mistake when some of the brethren and sisters set themselves up as judges of a man's inner thoughts and life. Josiah began to be visited by some inquisitors:

> two Sisters, viz. H. P. (Hannah Pain) and S. S. (Sarah Snow) came to examine me, and also to know of me when I was converted, etc. That was Saturday; next Monday S. S. a male (Solomon Searle) and the two Joseph Snows on the like Question of my evidences and Experiences and since that several more of the Church have been with me on the like occasion, and I do presume this is what they were prying into, . . . B. C. (Benjamin Cary) when I offered the two sermons he objected against for the Press, he refused, and when I proposed to him a Council, he replyed that all Councils would condemn him but yet he had something within him to justify him, smiting on his breast saying if deluded he was undone eternally. Oh! Queeso.

Such circumstances would try anyone's soul and particularly Josiah's, but to be catechized by women must have been about the last straw for one brought up in an all-male governed church.

The meeting which had been called pursuant to the notice posted and pulled down on Fast Day was held September 27, 1743. At this meeting they voted to adjourn for two days and to send messengers to their minister. These messengers, waiting upon Mr. Cotton, received for his answer a copy of the sentiments of Mr. Stone of Harwich as printed in the *Boston Gazette* for Tuesday, September 6, 1743, after reading of which he "folded up the same and gave it to the committee saying he should send no other answer." Joseph Snow, Jr., would call this a mockery of our "Lord and Savior the head of this church." Had they even been the words of the New Testament handed to a Providence man in the Boston *"Gazit"* they would still have seemed like mockery. Providence folks had gotten along a hundred years without caring what Boston thought or said.

No time was lost in the next action and on September 29 at their adjourned meeting they vote "to reject and depose him from the ministerial office and ask the Church to admonish him as a member and Brother;"

to which admonisition this Church ads her earnest and harty Prayer that your eyes may be opened and that your heart may be tourned and that you may give God glory making confession to the Christian satisfaction of this Church which mourns your sinfull conduct with all admonishing and forbiding you either to preach or offer yourself to the Communion of this or any other Church till duly restored.

There were eleven signers to the letter in which the above was contained and sent to "Mr. Josiah Cotton sumtime Pastor of the Congregational Church of Christ in Providence." They were: Benjamin Cary, Solomon Searle, Joseph Snow, Barzillai Richmond, Joseph Snow, Jr., John Pain, Peter Tefft, Jabez Ross, Jonathan Tayler, Samuel Tift, Alexander McCrary.

This was one less than had signed the "Warrant Notification or Situation as they called it in the morn of our Late Fast." The missing brother was Thomas Knowlton.

Why he did not sign this stuff—was that since his joyning with the Separates in two former papers he got dipped tho Baptized by me last May Oh! etc.

Four others are similarly disposed of by Mr. Cotton's comments after their names:

Mr. B. Cary 24 June 1745 did cross out his name. This 13 February 1743/4 Mr. J. Tayler of his own accord without ever having been sent for or desired came to my house and razed his name and mark and saying it was done by reason of Deacon Snow's importunity.

This 22 of December 1743, Mr. S. T. did of his own accord acknowledge his fault in signing the instrument against me and so crossed out his own name and saying it was done hastily at Deacon Snow's instigation. As to Mr. Ross, he went personally after signing the paper to Topsfield without my giving any notice to the Rev. Mr. Emerson there and was denied comunion because of marrying his wife's own sister, as did Deacon Peabody.

Cotton's reaction to the missive is further told in his own words:

Oct. 1, 1743: After sundown Saterday eve, I received this piece of stuffed nonsense, Ignorance and Malice, by the hands of S. Searle and B. Richmond. N.B. This is at least the fourth scrawl that I have received on Saturday evenings from our Separate Bretheren as tho' twas on purpose to discompose me from serving at the Altar on the succeeding Sabbaths . . . On the whole I mind the timing of things particularly.

As to the exact No. viz. 12 sighners of the late warrant I do not say that either of them is a Judas, but this that a quarter part of them, viz. J. T., S. T. and T. K. have neither of them heard me preach these 3 quarters of a year (saving J. T. one half day) yet they can be trumpt up to serve a turn, tho 1 lives 9 miles off, a second 12 and a 3rd 18) and tis said that B. C. lately questioned Deacon Snow's good status, yet they can improve him for a Tool being their chief Inditer without Britt should help him (ut puto.) But granting them to be in No., 11 or 12, that don't make them a major part of our Church which the son moderator and Father Clark must know . . . Oh! that this and all their other misconduct as well as ours in this day of difficulty and temptation may be forgiven us through the Lord J. Christ's blood. Amen.

Part of the reason for the quarrel and the dozens of others like it in the history of colonial America was the lack of more normal excitements. Life was drab and dull; full of hard work, lame muscles, cold winters, and hot summers. And if it was dull in Providence how much more so in Scituate. It was worth driving nine, twelve, and eighteen miles for such a stir. As always there were those who would come to church for a fight or a free supper who never would come to divine service. A good Western thriller in an air-conditioned movie house might have had salutary effects upon church life in the middle eighteenth century.

Church matters being participated in only by the men, we secure only fleeting glances of the women's part in all this; but they were having a part. Sarah Ames seems to have been the leading spirit, she of the Lion meeting who was carried away. By this time she seems to be taking a hand in exhorting and is defended by Joseph Snow, who says it is quite all right "if she felt herself called to take horse and go a hundred miles on end to preach or exhort." Josiah takes this particularly hard for she was one of the most respectable of his members, a sister of Nathaniel Ames of Dedham. It looks as if Josiah peached to Nathaniel about what his sister was up to, for we have the following letter:

To Rev. Mr. Josiah Cotton
in Providence

Dedham—Nov. ye 11, 1743.

Rev. and Worthy Sir:

I have heard of the Separation in your Church and am heartily sorrey that any that have my Blood in their viens should be of the party against you and as I think they are led by a Blind Enthusiastical Zeal, and Deacon Snow, to do as they have done, in this enclosed Letter to my sister Sarah Ames I have endeavoured to show the unreasonableness of those Principals which I think distinguish the

New Lights from the Orthodox profession of the Christian Religion and I expect my Sisters will either make their recantations from their errors or that their Ring Leaders will answer my Letter. Sir, I pray you to seal it up and send it to them as soon as you think convenient. I am Reverend Sir, your Friend and Servant

Nathaniel Ames

The damage had been pretty well done and it frightened both sides of the conflict into greater politeness, behind which there seems to be a genuine desire to heal the breach. By January, 1744, we find the part of the church under Josiah Cotton choosing a deacon to fill Joseph Snow's place and that of unfortunate Timothy Carpenter, and yet leaving the door open for their return. (Timothy was not of the Separates.) It is recorded "that t'was no ways to exclude either Deacon Carpenter or Deacon Snow but that with one heart and soul, we should be glad to receive them both again to their Places and office in our Church on their first giving Gospel satisfaction."

Two Benjamins were chosen, Marshall and Belknap. After considering it for three months: "in which solemn affair, Brother Benjamin Marshall for prudential reasons declines at present that important office;" . . . "After which Brother Belknap was pleased (after great condescention and humility in the Grace and Strength of our Common Lord and asking our prayers) to accept of the Deaconship, and accordingly the next Lord's Day was publickly invited to and entered in the Deacon's seat."

Perhaps the heroes of the whole unhappy episode should be Benjamin Marshall and William Compton. They were the ones most interested in making peace. When the final split came one would stay and eventually the other would go. Indeed by this time a movement must have been well on foot to locate a new church on the west side of the Salt River. This should have been to William Compton's liking for there he lived way out in the country pretty much alone. A church would mean more neighbors and better land values. But he was interested in the peace of the church rather than his personal prosperity. On March 15, 1744:

> Mr. Compton and Mr. Marshall were chosen as a Committee by the standing part of the Church (which are the major Party thereof, and have been so through the whole Controversy) to address the Separate Part thereof . . ."

But a week later—probably the Separates did not respond to the overture—the fat is again in the fire and Cotton secures a vote by which the Separates were "publicly admonished and rebuked by the minister in the name and by the consent of the Church and suspended fr the privileges of the special ordinances of the Chh of Christ."

According to Ezra Stiles, who had access to the missing pages of Josiah's records, this suspension of ten brethren and fifteen sisters was read by Mr. Compton and Mr. Marshall privately to the offenders on March 25, 1744, and publicly April 29. It was read yet again by Josiah himself with nine Separate brethren present on August 14.[2]

Among those who condemned the Separates this time was Joseph Snow, Senior's son-in-law, Matthew Short, and one of his wife's Providence relatives, Thomas Field.

By May, 1744, the Separates had been given the land for a church across the bridge (on which Beneficent Church now stands) and sometime before August, 1746, a meetinghouse was erected. But the spirited negotiations for securing either harmony or justification proceeded. There was also the question as to which party was the church of the founding fathers.

By 1745 the Separate group are seeking reconciliation. They have talked with George Whitefield and he apparently has given them sound advice not only on calling a council, but on their own behavior. They write:

Providence May 25, 1745

Mr. Josiah Cotton

Sir— Upon the advice of the Reverend Whitefield and others to call a councell we send this third time to yourself to know whether you will joyn with us to call in some of the neighboring churches which both parties shall agree to lay our grievences before in order to inable them to judg aright between party and party; for our part we find a freedom to confes anything we are cencable we have don that we ought not to have don and not only so but we desire to be made cencable wherein we have don amis in any thing what so-ever and also are willing to take the good advice of a Councell of the Churches of Christ. We pray God to direct us all in the way wherein he would have us to walk; in behalf of ourselves and those of our party we subscribe our selves your grieved brethren

Joseph Snow
Ebenezer Knight
Benjamin Cary
Solomon Searle
Joseph Snow, Jr.

The council was agreed to in a meeting attended by both parties in the meetinghouse:

. . . after solemn prayer (with which and a blessing we also broke up the said meeting) we and they mutually chose a Council of 5 Churches (in order to heal our unhappy divisions) to give us light and peace and their best advice, etc. Viz: The Rev. Prince & Foxecroft of Boston, Messenger of Wrentham, Williams of Lebanon and Mosely of Windham to come hither with one delegate apiece on the last Tuesday in September next. Q.D.C. Josiah Cotton. Pastor of the Church and moderator of the meeting.

Things looked hopeful, but alas, as the day approached, word was received that Prince and Foxcroft, the Boston ministers, would not be present. Thomas Prince, who had gloried in the Awakening, was unable to come and help put its unfortunate features back to sleep!

. . . their reasons were read before all and then we proceeded to make choice of 3 more Clergymen and their Churches to supply their vacancy (since they could not come) but our Separate bretheren were so partial, arbitrary and unreasonable that we could do nothing with them and ergo dismissed and disolved the meeting and the same day wrote to Mr. S. W. of Lebanon and S. M. of Windham not to come.

This seems to be the last attempt of the parties to get together. The mother church does not quite close the door until the new church is organized in 1747. On February 8, 1747:

Our Church this evening met by adjournment and joyntly voted two admonitions to be read and fastened tomorrow P. M. on our Separating Bretheren and Sisters. Viz: a second to the first lot of them and a first to the other sett of them, and also voted a draught of a letter to be sent to the pretended convienon of an Ordination in this town. Both of which votes are to be performed this week by Deacon Belknap and Brother Benj. Marshall and then we voted to disolve the said meeting.

The censure would stand until 1784 when Enos Hitchcock would say, "let bygones be bygones."

As in all such cases the immediate blame belongs on both sides. Most of the participants in the quarrel seem to have acted in good faith and sincerity. If the Snows acted with a weather eye on real estate, Josiah Cotton had something of the same thought on a much smaller scale when, seeing the personal storm clouds gathering, he made the memorandum:

In the year of our Lord Jesus Christ, 1745 & 1746, the Grand Comitee of our Society–Viz. Mr. William Antram, the Honorable Daniel Abbott, Judge Robert Biggs and Colonel Jabez Bowen were pleased (to prevent any after disputes that might arise) to give to me, their first minister, the sole right and propriety of that Pew next to our Pulpit stairs in our meeting house and do hereby forbid any after claims thereto by my successor or successors or any other person or persons that may after this chalenge itt as a ministerial pew as witnesseth my hand. Josiah Cotton.

The weakest member of the group seems to have been Benjamin Cary, whom Josiah describes as "a tool." He was one of those individuals, typical of most new movements, who seeing the good of the cause jumps in and becomes its worst advertisement by his failure in restraint. Such folks are naive and always see issues and people in terms of black and white. He was easy to sway. Joseph Snow, Sr., the deacon, whom the Separates chose as "ruling elder" in the midst of the quarrel, was a blacksmith and with his iron muscles there went an iron will. He was a domineering man, on the sour side, a product which New England raised all too frequently among her rocks and poison ivy.

Joseph Snow, Jr., from the beginning was a leader. His name is not mixed up with the caustic arts in which both sides engaged, but at his house and under his skull things were thought out. He knew ecclesiastical law and the New England Way, possibly receiving advice from able Elisha Paine, lawyer and New Light in Canterbury, Connecticut. In this period Joseph, Jr., was not as headstrong as his old age would discover him to be. He would admit his own faults or at least some of them. He based the procedure the Separates had followed first on the New Testament solution of such troubles, Matthew 18:15 (and for this reason repeatedly asked for a meeting of the church), and secondly on the Cambridge Platform of the New England Way drawn up in Cambridge, New England, in 1648, in answer to questions of the English Congregationalists regarding polity and procedure. Joseph Snow, Jr., probably knew this platform better than Josiah Cotton: he knew his way through it and even around it. In his own records of the events leading to final separation he admits that in parenthesis the Platform states that a church shall not depose its officer without calling a council.

But, we see the power of the church repeated in 6 section of the 10 chapter: that if in case an Elder offend incorrigeably the matter so requiring: as the church had power to call him to office: so they have power acording to order to remove him from his office &c: if it be objected: that this church did not come up in full with this paregraft in six section leaving out the perentheses: and deposing their minister before they had the advice of a councell so to do; to that objection this church answers in two perticulers: first what is inclosed in the perentheses was not a point of power but only a point of prudence. Probably sum may think it would have ben a point of prudence to have caled a councell before they had deposed their minister; others may think that it was more prudent to depose him first; which of these openions is right is uncertain; and cannot be known but by the event . . . no manifest duty should be neglected for an uncertain point of prudence.

There was a clear understanding expressed by Joseph Snow, Jr., of the power of a church quarrel sorrowfully to reflect on the good name of Christianity. One meeting was called by the Separates with this preamble, "We the subscribers of the Congregationall Church of Christ in Providence are senceable that it is mater of scandel to Religion: that we should call our selves a Church of Christ: and yett are got into two parties."

Manifestly the little church at Providence suffered from its isolation, Congregationally speaking. The calling of a "councell" was not easy and, as we have seen, when attempted the response was poor. In Massachusetts and Connecticut the council and consociation had much power, usually employed for the peace and harmony of the churches. In Connecticut the Saybrook Platform drawn up in 1708 introduced the Presbyterian idea of a permanent synod which they called the "*consociation.*" It was given legal status by the state to sit on the disputes of churches. Its advantage was that it prevented picked councils which was the apparent final cause of the breakdown of peaceful negotiations in Providence. Admittedly the consociation purchased peace at the price of liberty. They almost without exception decided against the New Lights in Windham County, Connecticut (Plainfield, Scotland, Canterbury, Windham, etc.). Gradually Connecticut dropped the procedure, although many of its associations keep the ancient name but act as an association to be called as a council on request of the church and organized for each such duty.

Both sides claimed a majority of members. In the anonymously written records of First Church the following appears:

> The Separate brethren had pretended they were the major part of the church. They were so confident of their being the majority that tho their number did not exceed Twelve, yet they promised and engaged, that if it could be made appear that the Standing part were the greater number, they would acknowledge that they had done wrong, and would return, and that what they had done should stand for nothing. Wereupon the Rev. Pastor proceeded to call over the names of the standing part of the Church which was found to be fourteen besides two that at that time missed being mentioned, and which would make the number 16. But notwithstanding their solemn engagement and promise, they neglected and refused to return.

Both lists appear to have been padded with "ringers." The division must have been practically even. The Separates had the more active brethren, the "standing part" possessed the more conservative folks who, at least by the absence of records to the contrary, must have behaved themselves pretty well.

Josiah Cotton was a good man, sincere and honest, but his stature was no greater than the best of his opponents. Even Ezra Stiles, who takes his side, says of him, "Mr. Cotton was a pious man and orthodox but an Opposer." One wonders if history might not have been different if good Sam Moody had accepted the call and come down from York.

This sad brief paragraph appears in the records quoted above:

Things having risen to so great an height, and the situation of affairs being so very uncomfortable Mr. Cotten resigned his charge some time in the month of July Anno Domini 1747—after having served in his Pastoral relation Eighteen years and Nine months. In which time he administered the ordinance of Baptism to one hundred and eighty persons, many of them adults:—And admitted to the Lord's table about fifty Six.

Nor did his unhappy time in the ministry end here. From Providence he went to Woburn, Massachusetts, where he remained until 1759, when he was again dismissed. From Woburn he went to Sandown, New Hampshire, where he remained the rest of his life, dying in 1780 at the age of seventy-eight. In those days ministers were settled in a pastorate for life and only unusual circumstances broke that compact. It took a council to decide if Jonathan Edwards should leave his pastorate at Stockbridge and go to the presidency of New Jersey College (Princeton). The same was true with Thomas Clap of Plainfield when he was asked to become president of Yale. One of the matters to be decided was what disposal to make of the "life settlement" given a minister when he assumed the pastorate. It was a kind of ministerial dowry. In the case of Dr. Clap the *legislature* appointed a committee at the request of Yale and the Windham church to decide this matter. They recommended and it was approved by the General Assembly that "inasmuch as Mr. Clap had been in the ministry in Windham fourteen years, which was about half the time ministers in general continue in their public work, the people ought to have half so much as they gave him for a settlement, which upon computation was about fifty-three pounds sterling."

The problem was not as great with Josiah Cotton's dismissal as we do not find that he ever received his "one hundred acres" which Joseph Snow, Sr., had tried to help him secure before the quarrel. He probably kept his title to the pew "next to our Pulpit stairs."

But whatever his faults, Josiah Cotton had succeeded in planting the New England Way in Providence-town. The storms which had been looked for from Jonathan Spreague and cohorts had been well guarded against and never developed. They had come from another quarter, led by a dyed-in-the-wool Bridgewater-Easton Congregational deacon.

His planting would go on to great growth, but for the time the quarrel would be costly for the mother church and the New England Way in Providence. Time and population would eventually have planted the West Side church without the unhappy break.

It is said that the sacraments were not administered for sixteen years. It was the very period when neighboring churches were growing rapidly. The Rehoboth (Rumford) church grew from one hundred and ninety-five members in 1733 to three hundred and twenty-five in 1743. In 1726 it had had sixty-four members.

For five years the First Church was without a minister and then called John Bass, who was not a happy choice. He had had a pastorate in stormy Windham County. Our friend Samuel Niles wrote a pamphlet against him. He resigned after six years to enter upon the "practice of Physic." During his first year as minister he, with Samuel Nightingale of the First Church and Deacon Snow, went into the distilling business! This was not such an unheard-of calling for the saints. In Hartford it was said that there were three Congregational pastors interested in spirits other than religious, "one of whom was said to raise the rye, another to distill it into whiskey, and a third to drink it." [3] The Nightingale-Snow-Bass venture was called the Concord Distil House on what is now Page Street on the West Side. Mr. Bass resided in this part of town. Thus leading representatives of the two churches found concord at last!

After three pastorless years the First Church was reduced to four members, two of whom were males, constituting the business body. On October 28, 1761, the trustee churches (Feofees) of

Bristol, Medfield, and Rehoboth were called in "at the desire of the remaining members of the Chh. of Christ in Providence to lead direct and assist them in the renewal of their covenant and the incorporating such others as shall appear to join with them." Among the brethren still carrying on were the two faithful Benjamins, Belknap and Marshall.

After another pastorless interval of four years, David S. Rowland came in 1762 and stayed until 1774. He it was who had been settled over the Plainfield Church in 1747 during the New Light controversy. There had been voted a £700 settlement and £400 salary, "the latter to be raised on the proportion of corn at twelve shillings pr. bushel; rye, at eighteen; wheat twenty-four; oats, eight; beef one shilling pr. pound; pork, two and also his fire wood." Mr. Rowland would have been "passing rich"—if he could get it. But the majority of the town were Separates who had opposed Mr. Rowland's coming. At annual town meeting the question would be put, "Will the town now proceed to pay Mr. Rowland his salary according to the covenant on town records?" Loud would the majority vote, "No!" "Year after year, Mr. Rowland was compelled to sue the town and follow the action through the several courts of the county before he could obtain a penny of his salary."

He was a good man for the Providence church, for here he would also have to chase his salary. When Deacon James Green appealed to Boston Congregationalists for financial help for the Providence church, he received this reply:

Boston, June 27, 1765, to Mr. James Green, Merchant,

Sir: I used all the influence I had with the convention to get something handsome to help you in paying your minister but could not prevail and the chief reason they gave was, they saw no end. That in several of your late applications you declared if they would help you then you would apply no more and that your applying now repeatedly was offering them affront. Furthermore, it was thought by some that Mr. Rowland was not so smart or popular a man as was necessary to make head against the several sects among you, though he might be a profitable preacher. I hope you will continue together striving for the Faith of the Gospel in nothing terrified by your adversaires tho you may be called to do beyond your power, remembering he that watereth shall be watered also himself. Have not time to add anything further but am, Your Friend and humble servant.

William Blair Townsend.

This judgment on Mr. Rowland by Boston should be weighed in the light of the fact that he was a Yale man! First Church never strayed from the Harvard path again.

Whatever his faults he was a man of great charity, for he wrote of the Separates of Plainfield who refused him his legal salary, "Although some things appeared among them at first very unwarrantable, yet considering their infant state it must be acknowledged by all that were acquainted with them, that they were a people, in general, conscientiously engaged in promoting truth, and Mr. Stevens, their minister, a very clear and powerful preacher of the Gospel, as must be acknowledged by all who heard him."

By 1774 the Benevolent Society, seeming to concur through "uneasiness" with Mr. Townsend's estimate of Mr. Rowland, asked him to resign. He may have been "not so smart" but his letter of resignation is a gem:

And now my bretheren I take this method to bid you farewell. Pardon my many imperfections, weaknesses and want of zeal and fervor in that most glorious cause in which I have been engaged among you. Farewell delightful temple of the Most High, that pleasant desk from whence I have often attempted to proclaim a Saviour's name. Farewell ye reviving choristers and faces of my once engaging friends, ye echoing walls farewell. Wishing you the blessing and direction of unerring wisdom I am your ill-used well wisher and humble servant, David Rowland.

Whatever his faults Mr. Rowland left the church much stronger than he found it, with some sixty families and thirty to forty communicants.

For about a year John Lothrop served the church. During the seven years of the Revolution there was no settled pastor in the First Church, although Chaplain Enos Hitchcock frequently visited the church and left his wife as something of a hostage for his return to become the pastor after the war. In 1783 he was settled over the church for life, which would mean a twenty-year pastorate full of the blessings of a great ministry to church and community.

As Enos Hitchcock learned the sad story of the split of forty years before, he made one of his first acts the final healing of that spirit of division which still existed. We can end the story of the quarrel with this happy record of the First Church:

At a meeting of the Church July 13th 1784 duly notified.

The Pastor laid before the members the ancient records of the Church respecting the suspension of "Mr. Joseph Snow and others" from the fellowship of the Church—the members, imprest with a sense of the great importance of Christian charity, and desirous of preserving the unity of the body of Christ.

Voted unanimously. That, in consideration of the fair character and exemplary lives of said "Mr. Joseph Snow and others," named, the censure formerly passed upon them, by the Church, be, and hereby is taken off—and he, with such of them as are now living, are restored to the full charity and communion and fellowship of this Church.

Voted also. That this Church is ready and willing to receive into their christian charity and all good fellowship the church under the pastoral care of the Rev. Mr. Snow, being desirous "above all things to put on charity which is the bond of perfectness." Col. 3:14

Voted also. That the pastor be desired to furnish the Rev. Mr. Snow with a copy of the foregoing votes.—which was done accordingly.

CHAPTER EIGHT

JOSEPH SNOW, JUN'R, PARSON AND JOYNER

At our safe and cool vantage point, two hundred years removed from the "great Quarrell," we are tempted to ask what it was all about after all. Two universal problems of the church were involved. The first, itineracy, had blessed and plagued the church from its beginning. The Apostolic ministry was an itinerant one, but Paul must have longed to engage in some kind of licensing system which would regulate Peter and Apollos with their contradictory doctrines. A settled minister resented the preaching of even as good itinerants as Wesley, Whitefield, and Asbury. They unsettled the congregations. There is always the human element which enters the picture. The parson who has been serving out fairly good spiritual diet Sunday after Sunday, year after year, is somewhat jealous of the itinerant who with a half-dozen well-polished homiletical bombshells carries the people away on wings of enthusiasm. Especially was this true among parsons who settled for life in a parish; they expected miracles, not to be performed over night, but by a steady and continued cultivation of spiritual things. On the other hand most ministers have been too jealous of their own pulpits. Few were as magnanimous as good Augustus Lord, minister of First Congregational Church, Providence, 1890–1932, who said, "I like to have a guest preacher. If he is better than I, my people should hear him. If his sermon is poorer than mine my people will rejoice in my return."

The problem was so great in Connecticut that the General Assembly passed a law forbidding preaching or exhorting "in any parish not immediately under his charge without express invitation from the minister or lawful authority of such parish."

Elisha Paine was arrested in Woodstock (then a disputed portion of Massachusetts) for itineracy and stayed in jail from February to May in 1743. He would not give bond because of the "contempt that was cast upon the truths of God's word by the warrant." It was the dirtiest prison he had ever seen. Begging a broom, he swept a place to walk in and experienced "the sweetest contentment in and resignation to the will of God." [1]

Fortunately Rhode Island could have no such speech-muzzling laws. Itineracy would continue to be a problem that could be solved only by the co-operation of the resident ministers.[2]

The other universal element was man's repeated yearning for a heart-warming religion. In New England the Calvinistic chill only increased such a desire. Yet for the untrained religious leader it is easier to produce hotheads than warm hearts.

Doctrinally there was little at stake. The great doctrinal wars would come in the next century.

Against these universal elements, local coloring was furnished by the hundred-year-old search for a true liberty, first in the Plymouth and Massachusetts Bay colonies and then in Roger Williams' settlement on the Moshassuc. The old arguments that had raged between John Cotton and friends on one side and Roger Williams (who had been expected to assist Cotton in Boston's First Church) on the other had carried over with John's great-grandson on one side and Joseph Snow, Jr., the "joyner" descendant of ship's carpenter John Alden, of the *Mayflower*, on the other. The rights of the minister and the rights of the people were again at issue. Douglas Horton has said, "John Cotton believed once a minister was ordained he was the will of God in the community." John's great-grandson had this conception of the priestly office nor has there yet been a complete solution of the dual responsibility of a parson who must hear both "thus saith the Lord" and "thus saith the congregation." The latter often means "thus saith the chief deacon."

To this problem the only adequate answer the church has ever found has been neither platform nor polity but the rule of charity. In this neither Cotton nor Snow had been as pure white as their names would imply.

The process of organizing the new church went forward slowly. The Snows maintained that their party was the church and on March 6, 1745, there is entered in Joseph Junior's hand:

It was considered that several members of this church had rent themselves from it: and venter to act as a church by themselves: separat from this church: it is therefore thought proper and expedient that the members of this church should renew their covenant solemnly before god: and passed a vote that every member should be examined concerning their knolidge and experiance of the work of grace and of their faith; and such as give an acount thereof as that in a Judgment of Charity they are counted true believers shall be admitted to sign the covenant and have a right to pertake and Bring their children under their care to Baptism & c:

Ten of the church were examined and signed. Seven of them were of the eleven who had signed the suspension and admonition that followed the September Fast Day and the "*Gazit*" incident. Three of the four absent names had been explained by Josiah Cotton's notations, two withdrawing from the Separates and a third moving to Topsfield. Peter Tefft was the only one unaccounted for. He may have been the one who lived eighteen miles away and that was a distance difficult to negotiate in March. The new recruits were Ebenezer Knight, John Johnson, and Thomas Dexter.

For its rule the re-covenanted church took the word of God and the Cambridge Platform, clearing up the articles "with the parentheses." It is remarkable that the two new elements introduced are the very form Congregational church polity took after its disestablishment in Massachusetts and Connecticut. They were inherent from the beginning but had needed the two forces of the Massachusetts and Providence experiments to give them practical expression. First, church government should be thoroughly democratic; the minister and other church officers were subject to the majority (of males, of course), and all were equal in voting power: "We can't think god send any to lord it over the conchences of his children." Secondly, it was a "gathered" church examining its members in a "judgment of charity."

In all this they claimed to be acting not as a new church but as the continuing church in Providence. Josiah Cotton and his adherents were thus the "separates." It was a device which would be used again by the chief actor a half-century later.

While there were further overtures to reunite the factions it must have seemed pretty clear to both parties that from now on there would be two separate Congregational churches.[3]

Daniel Abbott, who had sold the First Church its site and remained a part of that Society was perhaps the first to decide that it would be better if the two parties set up religious housekeeping separately. Someone had already started a building fund and on May 29, 1744, Daniel Abbott gave the lot of land the new church was to use down to the present day. The deed is beautifully worded:

Daniel Abbott

For, and in consideration of the Love, Good Will and Affection I have to the Congregational Way of Publick Worship in said Town of Providence. And have nominated, and appointed, Deacon Joseph Snow, Mr. Hugh Batty, Mr. John Paine and Mr. Joseph Snow, Jr. all of Providence above said, to have the Charge, Care, and Command of Erecting and Building a Publick Meeting House for the carrying on, and Preforming the Worship of God, in a decent manner, in that Congregational Way of Worship, and as a committee to receive in, and improve the money that is already subscribed towards the building said House and What more may be gathered and improved, necessaryly towards carrying on and Performing said work, all which Proceedings I am well affected with, and for the incurragement of accomplishing the said work I have given unto said J. S., H. B., J. P. and J. S. Jr. and to such others as have already subscribed towards the charge of Building said Meeting House,

A certain small lot of land to set the said house upon, the which is situated, lying and being near the Dwelling house of the said Deacon Joseph Snow in Providence aforesaid and bounded etc.

It was unusual to nominate not only the trustees of the land but to name them as the "building committee." Daniel Abbott's affection for the Congregational Way may reflect his concern that the Way should become two-laned as rapidly as possible in the interest of its peace and welfare.

Daniel Abbott was the son of Daniel Abbott, who in the King Philip's War was one of those "who stayed and went not away," along with Roger Williams, Thomas Field, Zachariah Field, and others. Courage to meet the threat of the Indians may have given a goodly heritage to meet in a statesmanlike way the threat of the warring saints.

No town fathers worked harder for the progressive betterment of the settlement than did the Daniel Abbotts, father and son. It was their vision which secured the building of Weybosset Bridge, the demand for a townhouse, and a public market-house. As has been noted, the Daniel Abbott of this period had signed a petition for an Episcopal missionary, had sold the land for the First Congregational church and joined that society, and now gives the land for the daughter church.

By February, 1745,[4] the church of the "new Measures" as some of the New Light churches were called, was completing its organization to a degree where it would be safe to admit the ladies; several are propounded after giving a spiritual account of themselves. By the end of the month the new enterprise had a total of thirty-five members as nearly equally divided in sex as that number will divide. It was a good beginning. Among them were a blacksmith, a carpenter, a hatter, a furrier, merchants, shipmasters, farmers, a distiller. It looked a little as if Hugh Batty had been hand-picked by Daniel Abbott, having been made a trustee before he was a member. New member, Stephen Rawson, may or may not have sensed that the new church would some day develop his good spring into a profitable "fountain." Thirty years later Joseph Snow would take as his text for Stephen Rawson's funeral sermon, "And devout men carried Stephen to his burial and made great lamentation over him." Many would prove devout men, a few would backslide. Several would serve in town and state offices and the first member to be received after the church should be constituted would be the Revolutionary governor, Nicholas Cooke. His wife, Hannah, was among the first signers, as were Elizabeth and Sarah, the respective wives of Joseph Senior and Junior. The Ames sisters were also there, those who liked exhorters, as was Elizabeth Compton, who had brought her letter to First Church from Dr. Prince's Old South in Boston.

But where were the professional men? For the most part Providence possessed none. Schoolteaching was not yet a Rhode Island profession; college professors were yet to come; there were a few doctors and some of them would soon be members; lawyers and bankers were nonessentials. The banker would finally be socially accepted, but the lawyer would have a tough time of it. Old Samuel Thurber wrote:

As for lawyers, I never had much to do with them as I ever had a contemptible opinion of their trade. I recollect one by the name of John Aplin . . . He like some others of the trade became very avaricious. A very important case presented, both sides wanted him, he so engaged and received a fee from each. This was discovered; he consequently up keleg and scud for Connecticut.

The question of a settled minister for the church across Weybosset Bridge was now looming before them, as they became increasingly conscious of being a separate church body. In the spring of 1744, Joseph Snow, Jr., was "approved of an desired to preach." As a continued separate existence seemed increasingly likely, they were considering a year later "what the church should think proper farther in order to a regular settlement." It would seem at this time that neither the Snows nor their friends were thinking of young Joseph as the permanent minister. On March 9, 1744, the following letter was written to the leader of the New Lights in Windham County:

Dated Providence, March 9th, 1743–4

Mr. Elisha Paine:

Rev. and Dear Sir:— These few lines are to make known to you, that we, the subscribers, members of the Congregational church and society in Providence, have chosen yourself for our minister in the Lord; and do, by these presents, call you, Mr. Elisha Paine, to the pastoral office among us, to be ordained over us according to the gospel, and we hope that the same God that has inclined us to give you this call, will incline you to accept and take the oversight of us, according to the gospel. 1st Pet. 5th Chap. 2nd and 3d vs. And if so, then by these presents, we promise that we will be mindful of our duty towards you, as God shall enable us, according to the gospel, and in particular the 6th chap. to the Gal. 6th v., and the 9th chap. 1st Cor, 14th v., during the time that by the providence of God we shall stand so related.

Witness our hands, &c.,[5]

Elisha Paine of Canterbury was well thought of in Windham County, "universally conceded to have the best sense of any one in those parts." While he was in jail his brother ministers, including Eleazer Wheelock, soon to be founder and first president of Dartmouth, and Samuel Mosely, who had consented to come to the council in Providence which was not held, gave him a character reference:

> From the knowledge that we then had of him, we were of the opinion that he was qualified and that it was his duty to preach the Gospel. And we think it our duty to give our testimony for him, that he is, so far as we know or have ever heard, of a regular Christion life and conversation; and we esteem him sound in the faith and of good understanding in the doctrines of the Gospel of Christ.

He would have made a heroic first minister of the church but as far as the quality of "good sense" went, the new church was to be well endowed with that. But Elisha Paine declined the call.

Increasingly the little company found themselves being willingly led by the younger Snow, who was just entering his thirties. They admired the older deacon, who was something of a one-man thunderstorm, but they found themselves won to and willing to follow the son. The funds for the new building did not come in as fast as was hoped and it looked like a long time ahead before a meetinghouse would stand on the land given by Daniel Abbott. But young men do not wait, and under the enthusiasm of Joseph Snow, Jr., they organized themselves into a woodsmen's bee. Trees were felled on the Abbott, Snow, and Field lands, their owners gladly giving the timber for a house in which to worship God; incidentally their land would bring better prices with the timber cleared from it. Day after day half a dozen Snows and some Richmonds, Searles, Batteys, and others devoted all the time they could spare to the felling of trees, the hewing of timbers, the quarrying of stone. The foundation was set thirty-six by forty feet. Good ship's carpenters helped set the huge sills, hewn a dozen inches on the side. Other timbers were cut to pattern and piled in order on the ground. And then came that great day in the summer of 1746 when the meetin'-house raisin' took place. Elizabeth Compton's kitchen was full of the feminine Snows, Hannah Cook, Mary McCrary, Thankful Cary, Zeruiah Field, and many others. And from it the smells of good victuals spurred on the men as the frame was "reaised."

When it was well on its way towards completion, Daniel Abbott was so well pleased with the venture that he said this church must be a true New England meetinghouse and have a village green in front of it. The green remains today as Abbott Park.[6]

The common and church, built well in advance of permanent homes, were truly the New England Way which Providence had not hitherto experienced. It made the growing West Side settlement more community conscious than the East Side had ever wanted to be. It was another step in adding the good things of Massachusetts Bay which individualism had neglected in Providence. The new community on the West Side would represent physically a compact togetherness rather than a strung-out independence as did the settlement along Towne Street and Back Street on the other side of Weybosset Bridge. One day there would be a movement to incorporate the new venture as a separate town.

The opinion began to be expressed that a man who could take the lead in framing the physical structure of the new church, making it sound and New England weatherproof, ought to be the one to build it into a spiritual house. Later, in constituting a new church back in the Snow's home town of Bridgewater, Joseph, Jr., would write asking "whether you are fitly framed together and built up a spiritual house upon the foundation of the apostle and prophets, Jesus Christ himself being the chief corner stone."

Joseph had done considerable of the preaching since "he was desired to preach" but being both young and a layman, others, particularly Old Joseph and Benjamin Cary, felt perfectly free to exhort on an equal basis. But now the church was ready to ask him to become its spiritual leader, and on October 20, 1746, they "mett and made choyce of Joseph Snow, jun'r to be their minister."

For a year and a half they had met many times and kept a Fast Day for guidance on this great decision. But it was not yet settled. Months went by and Joseph, Jr., gave no answer. We can well imagine that there was opposition. The Comptons of Boston and the Snows themselves would wonder if you could be "fitly framed together" without a Harvard graduate as pastor. Josiah Cotton had helped shake their confidence in this unbroken rule, but not completely.

Finally the people grew restless and asked for an answer.

He was not as yet ready to give them an answer; notwithstanding the repeted fastings and prayers made by him and the church that his duty might be mad plain to him on that Respect they appointed the next fryday the 23 day of January (1747) to be kept as a fast and mett together and spent the day in supliation and prayer that his duty might be made plain to him: and in the close of the day he gave them his answer and accepted of their call: to take that charge upon him: desireing their prayers for him that he may be found faithfull: then they rejoyced sung &c. praised god and prayed and adjourned the meeting to the 26 day.

On that day they "appointed his ordination to be the 12 day of february 1747 and agreed to send to 5 churches in Conetticut: namely to Canterberry; plainfield; Mansfield; Norwich and Stonington: and of them churches came Elisha Pain, Solomon Pain, Thomas Stevens, Simon Spaulden, Mathew Smith and Oliver Grant."

On February ninth, Josiah Cotton wrote a letter to Deacon Marsh, Solomon Paine, Mr. Denison, and Thomas Stevens, all of Windham County, protesting Joseph Snow's ordination as "a bold intruder or novice in the Priest's office." The letter may have led to the absence of Deacon Marsh and Mr. Denison or it may have been the roads.

Many would remember the ordination of nineteen years previous, the greatest ever held in North America. This time no great names of Boston divines would appear on the roster. The ministers and messengers would come from the New Light groups of Windham County and they would be accompanied by no "bands-men." Coming in over the Great Roade to the Connecticut Government, they would not even need to know that the older part of the town existed; horseback would be the most comfortable mode of travel over that particular road, and the rest and refreshment at Solomon Searles', the Compton's, and the Snow's would be indeed welcome.

Thomas Stevens was one of the leaders in the separate church in Plainfield. His father was a tavern keeper. Matthew Smith was the minister at Stonington.

Samuel Drown was chosen to represent the church in the laying-on of hands:

> February 12 1747. and after we had appointed every man his work in said ordination; we all repared to the meeting house; which was thronged with people and after a Decent silence: the Rev. Solomon Pain began the exercize by Prayer; and sung a psalm: and then the Reverend Mathew Smith preached a sermon from the 24 chapter of Luke from the 44 verce to the 49 vearce which was attended with great solemnity: after sermon Joseph Snow jun'r gave a Relation of his convartion: and of his cal to the work of the ministry: and the churches confission of faith and covenant was read before assembly: and then proceeded to imposition of hands: then Thomas Paign gave the right hand of fellowship and after singing another psalm the assembly was dismist by the pronouncing a blesing.[7]

John Alden of Plymouth Colony fame had shipped on the *Mayflower* not as a Pilgrim but as the ship's carpenter. He found the business of religion exciting enough to lead him to stay with the colony. In much the same way his descendant, Joseph Snow, Jr., had cast his lot with the people of Providence as a "joyner" not of churches but of wood. He too finds the business of kingdom-building as exciting as house-building and by a strange sequence of events came to be the first minister of the first church across Weybosset Bridge, on the west side of the Salt River in Providence, the most truly Congregational-Separatist church in New England.

CHAPTER NINE

WEST SIDE SAINTS AND SINNERS

THE SEPARATION was complete, the meetinghouse was built, a covenant and confession of faith adopted, and a parson chosen and ordained.

The ordination had been on Thursday, February 12, 1747. The next Sunday found Joseph Snow, Jr., the minister of the church in his own right ecclesiastically; on a par with Josiah Cotton and all other shepherds of the New England Way. The congregation felt proud of one of their own number raised to the high office of minister, but Joseph's feelings must have been a surprise to himself. For three years he had been a leader of the congregation and to him the people had increasingly turned. The two Josephs, father and son, had been the most frequent Sabbath exhorters. This was not the first time the younger had stood at this new "desk" which had been fashioned with his own hands. But today it was different; he now spoke as an ordained minister of Christ; gone was some of the cocksureness he had felt when he had led the revolt against the church on the hill. If only the simple pulpit would fall apart and let him repair it with the skill of his hands instead of ornament it with the wisdom of his mind and the eloquence of his tongue. But fall apart it wouldn't, for he had built it like the bridge on a ship to withstand all of the storms which might come.

Nor was there a sense of ease acquired by the newly ordained parson on the following Sunday, February twenty-second.

Preaching to one's mother and father, brothers and sisters, in-laws, one's own children, familiar neighbors, and business associates was difficult enough, but to perform the priestly offices of the ministry was even more serious. For the first time the sacraments of baptism and the Lord's Supper, "the two outward Seals of the Covenant of Grace," were to be administered. Three children were baptized; two of them belonged to the minister and his wife, Sarah, and the third was Anna, the daughter of "Elizebeth Comton." Lidia Snow was three years old and Susanna sixteen months. As Joseph took Lidia in his arms, he wondered why his breath was so short and why he felt so warm on a February morning. His calloused right hand felt awkward as he dipped it in the pewter basin which he had probably brought from his father's house. The child whom he held so easily at home seemed a great burden at church. He wished he had watched Josiah Cotton's technique more carefully when he had baptized the older Snow babies. As he said, "in the name of the Father and the Son and the Holy Ghost," he found himself as out of breath as if he had lifted a great timber. But so thoroughly did he stamp Lidia's name upon her that she never changed it, dying in her thirty-first year unwed. Susanna, being the second child to be baptized, received lighter treatment. She would become the wife of Dr. Samuel Carew and live just below her grandfather's house at the corner of Abbott's Parade and Weybosset. Thus appropriately the first two children baptized in the new church were Snows. Hundreds with Snow blood under the names of Snow, Searle, Carew, Wardwell, Short, Barstow, Crapon, Dean, Lippitt, Gladding, Sampson, Field, Paine, Munro, Potter, Olney, Mumford, Andrews, Simmons, Jenckes, Rogers, and many more would follow in line—children of the minister's brothers and sisters, children's children, and children's children's children.

Joseph's wife, Sarah Field Snow, had been baptized April 25, 1725, by good Samuel Moody, among the first in Providence to receive Christian baptism from a minister of the New England Way. For those who remembered, it would have seemed that the baptism of her children as the first in the new church fulfilled all the requirements of tradition.

On the same Sunday there was an adult baptism and this, too, augured well for the quality of the church. It was no less a person than young Nicholas Cooke (Nickolas Coock, in the records) who would become a leading citizen during the Revolution, serving on most of the protest committees in the rapid succession of which Rhode Islanders were at the fore. He would be chosen the first governor of the colony after the break with the mother country and the deposing of Governor Wanton. There is no indication in the records but that his baptism was administered by water from the same pewter bowl as that used for the three children, but years later Nicholas Cooke was to claim that he was immersed. According to Isaac Backus, when "Governor Cooke was chosen member of the College Corporation and some scrupled whether he could properly be denominated a Baptist, because he was a member of a Congregational church, he informed them that he was ever a Baptist on principle, and was baptized by immersion, and should have joined the Baptist Church in Providence, if such doctrine had been preached therein then as there was now."

Could it be that politicians of that day of even the high caliber of Governor Cooke might forget or mistake sprinkling with cold water in February for what his Baptist critics would call the "real thing." Many of the West Side church were immersed in the Providence River, but something tells us that Joseph Snow, with his Massachusetts upbringing, did not undertake that particular phase of his ministry on a February Sunday right after his ordination.

On the same Sunday the Lord's Supper was administered for the first time. Possibly the bread came from Elizabeth Compton's kitchen; the wine may well have been elderberry. It was the first sacramental act of the deacons, who had been waiting a year and a half since their election to "deac." They were Benjamin Cary and Barzillai Richmond, with Joseph Snow, Sr., as ruling elder. Benjamin Cary had earned the office by his leadership in the quarrel and that was all that could be said in his favor as a deacon. Fortunately for the peace of the new church he would ultimately remove to Plainfield. But Berzillai Richmond set the pattern for the many deacons who were to follow, men who knew something of the meaning of religion, could be relied upon in church and community, would be opinionated but loyal to the end. He would hold the office until his death, an even half-century.

The Confession of Faith and the Covenant consented to by the minister and people at the ordination of Joseph the previous week was that day read and consented to by Nicholas Cooke and renewed by the congregation. One might catch in young Joseph's tones as he propounded the Confession of Faith some of the stern tones of his idol, Gilbert Tennent: "We believe that this God hath forseen and permited Sin." Contrasting softer tones which he may have heard in George Whitefield would be heard as he read of God's Grace, "that God hath not Left all mankind to perish Eternaly; but of the Riches of Free Grace Elected Some to everlasting Life."

The interpretation of the word "Some" would always remain a temptation to his type of temperament; at times it seemed easier to classify almost everyone with the "Some" not to be saved, than with the elected "Some." An embryo carpenter-theologian would be forming back of the words, "God that is parfictly three: and parfictly one. One in Assence: three in Subsistance: one in nature: three in Person." His hands would involuntarily grasp the Book as he read that the word of God is "a suficiant Standard both for our tryal and walk."

But in the Covenant, warmer tones would rise. Against the background of discord the sense of fellowship with this group was heightened and prized. For more than three years the little band of thirty-five had been knitting itself together through the trials of the quarrel and the adventures in new and high undertakings. (Nicholas Cooke made an even three dozen with a dozen and a half of each sex.)

And now they renewed the covenant already made: "We do unfainedly Rezine up our Selves and ours to the Lord Jehovah Father Son and Holy Ghost: and avouch him this Day to be our God: Father Saviour and Leader: our portion hear and forever."

They pledged their allegiance to Christ and his gospel, to the holding of regular communion with the whole "Regular Misticul body of Christ." And then there followed the three promises which would make the church more than a polite association. It would make it vitally concerned with the conduct, the welfare, and the lives of one's own family and each fellow member:

> We do solomly promis by the assistance of Gods Holy Spirit: mutually to watch over one another in Brotherly Offices of Love and tenderness by Reproofs and admonitions as Christ hath injoined us according to our Several places.
>
> We will oppose all Sin and error in our Selves and others as fer as in us Lyes: all Carnal Mearth or Recreation and wantonness idleness sensuality and all other sins forbiden in the Scriptures Renouncing the divel the world and the flesh: and all appearance of evel for Christs Sake:
>
> we will by Gods assistence be carefull to bring up all under our care in the nurture and admonition of the Lord.

Joseph Snow was building better than he knew. He and his followers had gone over hurdles and avoided pitfalls which wrecked many of the churches which came out of the Great Awakening. Bridgewater and Easton Congregationalism had triumphed against the excesses that such a movement usually brought forth and Providence tradition had corrected the tendencies of a Harvard-trained ministry which forgot that a Massachusetts clerical highhandedness was not a part of the pattern of religion in Rhode Island.

Some of the New Lights even in Providence went to excesses, if we are to follow John Checkley of King's Church who wrote in 1751:

> The infidels and the New-Lights rage most furiously against the Ordinances of Christ being necessary to Salvation. The Enthusiastic New-Lights affirming nothing necessary but what they wildly call Conversion. That is screaming and tumbling about on the Floor at once; oftentimes in their private and sometimes in their Publick Meetings; always screaming, and sometimes in a most hideous manner, calling upon People *to come to Christ, come to Christ, come to Christ.*
>
> This is what these horrid Enthusiasts call Conversion! On the other hand, the Infidels who laugh at these mad Pranks (and well they may) declare for the Religion of Nature, disclaim all revealed Religion, and affirm nothing necessary to an happy hereafter, (if there is an Hereafter which they say they very much doubt) and loudly plead (I say) that nothing is necessary to Happiness in another World but Morality, which, however tho they talk much about it, they practice but little of it.
>
> Thus from the Atheistical & unbelieving on the one hand and the wild Enthusiast on the other, I have extream hard Service.

None of these excesses were the teachings of the leaders of the Great Awakening, but belonged, rather, to the poorer type of exhorter who followed in their train somewhat as does a cheap side-show at a respectable county fair. The Ames girls might well have been interested in this greater demonstration of piety and perhaps on occasion forsook Joseph's flock for such antics, but the church's earliest records indicate that the horror of rolling ancestors is not a part of the West Siders' heritage.

There were older influences to be encountered than those of

the New Lights: the Baptists and Quakers. Again and again Checkley writes to the London Society for books on Water Baptism. In 1743:

> I most earnestly desire some Tracts upon Baptism, the hindering of people coming to that Ordianace being the point the Infidels mostly favour at present, I having baptized but four Children this last half year.

Here we find the first illustration of the necessity of conformity with the traditions of a community by those who invade it with an entirely different set of practices. Providence Plantations, while sheltering many sects, had been chiefly stamped by the Baptist and Quaker dies. All subsequent groups had to take account of this fact and modify their own practices. The roots of a community, even of as diversified a town as Providence, lie deep and determine the direction of the tree's growth even after three centuries.

That influence shaped the sacramental form of the "sprinkling churches." Checkley records, "Baptized a Quaker and Antipedobaptist both of whom (at their Desire) I baptized in the presence of many People by total Immersion. To a child I formerly gave Clinic Baptism." Up to 1800, Beneficent Church immersed at least half of its members and as late as 1832 was purchasing nine baptismal robes.

Another good Baptist tradition which the West Side Church adopted was that of monthly communion. As far as we have ascertained, Beneficent Church is the only Congregational church which observes it monthly, down to the present day.

Some of the New Light churches went to extremes, as described by John Checkley; many others became affiliated with the Baptists. Isaac Backus, the Baptist historian, was a product of Whitefield's preaching and a convert from the "established order." The great strength of the Baptists in the South was born out of this revivalistic period. The Congregational Separates movement, which in New England reached its height in Windham County, waned, but left its effect in Connecticut in persuading the churches ultimately to abandon the Saybrook Platform of 1708 and follow the Congregational pattern rather than the Presbyterian. Beneficent endured as a Congregational church, due to the Massachusetts churchmanship of the Snows, the liberality of the Providence tradition, and the real-estate boom which it started.

Nothing could have given Joseph Snow, Jr., a greater kick in these early years than the opportunity to go as a New Light missionary to his ancestral town in Massachusetts with the happy by-product of bringing into the New Light ministry Isaac Backus, who was destined to be one of the immortals of the Baptist church. Collectors today will pay just about any price for his three-volume history of the Baptists.

A new precinct, Titicut, had been organized in 1743 out of a portion of Bridgewater and Middleborough, for the purpose of establishing a new church of the congregational order supported by taxes. Joseph Snow, Jr., as a product of the town, found opportunity to advise in the matter of separation of church and state, and the forming of a truly Separate church or a church of the "new measures." He visited the community several times and finally took with him Isaac Backus, who records the story. On December 18, 1747, they went to "the house of Seth Hayward, a christian brother in Bridgewater, where they were kindly entertained.

(On the next day, we) visited several other Christians in the town, and had freedom in conversing with them. They appeared to be in reality hungering after gospel food. Towards night we came down to Titicut to brother Samuel Alden's, where brother Snow, who had labored in the place before, was welcomed with much rejoicing.

After a little, I went out abroad and was enabled to bless God that He had helped as hitherto. When I had come in, and we were seating ourselves to partake of food, these words came into my mind with great light and power: "Say not ye, There are yet four months, and then cometh harvest? Behold, I say unto you, Lift up your eyes, and look on the fields; for they are white already to harvest."

By these words I was led to discover in this place a large field all white to the harvest. Other men had labored here in years past, and the Lord had wrought wonders by them, but now my soul was constrained by divine light, love and peace to enter into their labors. My heart was so drawn forth toward God and in love of this people, that I felt myself willing to impart unto them not only the Gospel but my own soul also. Thus the Lord bound me to this people ere I was aware of it and before I knew any of them personally.

The next day they began a series of meetings and in ten days Joseph and Isaac preached alternately twenty-four sermons.

Monday, Dec. 28. This morning the Precinct Committee came and requested me, in case I would be examined and approbated by the neighboring pastors, to preach to them as minister of the parish. I replied that I was clearly convinced of its being my duty to preach to this people for the present, and that I cared not how many came to hear; that I was willing to be examined by their ministers, and to give them the reasons of my hope and my practice; but that I should not consent to their proposal with any such understanding as this, that the precinct instead of the church had a right to lead in the choice of a minister, nor should I leave it to man whether I ought to preach the gospel or no. This answer did not please them: yet they requested me to preach to them for a while. I afterwards found great reason to bless God for enabling me to be steadfast, and to escape the snares which men were laying for my feet. If I had yielded to their scheme they would soon have sent me off.

By April of the following year a New Light church had been formed of thirty-four members with articles and covenant peculiar "for their high toned spirituality, Calvinism, and republicanism." Mr. Backus had been chosen pastor and his ordination was set for April thirteenth. And now comes the clash between Massachusetts Congregationalism and Joseph Snow's Rhode Island pattern:

While the church and council were occupied with matters preliminary to the ordination, Benjamin White, Esq., rode up among the throng of people, and in the name of the Precinct Committee, of which he was a member, forbade all the proceedings. Yet this prohibition was disregarded, and Mr. Backus was solemnly ordained and set apart to the ministry of Christ and to the pastoral care of the church in Titicut.

It may not be amiss to add, that the Precinct Committee had previously, about the first of March, revoked their invitation to Mr. Backus to act as preacher for the parish. And the spirit which animated them may be inferred from the following circumstances. No compensation was made him for the services which he had rendered. His own language is this: "They never offered me a farthing for my preaching two months at their request." . . . "Directly afterwards," he adds, "they called a precinct meeting and taxed me five pounds." This tax was for the support of religion in the place, and Mr. Backus, who was conscientiously opposed to the maintenance of religious worship by the civil power, refused the payment. The result is given in the following memorandum. "Monday, February 6, 1749. This morning I was seized by the officer, who threatened to carry me to prison for the precinct-rate; but, glory to God, he gave me a sweet calmness and serenity of soul, so that I was able not to fear the officer, or treat him with any bitterness. I told him that they were going on in an unscriptural way to support the gospel, and therefore I could do nothing to countenance them in such a way. He told me that if I would not pay him he would immediately carry me to jail; but just as he was about to drag me away, there came in a man, Capt. Abiezer Edson, who called him out and paid him the money, so that he was forced to let me go." . . . "After they had imprisoned one of our brethren, and made distress on one of my hearers, it appeared upon trial in our county court, that said tax was voted at an illegal meeting. Yet they sent an agent to Boston and obtained an Act of their Legislature to make it legal, and the supreme executive court turned the case against my hearer upon said Act. Thus was judgment turned into wormwood; and this is the natural effect of the use of the sword to support religious teachers." [1]

Isaac Backus with this stormy start remained a lifetime in this parish, which eventually became a Baptist church. A half-century later he would take up his pen in defense of his patron, Joseph Snow, Jr. The incident at Titicut is, as far as we can ascertain, the first instance of a Providence missionary to Massachusetts insisting on the Rhode Island model of separation of church and state which later would become a national pattern.

Settled down in apparent peace and harmony, Joseph Snow's flock back in Providence was soon to be tried in its ability to deal in "Reproofs and admonitions." On March fourth, less than a month after his ordination, one of the saints was needing admonition. It was Keziah Knowlton, who had been the second woman after Sarah Snow, the minister's wife, to sign the covenant. She was found intemperate, but after a considerable time was restored again "upon a genuine confission."

Three of the more troublesome heritages from the mother church soon moved away. Deacon Benjamin Cary went to Plainfield; Sarah Ames to Killingly, and her sister, Anna, to Canterbury. It would seem more than a coincidence that they went to the centers of the New Light movement. It may be that they were disappointed in the course the new church had taken and went to the country of the "Lion of Plainfield" for a more lively religion.

The first twenty-two years of the new church's history are recorded in only twenty-one pages of Joseph Snow's "clark's" book, but they indicate periods of high excitement without great growth in church membership. Eighteen children were baptized that first year after his ordination, but only two members were received, Nicholas Cooke and Mary Dexter, making a total of thirty-seven from the beginning. In the next ten years about forty were added and by 1764 the total membership was ninety-two, less than four additions a year. Then in 1764 there was a great spurt; seventy-seven joined in that one year and twenty-three more the following year.

Two of the original eleven saints brought trouble to the church in this period. John Paine apparently was longing for the good old days of ecclesiastical excitement and went to Rehoboth to exhort. Here he announced that one of his fellow members in Providence, Daniel Branch, and apparently two members of the Rehoboth church, Jonathan French and Thomas Perry, had been cut off from the church by the Holy Ghost and been delivered up to the "Buffiting of saton." Some of the brothers stood up for John Paine's interpretation of the workings of both the "Holyghost" and "saton," and feeling ran so high that the Lord's Supper was omitted:

> . . . at last on a saterday the second day of february 1752 those of the Breethren and sisters that ware so offended with the other of the Breethren that they could not tell how to sett down with them att the sacrament Came into this Conclusion: that if the church as a body would do so much for the declaritive glory of god as to declare against the antinomian spiritt and against the Conduct of the said John pain: also considering that the lord had now lett so much lighte into this church that by the help of the holy spirit; the antinomian spirit could not Rule this Church. In the Evening of the said day the church was caled together on that acount and sum of the Brethren did then declare for said John pains disapline; that it was good: namly Nicholas Cook Berzilai Richmond Benjamin Cary & Nathaniel Jacobs them foure & no more; and the Rest of the Brethren there present did declare that in their opinion his manner of disapline was not acording to the Rule of the gospell and consequintly not good namely Joseph Snow pastor hugh Beatee Benjamin Cushing Alixander McCrary Isaac Cary Joseph Snow and Stephen Rawson.

Many issues were settled by divided votes which sometimes

left hard feelings. They realized that the problem of Christian democracy is what happens to the forty-nine (or less) per cent whose will is not accepted. We find an attempt to meet this:

> It was objected by Some that the Church in som of their former Acts: had been too arbitrary: that when a vote was obtained by the majour Part of the Church the miner were compelled to sumit: which brought great tryalls and temtations upon them which thing the Church Deliberately considered and unanimously agreed that if the Church as a Body or the majour part of the Church was of one judgment and the miner of another: that in order to make it a church act: the majour should first Labour with the miner with Light and Love that if possible it may be a unanimus act; but to act otherways is rong.

Here was more good Quaker influence!

The other saint to slip was Alexander McCrary. He, too, over-indulged in the product of the two divines and deacon down on Distil House Lane. After his first admonition he "made so much of a confission that the church allowed him a longer time for tryall." But the habit did not conquer easily and this letter was written to him:

> The Congregational Church of Christ in providence
> to our Brother Alixander McCrary
>
> Dear Brother with ardant desires of your Reform we send you this our second letter of admonition for the sin of intemperence in the use of strong drink . . . (we) call your conciance to witness against you if it cannot clear you before god who is the sarcher of all harts; . . . and if you neglect to hear the church we are in conciance to proceed and cast you out and cut you of from all the privileges of church felowship; we therefor in christ sted pray you to be reconsiled to god by making a harty confision of your sin and behold Bowels of christ how shall I give you up &c are in the Eliventh of Hosea 8 vearce; that god would give you a Repentence unto life is the harty prayer of your greeved Brethren upon which we now with

open armes and hart are Redy to Receive you and Bare your Burdens as our own; so we subscribe your Brethren

Joseph Snow in behalf of the church

It received a reply as contrite as could be asked for:

A confission writen with his own hand and sent to the church providence Aprill 12—1759

I the subscriber being of the church in providence under the pastoral care of Joseph Snow and now under admonition of the said church do make this acknolidgment that I am a worthy member in my great lord and gide as I trust I am in him; but in myself the most dreadfull creture Ever that hoped in him; I confis that there is no sin but I am gilty of; in perticuler the sin of intemperance of which I have ben justly Reproved by this church and have promised to guard against it and have: and in the fear of the Lord do now promise to guard against that sin in perticuler as if there was not another; my breethren I know it is my constitution sin; and I beg your prayers for me hopeing that yours and mine may meet in Heaven: in the fear of god I call myself your Brother in Christ.

Alixander McCrary

No further recurrence of discipline is noted in the records and we may conclude that Alexander worked for the glory of Joseph Snow's meetinghouse rather than Deacon Snow's "distil" house.

We have little knowledge of Joseph Snow's capabilities in thought and composition except from the "clark's records" and a few letters. Most of his epistles are vitriolic when he is waging a verbal war. That there was another side of his nature is shown in the letters of discipline which he wrote and particularly in a letter of entreatment seeking to retain in the fold another charter member and the first West Side settler, Elizabeth Compton. Elizabeth, who had come out of South Church, Boston, into

Josiah Cotton's church and then had come with the Snows down the hill, was flirting with Episcopacy after a twenty-year stay in the meetinghouse under whose shadow she lived. Sickness had played a part and she was not long for this life. But Joseph was as tender in seeking to keep his flock from further wandering after its desertion of the hillside pastures as he had been persuasive in leading it down the hill. In this letter Joseph shows himself skilled in the art of ecclesiastical debate, a good Bible quoter, and much more of a literatist than his spelling prejudices one to think.[2]

The first part of his letter to Elizabeth deals with the nature of the church and contains the fruit of many debates and much mind-searching concerning the ecclesia of England, Massachusetts, Providence, and the New Testament.

Dere sister we are surprized to hear by our Breethren sent to you to desire you to come and give us the Reasons of your abcenting from us that your Reply to them was that we ware not a church or no visible Church of Christ and so would not come; we think it our duty to lay sufficiant matter of conviction before you: and Reprove you for your conduct which we hope god will make Efectuall as followeth, first that the matter of a visible church are a Number of saints by calling, such as have not only the Knolidg of the principles of true Relidgon but Renounce grose and open scandals; but also profess faith in Jesus Christ and Repentance and walk in Blamles obediance to the word of god so that in a Judgment of Charity may be counted saints 1 Cor 1.2

Dear Sister our mouth is open our harts is inlarged; could it then Ever Entred into our Harts to think you could possibly in any measure Joyne with those that dispise the said work of god; and Neglect the fellowship of this church which is and has been so dispised by the wourld and atacked by Enimies: yett upheld by its foundation Bult up by the power of Soveraign grace, still praising god and haveing favour with all the people (acts 2-47); a church, (not to spake dispising of any other visable church) acording to the apostles discription; a visable church, if there is any now on earth; it is true the church of Corinth is not the Church of galatia nor the church of golatia the church of Ephesus nor the church of Ephesus the church providence but they ware all the visable churches of christ; at least the former were so in there day; but they ware all defective, at least sum of there members But the apostole cals them churches of christ and Rights to them to Reclame them that ware out of the way; and what he wrote to one church or to any of there members one or more is aplicable to another under the like mistake.

Then he appeals to her loyalty to the years of struggle together in the church:

you have ben a member of this church of christ upwards of twenty years: and you must still Remember that heretofore you have endured with us in our temtations: you can witness how smale and weak our begining was; we ware Reviled but we Reviled not again; being defamed we intreated; we ware made as the filth of the world: we ware persecuted and had Evell spoken against us falsely for Christs sake; but we Rejoyced and ware Nothing terrified by our advarsaries: which to them was an evident token of perdition but to us of Salvation and that of god; for unto us it was given in behalf of Christ not only to belive on him but also to suffer for his sake: farthermore you can witness tho our beginning was smale yett we are greatly incresed not withstanding all the opposition; what wonders hath god wrought among us for more then twenty years past. o what a Nomber of hardened stuburn sinners has ben Bowed to the soveranity of god. how often have you Rejoyced with us when the lord was pleased to power down his Spirit his Blessed Spirit upon us when sinners ware convinced and convarted and Saints Sweetly Refreshed and Comforted and Strengthened in faith and love patiance and Every grace; oh what Humbling self abaseing vews of Christ crucified has ben transforming to our one Soles and aditions made to the church of such as we hope shall be saved; thus the Kingdom of Heaven as a grain of mustard seed has increased: did you not then, as we, hope? you did withall your Hart Rejoyce with us; and give all the glory to god that loved us and gave himself for us; where is that Blessedness you once spake of?

The last part of the letter is a clever dialogue which he stages between the Apostles Paul, James, and John and Elizabeth:

> Pray dere sister let us all give deligent attention to what answers the apostle makes to you, a member of one of the above mentioned churches who at present hath abcented from us;
>
> Paul, ye did Run well who did hender you that you should not obey the truth; this perswasion cometh out of him that calleth you:
>
> Sister, I have ben a suferer for many years:
>
> Pall, ye have suffered so many things in vain if it be yett in vaine:
>
> Sister, but I had not so much lite then as I have now;
>
> John, but if we walk in the lite as he is in the lite we have fellowship one with another;
>
> Sister, but I have better instruction now; sum of my teachers appear to me as fathers and Pal saith Covit the best gifts.
>
> Pall, and yet I shew unto you a more Exlent way;
>
> Sister, but I have incresed in knowlidg by these fathers;
>
> Pal, Knowlidg puffeth up but charity Edifieth; . . . indeed bare with me for I am jealos over you with a godly jealocy I fear lest . . . as the Serpent begiled Eve through his subtelty: so your mind should be corupted from the simplicity of the truth that is in Christ.
>
> Sister, but my teachers are both larned and I think Established and are emminant in defineing faith which is very Nessary:
>
> James, but if ye have Respect to persons ye commit sin and are convinced of the law as transgressors: se then, by works a man is justified and not by faith only:
>
> Sister, I Exercise conchance in what I do:
>
> Pall, I Exercise myself to have alwayes a conscience void of offence towards god and towards man: wherefore ye must needs be subject for conscience Sake: give none offince Nither to the Jews nor the gentiles nor to the church of god.
>
> Sister, Should we not Receive the lords Supper Every first day of the week?
>
> Paul, as often as ye eate this Bread and drink this Cup ye do shew the lords deth tel he come:

The letter then closes with a strong but tender appeal to Elizabeth Compton to return to the fold:

and now Sister we look upon these appostles words to be binding and we belive our lords saying what soever ye shall bind on Earth Shall be bound in heaven: therefore upon the whole Dear Sister how many years have you ben a member of and a partoner with this church in our trials and favours as afore said, how often have we mett together in all the Blessed Docktrins of the appostles how often have we mett together in the Blessed fellowship of the gospel: How often have we mett together in Breaking of Bread and how often have we mett together in prayers; which Now we refer to your conscence in the most solem manner before god angels and men: oh how often have you Recognized your covenant with us you your self is witness: therefore being by the law of god bound in our consciances in faithfullness and love to your one soul: we joyne with the apostles as above and admonish you to Retorn to the Church of Christ which he hath purchised with his own Blod from which you have absented and that you no longer persist in the neglect of that command of our lord do this in Rembrance of me:

these Dere Sister in love with a Real and Earnest desire you may yett be Recovered from all mistaks and Restored to us and we to you; that we may yett injoy the divine presence alltogether as much and more then Ever here to fore, tell we are all prepaired for the Church triumphant, which is the prayer of your Efecionate Brethren in the lord

Amen

It is our best example of the other side of Joseph Snow. Surely he knew the "Brotherly Offices of Love." The letter is also the nearest thing we have to a biographical account of his trials and joys in the early days of the church and his own opinion of the rightness of his cause. But it was without avail and Elizabeth apparently spent the rest of her life in the communion of King's Church. After her death her husband, William, married again and his new wife, Allettier, did the neighborly thing and joined Father Snow's church. William himself had never joined, possibly becoming cynical after his rôle as peacemaker had failed in the First Church.

One of the choicest of all of Joseph's letters of admonition was the one to Jemime Bell, another imbibing sister:

July 4, 1763

The church of Christ in providence to our sister Jemime Bell sends greeting

we here send you our second adminition hoping that the spirit of god will assist us in our indavours to Reclame you from your abominable practice of Drinking of strong licquer to access: you are now in the Brawd Rhoad that leads to distruction Oh consider your ways and Repent and turn your feet into gods testimonies or you will be a pertaker of gods wrath; god has said that Drunkards shall have their part in the lake that Burns with fire and Brimston Oh Dear sister Realize the Dreadfull stat of those that have such a portion; consider that you are now in the way that lead directly to that Dredfull lake of fire and Brimston; make a full stop now and go no farther in that way: though drinking strong lyquer be as dere to you as your Right eye & as your Right hand—cut it of and pluck it out and drink no more strong lyquer; for it is better for you to go to heven haveing but one eye & one hand then to go to hell haveing two eyes and two hands; dont force this church by the spirit to cast you out of church felowship: consider that what this church doth here on Earth in that Respect will be confirmed in heaven if it be don by the influence of the true spirit; o that god would please to bless our indeavours so that you may Retorn with the prodigall & Have your soul Refreshed: beter then with a fatted calf:

Joseph Snow Ruling Elder

Sometime afterwards, the said Jemima was cast out of church.

Here Joseph did not have as good results as with Alexander McCrary. Apparently Jemima remained of the "nomber of hardened stuburn sinners."

New members "were required to take the Broad aisle; when

they were cut off by discipline it was customary to read such out of the Church as publicly as they were read in." As we read the records we marvel at the patience which those who insisted on discipline exhibited in their labors to reclaim straying sheep.

All manner of problems were brought before the church, such as the case of Elizabeth Rogers who in 1768 stole her neighbor's clothes. Perhaps they had been hung to dry on the fence and to Elizabeth seemed more on her side of the fence than on their owner's.

The town records report one of the concerns in 1757 was a request by the members of the Presbyterian Congregational church that Samuel Westcott have a license to keep a tavern near the meetinghouse. It might have been either of the churches; the request has the earmarks of a judgment upon the dry sermons which were occasionally preached.

A peculiar case of discipline came before the church in 1768 when a Brother Smith was complained about for making his home at the Mason's in Rehoboth, a family which was "on the town." The Rehoboth brethren had complained of the conduct of the Beneficent brother. He was urged to leave his new-found abode, but finally for his "still neglecting to hear the Church and for his disorderly walk he is rejected and cast out of the church."

By 1770 some of the new freedom was expressing itself in grosser immorality. Members of both sexes were tried for fornication; two repented, another "confessed and promised to make gospel repairation unto the unhappy Partner of his Sin." But, failing to do this, he was rejected.

Another saint was taken by death from the company in 1774. It was Deacon Stephen Rawson. His life had been like his fountain, a source of refreshment and cleansing to those about him. It became necessary to "chuse a dacon in his roome." Brother Henry Bacon was elected. He was examined before the church and it was manifest that he professed "to believe that through the atonement of Jesus Christ the whole human race here after will be etarnaly saved." Laboring with him had no effect. He was "admonited in wrighting." It was the first appearance of Universalism in the company, but would not be the last. But freedom was in the air and the deacon served with his unorthodox views until 1791, when infirmities kept him from further service.

In 1775, Deacon Ebenezer Knight, charter member and the first "country merchant" on High Street, died.

The decade before the Revolution was full of excitement. Rhode Island's fiery governor, Samuel Ward, was the only New England governor who dared refuse to take his oath to enforce the Stamp Act. Nicholas Cooke had been one of the Rhode Island committee with Stephen Hopkins to draft a protest in 1765. In 1766 the act was repealed.

There were also demands for freedom among the saints in the church. William Richmond, son of Barzillai, had not responded kindly to being called up for declaring that there was no need of conviction before faith and that "all conviction before faith was of the same nature as the conviction of the damned in hell." This was in 1766. Two years later we find a vote that "being satisfied with Brother Richmond's gifts, manifested their freedom for his improving his gift by way of Doctrain and Exortation both at home and abroad." It looked as if William had carried his demand for freedom in the church.

Some of the saints were falling asleep. Sarah Field, wife of Joseph Snow, Jr., "dyed" July 19, 1753, at the age of forty-three. She had borne nine children in twelve years, only four of whom outlived her. She had stood loyally at her husband's side during the years of hard work. Her eldest daughter, Sarah, the first to be baptized in the meetinghouse, died three months before her mother. Joseph mourned his wife's memory for eight months and married Rebecca Grant of Boston. She would bear him four more children, among them Samuel, the most illustrious of the parson's offspring. He was at Rhode Island College at the outbreak of the Revolution, entered the army, and became a captain. In 1780 he was back at college and graduated in 1782. He married Frances Wanton, great-granddaughter of Chief Justice John Gardiner. Later Samuel Snow would engage in the China trade and become first United States consul to Canton, on the appointment of President John Adams.

Deacon Snow's wife, Elizabeth, outlived her daughter-in-law (and cousin—both were Fields) fifteen years, dying April 15, 1768, at the age of seventy. She, too, had mothered nine children; only the three sons, Joseph, Jr., Daniel, and James were living to mourn her death. The old deacon would follow her in five years at the age of eighty-three, but in the meantime he felt that the admonition, "it is not good for man to be alone," applied to old Josephs as well as young Adams, and he married Marcy McClanell, one of the charter members of the church who had signed the covenant directly after his first wife, Elizabeth. "Marcy" outlived her husband by nine years. Marcy was a widow, whose grandchild, Eliacum Hand, her future stepson had baptized in 1750. Since the formation of the church she had been a devoted member.

Either before he reached the decision to remarry or else because of it, and also that he might assure his children of his loyalty to them and their mother, the aged deacon gave much of what remained of his Westminster Street property to Joseph, Jr.

Others of those early saints were getting old also. Solomon Searle had remained loyal all through the years and had served as sexton since the church was built. Death overtook him in 1774, when he was just getting a new business well under weigh. He had purchased a horse and cart and carried the neighbor's corn and rye to the old gristmill for grinding. He received three coppers a bag. Ebenezer Knight, of the original ten, died the first year of the war. Three of the ten besides Joseph Snow, Jr., lived to be fifty-year members of the church: John Paine (we hope he grew milder), Barzillai Richmond, and Thomas Dexter.

A familiar town's figure which also stood for liberty was mourned in this same period. It was Manna, the freed slave of Gabriel Bernon; he had opened the first oyster-house on Towne Street and been widely popular.

Joseph was frequently called on to go to ordinations and services for constituting new churches. In 1785 he had the prayer at Israel Day's ordination in South Killingly. Ezra Styles says that most of the ministers there were lay-ordained, except as the apostolic succession had been unwittingly maintained by the participation of Rev. Mr. Dennison, who had joined the New Light group. Mr. Dennison seems not to have been at Joseph Snow's ordination but those who had had the laying on of hands from him were there.

Joseph Snow, Jr., had become an humble prophet of a new and better brand of Congregationalism, in which things must be done decently and in order without offending the freedom of men. He even sought to solve the inherent problem of democracy by holding up the rights of the minority. His ultimate solution was in his definition "the matter of a Visible Church are a number of saints by calling," "fitly joined together," ruled by God, and a spirit of charity.

CHAPTER TEN

A VILLAGE IS BORN

SIDE BY SIDE with the ecclesiastical adventures of the Snows went their real-estate exploits. To plant a New England village a half-mile west of the Greate Bridge in Providence was no mean undertaking. President Dwight said of the colonists and their many village plantings "a more hardy effort begun with more discouraging prospects and executed with smaller means, more unruffled patience, and more immoveable perseverance has rarely been made by man."

When Deacon Snow arrived in Providence there were a dozen houses west of the bridge. John Howland lists six owners in 1721: Dr. Hoyle, Ebenezer Knight, Deacon Cary, the old Mathewson house (northwest corner of now Union and Weybosset), Nathaniel Jacobs, and Job Sweeting's (now Grosvenor Building site). He thinks there may have been a few others. In 1739 a bridge was constructed across Muddy Dock (Dorrance Street) to connect Weybosset and (then) Broad Street. Previously this had been a fording place.

The Snows and Fields would change this West Side scene. "As expansive as the Snow-Fields" was a good real-estate proverb of the day.

Deacon Joseph Snow had no intention of depending on father-in-law John Field's large land holdings on the west side of the river. With the proceeds from the sale of his Easton holdings to the minister as a parsonage estate, Joseph, Sr., immediately purchased from Captain James and Elizabeth Arnold of Warwick some of their family's original grant on the west side "neore s^{d} Providence Town." It extended along the south side of what is now Broad Street, east from Claverick to what would become the site of Beneficent Church, ending at "an old stump at the head of the valley." [1]

Altogether Joseph Snow purchased seventeen lots of land. In his most optimistic moments he saw all of this land quickly resold at a good profit, plus opportunities for himself and sons to build houses upon the land they sold.

The early resales were not of a land-office character. His first customer was William Whitney, apprentice to Richard Waterman, the town clerk, who recorded the many Snow deeds. In May, 1740, he sold the lot next to the future site of the church he would help found (where the newsstand now is) to William Compton, joyner, and thus began the development in the vicinity of the future church and common. The lot, which is only forty by forty, brought sixteen pounds, which is rather good profit on land bought from four to forty pounds an acre. The sale price was at the rate of over four hundred pounds per acre. William seems to have been a little gullible, coming from Boston. It may explain why he was not as immediately co-operative in the Separatist movement sponsored by the man who dealt in West Side real estate at fancy prices.

But it worked the other way eventually with Matthew Short, Jr., "nailer." Although Joseph's son-in-law, he had been a loyalist at the Cotton Church. With his purchase of land in 1741 from Joseph Snow, he eventually became a member of the new church.

The real boom did not set in until the planning of the new church, the erection of its building, and the gift of the common. Then the West Side of Providence went New England. Life grew up not around the mill but around the church and tiny village green.

House lots were purchased and built upon. The men who raised the buildings from cellar to roof-tree were Joseph Snow, blacksmith; Joseph Snow, Jr., joyner; William Compton, joyner; James Snow, house carpenter; Matthew Short, nailer; Daniel Snow, mason; and Solomon Searle, helper. On Sunday the same people met in the meetinghouse as minister, ruling elder, deacons, and sexton.[2]

The 1746 Abbott deed speaks of Solomon Searles' house built on land "I gave" to him. It would be of interest to know the reason for Daniel's generosity to good Solomon who would serve many years as the church sexton and live to a ripe old age.

President Dwight did not know Joseph Snow, John Field, and Daniel Abbott or he might have qualified his statement that land in America is like water to the European, "valuable in itself but too abundant to become the subject of price."

Joseph Snow, Jr., came into the real-estate picture in 1740 and purchased two acres of land for £95. On it he built a house which three years later he sold to Ebenezer Knight, Merchant, for £200.

Because Daniel Abbott's land was such a peculiar-shaped bite out of the Snow holdings, the problem of straightening the lines of the West Side church property plagued the officers of the church for a hundred and fifty years. Purchase after purchase and swap after swap of little slivers of land were made. Both the meetinghouses of 1746 and 1810 were built hanging over the edge of their legitimate sites, resting on other peoples' land. There is no record of any legal dispute arising or any exorbitant prices asked. Neighboring owners accepted reasonable amounts for land, and finally the meetinghouse foundations rested on church-owned land.

During its two hundred years, Beneficent Church entered

into nearly half a hundred legal agreements regarding its property, exclusive of the sale of pews and burial lots! William E. Richmond never worked harder for ten dollars than he did in 1847. That was his pay for searching the records and making a report in relation to the boundary of the meetinghouse lot.

The purchase of the Arnold and Peleg Williams' lands put the squeeze play on good Daniel Abbott who suddenly found his holdings entirely surrounded with the property of Joseph Snow. It may have helped him to make up his mind to the generous offer of the land for the church and common. But he was a Yankee too and held out a little more than a quarter acre from the gift. This he sold to Joseph for fifty pounds. Not a bad deal for Daniel! It was the land around the east and south sides of Abbott Park. It was on this property at the corner of Weybosset and Abbott Park (now Summerfield's or McGee's Furniture store) that Deacon Snow erected his own house. The rest he sold as house lots to his sons Daniel and James, on the site of the Plantations Club and Waite-Thresher building, and did not cut the price.

Here Daniel and James settled down with three of Solomon Searle's daughters as their respective wives. Daniel married Elizabeth in 1749 and Sarah in 1767; James married Hannah in 1755. Solomon's house lot was only 32 x 30 x 30 x 20 (site of the Dr. Krom room in the present meetinghouse). It was a handy location for the first church sexton. Deacon Snow's daughter Susanna married Dr. Samuel Carew and they settled down the street, two houses below her father, with Deacon Richmond's house intervening.

Real estate was booming sufficiently by 1749 for the town council to grant a petition for the laying out of a highway from the "parting of the Paths by Dr. John Hoyles house (Broad and Weybosset) southward to Pawtuxet Line."

In 1749 the biggest land deal of them all had been launched, when widow Elizabeth Mathewson was empowered by the General Assembly to sell her husband's property to pay his debts. Her husband, Nathan, had died in the Cape Breton Expedition. Joseph Snow organized a company to make the purchase of the large Mathewson estate, now bounded by Weybosset and Westminster, from what is now Clemence Street (then Sugar Lane) to Cathedral Square, containing close to ten acres (today center of Providence's highest priced commercial land). With him in the company were Joseph Snow, Jr., joyner, Barzillai Richmond, hatter, and James Brown, shopkeeper. With the exception of James Brown, it was a New Light enterprise. Joseph Snow is not denoted as "blacksmith," but "Esquire." He had earned the title, for in this deal he raised £1600 in "bills of public credit old Tenor." Joseph Snow, Jr., is still referred to as "joyner" rather than "Clark" or "minister," although it was two years after his ordination. James Brown was probably the eldest brother of Nicholas, Joseph, John, and Moses; named for his father, he succeeded him and his uncle Obadiah in the shipping business, but only for a few years, as he died in 1751 still under thirty.

The following year the land company divided their holdings. Whether Deacon Richmond and Merchant Brown found it difficult to join hands with two strong individualists such as Joseph Snow and his son we do not know. James Brown took the base and apex of the triangle. Joseph Snow, Sr., and Joseph, Jr., took the central block of land and divided it by "Snow's Lane" (now Snow Street), the deacon developing west of the lane directly across from the meetinghouse, and the minister between the lane and what is now Mathewson Street. Barzillai Richmond came out of the deal with an irregular-shaped piece between Merchant Brown and Joseph Snow, blacksmith.

Ultimately much of Joseph, Senior's, holdings would be given to his son, Joseph, Jr. The minister seems to have had at least three dwellings. Before 1739 he lived on the south side of Weybosset Street, about where Walker Electric Company now is. His brother-in-law, Dr. Samuel Carew, succeeded him here and Joseph, Jr., built on the site of the future distil house on Distil House Lane (Page Street); after 1750 he built his home at the corner of Weybosset and Mathewson, on the site of Liggett's Drugstore, with his garden extending along Middle Street (Chapel) in back of his house.

The young parson lost no time and led a movement of landholders in 1751 to give the land for what is now Westminster Street (Providence's main artery of commerce), "in consideration of the love and good will which we have and do bare for and towards the inhabitants of the Town of Providence, their interests, advancement and advantage and growth and for the benefit of all his Majesty's subjects in general." The road was laid out from what is now Cathedral Square to Waterman's marsh and through the marsh to Jacob Whitman's Turk's Head, but was built at first only a portion of the distance.

Various names were used for the street. At first it was unnamed and so was called New Street, then Back Street, as Benefit Street had been called a hundred years before. Finally Joseph Snow, Jr., with all of his Calvinistic hopes for the new village, named the street Westminster. His congregation who lived and worked upon it would hear frequently of the Westminster Confession. There would also be a romance about a name which bespoke the hopes of a growing village centering around the "West Church." A Westminster Congregational church would one day be built upon it, become Unitarian and move off the street, and yet because of happy associations retain the good old Calvinist name. It would remain for a modern generation unconscious of history and theology, to set their fathers' teeth on edge by calling it "Westminister."

The street thus named extended only as far as Turk's Head

at the junction of Weybosset. Here it joined Market Street to cross Weybosset Bridge. The builders of the first houses upon the street followed an unusual agreement. They uniformly built four feet back from the street bounds. It was a brand new idea, containing much foresight. This cleared the way for the petition of 1784 to widen the street to forty-eight feet:

That the inhabitants who have built houses on said St. have by universal consent left 4 ft. on each side of the St. for the purposes of widening the same, so that the St. between houses already built is 48 ft. wide. As there are considerable vacancies yet to be built upon some of them may fall into the possession of less generous minds who may not conform to the laudable custom of those who have already built on said St. and put their buildings quite up to the line of the St. as it was originally laid out while if it should be done would not only be to the prejudice of those who have already built, but would mar the beauty and uniformity of said St.

But the petition had not quite stated the facts. Down at the junction of Weybosset, the houses of Jacob Whitman and his neighbors had been built either without compliance with or previous to the "laudable custom." The town council's committee was weak-kneed and allowed the street to "bottleneck" at this point to "as wide as may be without obliging any person to remove their building." Townsfolks grumbled about it for twenty years, some saying nothing could be done until old Jacob Whitman went to his reward and the Turk's Head passed into other hands. This at last came about in 1802 but, alas, there was Jacob, Jr., now to deal with. Courage and determination were found in 1806 and it was ordered that the street at the bottleneck should become forty-eight feet wide. Property owners William Taylor, Peter Grinell, William Lee, and Levi Ham were public-spirited and agreed to the widening, "provided the buildings should not be removed until they should be taken down by the proprietors thereof or be destroyed by accedent."

But Jacob, son of Jacob, lived up to expectations. He held out as long as he could and finally compromised with progress when the town raised its offer from two hundred to three hundred dollars for damages. The others did not ask for or receive damages. Jacob, sitting in his large garden under his huge white mulberry tree, would rub his Yankee hands together in pleasure that he had not lost the battle for nought, nor had he failed to carry on the family tradition.

The first house lots to be sold were on the north side of Weybosset Street. It still took an adventurous spirit to live on New or Back Street.

The block now bounded by Westminster, Mathewson, Chapel, and Snow streets was Joseph Snow, Junior's, particular joy. The larger part of it was for years "Rev. Joseph Snow's garden." In dry weather the garden could be watered from the brook which ran through the south side of the lot. The deeds allowed one to three feet for "run of water" at the edge of the lots. The aisles of Grace Church still show the effects of the uneven ways of the brook. Where the Albee Theater now stands was developed as a potash lot by Joseph Snow, Jr.

Mathewson Street was first called Cross Street, connecting Old Street and New Street (Weybosset and Westminster). Soon it became School House Lane, for now that the West Side community had centered itself in New England fashion around the church and green it must have a school. Samuel Nightingale was the leader of the movement and organized a group of proprietors to buy land and erect a school. The lot was small, thirty by forty-two feet, located on the southeast corner of the block (site of Grace Church parish house). Four feet of it extended into what is now Chapel Street. Purchased in 1761, the schoolhouse was built in 1763. The hopes it expressed were greater than their fulfillment. Education was not one of the commodities which found ready acceptance, even in the West Side community, where Providence ideas made a healthy struggle against New England traditions.

The back corner lot (Westminster and Mathewson) was occupied by the house and barn of Nehemiah Ward, who was followed by Joseph Bennett, Benjamin Hoppin, Paul Allen, and John Brown as subsequent owners. In 1795, Providence's first theater company was organized and purchased a portion of this corner lot. John Brown was the largest stockholder and Jeremiah Olney was treasurer. John Mumford and Bennett Wheeler of the West Side Meetinghouse were among the purchasers of shares. They may have crossed the street when they saw the parson coming.

The first plays were produced in September, 1795, and were "The Child of Nature," and "Rosina or the Reapers." A traveling Scotch company had presented plays in Providence in 1762, the first theatrical production in New England. Between this date and the erection of the theater there had been a statute of the General Assembly forbidding theatrical productions. Subsequently there would be strong church statutes on the same matter, from which many of the flock would stray.

Grace Church purchased the lot in 1832 by buying out the thirty shares which in the three decades had become quarter shares in some cases of inheritance, and had been scattered among a hundred or more holders of half and quarter shares.

Samuel Nightingale, Harvard graduate slated for the ministry, had used the excuse of health from following his profession. He was a real community leader. A member of the First Church on the hill, he resided and found his other interests in the West Side community. We have already mentioned his leadership in building the schoolhouse. Looking around for other essentials for a community and a good investment as well, he decided no community was complete without a distillery. He chose as his partners in the undertaking Deacon Joseph Snow and Rev. John

Bass, who had given up as the successor of Josiah Cotton, deciding that he too was not for the ministry. They erected the Concord Distil House south of Weybosset Street on "Distil House Lane," now Page Street, next to the dwelling of Samuel Nightingale, which was at the southeast corner of Weybosset Street and the Lane. On a summer night Samuel could smell the fumes of his profitable business as he meditated upon theology.

Later Samuel bought out Joseph's and John's interests and began to lay the foundation of the Nightingale fortune which within a few decades would, among other things, build the mansion on Benefit Street which today is the home of John Nicholas Brown.

Miss Kimball writes, "Each Sabbath morning found him shaking the dust of the Snow Neighborhood from his polished shoes with their shining silver buckles" to climb the hill to the meeting house at the head of Presbyterian Lane. But during the week there was "concord" on secular matters and material spirits at the Distil House.

An interesting engineering undertaking which may well have arisen partly from a desire to increase the efficiency of the Concord Distil as well as to take care of the drainage problem in the low point of Weybosset Street was the development of a series of "docks" or ditches. The first of these was dug along Distil House Lane in 1752 and was known as Grate Dock. Tradition has it that it was used not only for drainage but at high tide served as an artery of commerce. Barrels of molasses were unloaded at Long Wharf (near the present Custom House Street) and floated to the distil. After their contents had been processed into rum they would be floated back on an ebb tide again to be loaded on shipboard.

A second "dock" was dug on the parallel street (Garnet) in 1757 and was known as New Dock. This was an ambitious layout with the fourteen-foot dock bounded on either side by a twenty-foot street, thus making the first parkway or boulevard in town. Muddy Dock (Dorrance Street) was dug in 1762.

In addition to Joseph Snow's blacksmith shop, the carpenter shops of Joseph Snow, Jr., and William Compton, the quarry from which Daniel Snow would gather his foundation stones, the clay bank for bricks (now the comfort station on Weybosset Street), and Matthew Short's and John Angell's shops for the making of nails, there were many other industries coming to the West Side.

By the 1750's the name of the Eddy family is prominent in the West Side church and down in the new shipyard. Ezek Eddy was a boatbuilder and Ichabod a blacksmith. Stephen Wright and others are listed as ship's carpenters when they buy house lots from the Snows.

Richard Seaver bought the southeast corner property at Chestnut and Weybosset (now occupied by a drugstore) before 1756, which gave it the name "Seaver's Corner" for a century. He and Richard Bacon were chaise makers. Richard and his wife, Hannah, joined the church "next door" September 22, 1757. Other sample trades of West Siders were Daniel Branch, "taylor"; John Aplin, attorney-at-law; Grindall Rawson, shop joiner (possibly cabinet maker); David Smith, cordwainer; Paul Ten, sheriff; Stephen Rawson, gentleman; Thomas Perry, yeoman.

Farther out from the church center there was a slaughterhouse, Calvin Dean's tanyard, and a ropewalk. The day would come in the 70's when houses would have running water from the fountains of two of Joseph Snow's church pillars, Stephen Rawson and Deacon John Field. Knight Dexter, on the road to Meshanticut, and Christopher Olney, on the road to Connecticut Government, would become large landholders. New horizons of travel and business would be lengthened with the building of the Tar Bridge across the Woonasquantucket.

As community consciousness grew in the "Snow-Fields," with it grew the feeling of rivalry with the community on the east side of the river. Composed of older families, the political life was too much in their hands, and they were the conservatives in foreseeing progress, so thought the West Side folk. While the East Side was content to wander in an irregular course along Benefit Street, dodging family graveyards, the West Side had laid out its streets in a straight line and buried its dead in one neat acre, the Dr. Hoyle church lot, as befitted a New England community. Feeling and community pride rose so high that in 1770 a petition was submitted to the General Assembly, asking that the area on the west side of the Bridge should be set off as a separate town, to bear the name of Westminster.

Miss Kimball writes of the petition:

The number of inhabitants is estimated at twelve hundred, "among whom are at least one Hundred Freemen . . . altho it is but a few Years since building Houses took Place there." The people are described as "Tradesmen chiefly . . . (who) by Diligence and Industry . . . surmounted many Difficulties to effect a Settlement. They levilled several Hills which stood in their Way, filled up sunken and low Places, laid out and made divers commodious Streets and Lanes . . . and have Reason to hope, that with a Blessing on their future Industry, they will in a few Years become Very Populous."

Furthermore, it is alleged that "Nature herself hath interposed, and divided them from the old Settlement by an Arm of the Sea . . . (and) Besides this Detachment . . . the Interests, Views, and Occupations of the Inhabitants on either Side of the Water, and their Modes of getting a Living are so distinct and different, that an united Force of the whole for the public Service, can never be expected." And here the petitioners, in sorrow rather than in anger, "beg leave to remark that they have in many Instances been aggrieved by their powerful Neighbours in the Other side of the Bridge, the Particulars whereof they forbear to mention from a Tenderness to them, and Love of that Union and Harmony which ought to be kept up in any Community." Nevertheless, all past injuries shall be overlooked, and past contentions buried in oblivion, if only "all that part of the Town of Providence lying westward of Weybosset Bridge, and the Harbour or Bay, may be incorporated into a Town, to be called and Known by the Name of Westminster, or such other Name as the Assembly shall think fit." "Weybosset" was the name first selected for the new civic entity, but the word was carefully erased, and "Westminster" written in its stead.

Even the petitioners were not aware of the deep underlying currents which had led them to want to become a separate town. The surface and immediate reasons they had rightly analyzed: differences in occupation and ambition and weakness in political power. But underneath was the fact that the Roger Williams brand of individualism, now much less poverty-stricken, had become a self-satisfied if not smug way of life on the east side of the bridge. On its west side the experiment to make a synthesis out of freedom, culture and enterprise was more lively than anything Roger had ever witnessed. The fate of the school on School House Lane showed many that in just the matter of education something besides individualism was needed by those who could not afford private tutors for their children.

What Joseph Snow, Jr., had done, often blunderingly, for religion, needed doing for the other aspects of town life. But fortunately for the future it would be accomplished by a slower process than "twin-town" legislation.

Defeated in their petition, the spirit of the West Side folks was not daunted and they set out to make life comfortable. Soon many housewives would lead their East Side friends into the kitchen and proudly display the magic of the spigot which, when opened over the wooden sink, would yield the purest stream of water ever seen. Some were fed by the Field fountain directly in back of the church and others by the Rawson fountain north of the church.

There was good-natured rivalry between the patrons of each

as to the relative merits of their waters. The chances are they were both from the same vein. The "fountains" were proof of Yankee enterprise. They were also testimonials of the particular resourcefulness of Father Snow's flock; the fountains were part and parcel of the Snow real-estate-religious-development on the West Side. The land for the Field fountain had been given by public-spirited Captain John Field. A log aqueduct three-fourths of a mile in length had been constructed by Joseph Bucklin and Nicholas Clark in 1772, said to be capable of carrying a hundred gallons a minute. The families served by it had written a letter of thanks to Captain Field: "We are supplied with fresh water in a more convenient manner than any of the inhabitants of the colony."

Deacon Field had no more cherished possession than the silver tankard presented him by the Field Fountain Society. In his will he left it to his wife and "on her decease it shall be lodged with my son Daniel (and then) it shall devolve to him or her of my Heirs who shall then live nearest to the Fountain out of respect to the Society who so generously and politely presented me therewith."

In October of the following year, the "Rawson Fountain Society" was incorporated and dug a reservoir for its spring "Thirty feet in length, thirteen and a half feet wide and about ten feet deep." Special machinery was invented on the spot for boring the logs with a four-inch bore. The log pipeline was a mile and a quarter in length. Religion has often found streams of living water a choice symbol of its task and treasure. It became realistic to those early worshipers in Father Snow's meeting and must have stayed in their imaginations, for a century later we discover a beloved deacon (James G. Woolworth) of Beneficent, who had married a descendent of Stephen Rawson, inventing a water filter! It was in general use in Providence homes up to the building of the Scituate Reservoir.

Following the Revolution, there was yet another piece of real-estate development in which Elder Snow and his West Side flock took the lead. In the area now bounded by Broad, Chestnut, Friendship, and Foster streets there had been constructed Fort Sullivan. The Snows, Richmonds, and Fields used the fort and much of the hill on which it stood to create more house lots by filling in the marshland along the river; thus forts were beaten into gardens in which the peaceful plowshare could ply its profession.

Not only did the Snow lands increase, but so did the Snows. Deacon Snow sired nine children and Joseph, thirteen—nine by his first wife, Sarah Field, and four by his second wife, Rebecca Grant of Boston.

From Joseph Snow, Junior's, marriage in 1737 there are eighty-nine Snow marriages recorded in Providence. They marry the Searles, Fields, Gladdings, Olneys, Jenckes, Paines, Wardwells, Bosworths, Barstows, Lippits, Greenes, and many others, until it sounds like calling the church roll.

As Deacon Snow became in age and appearance the West Side patriarch, he could stand at Abbott Parade and see in every direction lands which he had owned and sold; there were other lands which had belonged to his father-in-law, John Field, and some of them had come to his wife, Elizabeth. There were the holdings of his son, the minister, and the houses of his other children. Most of the houses in the community contained hinges and cranes from his forge and in their cellars a product from the distillery of the three Congregational leaders. Up the road in John Hoyle's acre were the graves of many who had stood at his side in the building of the meetinghouse-centered-West Side village. More than any single individual he had been the founder of the church and creator of the community which his son had wanted to name Westminster. Perhaps the old man would have preferred "Snowfield."

CHAPTER ELEVEN

THE BAPTISTS PLANT A COLLEGE AND HOLD COMMENCEMENT

WHILE THE Congregational churches of Providence were being led by the humble mind of Joseph Snow and the rather ineffectual ministry of David Rowland, two of the most brilliant Congregational lights in America were holding forth at Newport in the 1770's. Ezra Stiles, who was to become president of Yale and write voluminous diaries, came to the Second Church, Newport, in 1755 and remained until the outbreak of the Revolution. Called the "most learned American of his day," his greatest weakness seemed to be that he knew it. Samuel Hopkins became the pastor of the First Church in 1769 and remained until his death in 1803. His was a great, gentle, and courageous soul yet he became the center of controversy as the father of "Hopkinsianism" which would be warmly defended and attacked during and beyond its Newport founder's life. His installation sermon at Newport had a choice text, "I ask for what intent ye have sent for me."

It is Ezra Stiles who gives us our first estimated religious census of Providence. He tells us that at the time of the upsweep in membership in Father Snow's church (1764), Providence contained "five hundred dwelling houses, and about four thousand inhabitants, or half as big as Newport . . . I estimate one hundred families real Baptists; one hundred and forty political Baptists and nothingarians; one hundred and forty Mr. Snow's congregation, two-thirds Baptists, one-third Presbyterians; sixty Pedobaptist Congregationalists; forty Episcopalians; twenty families, Quakers; a few Sandemanians, and about twenty or forty persons Deists."[1] Thus Joseph Snow's congregation was by a considerable margin the largest in town.

Not in vain had the Snows combined real estate and churchmanship. Westminster Street, which they had opened and given to the city in 1751, was beginning to present a short row of houses.

Other growing pains of the town were demonstrated by the setting off of Cranston from Providence in 1754, Johnston in 1759, and North Providence in 1765. In all, Providence would give away eight towns. The success of these petitioners had encouraged the petitioners for "Westminster"; they, too, had come close to independence.

In spite of this growth in population religion in the 70's was far from enjoying a healthy state. James Manning, first president of Rhode Island College (Brown University), wrote to an English benefactor, "The state of religion is generally at a low ebb amongst us. May the Lord revive it. Would your English people be scared at an American Indian?" The juxtaposition of the two subjects is hard to account for. Possibly he felt that the state of religion needed a few war-whoops to pep it up. A decade later he writes, "I think the aspect of things is more favorable in our churches, public worship better attended, the ministry better supported, and more appearance of a revival of God's work. Even poor Providence seems to share a little. I baptized one young man last Lord's Day and some more are under serious impressions." "Poor Providence" had been doing rather well, considering her past, before Mr. Manning arrived on the scene. He and his college did bring an influence to the community which gradually changed much of its thought and direction.

Among other things it brought to the Baptists their first minister who was a college graduate since Roger Williams deserted them. He served a stormy internship. An hundred-and-thirty-year reign of home-talent parsons was not going to end without strong protestations. Samuel Winsor had been minister of the church for over ten years and asked for help, "considering his remote situation from town," and Manning was chosen in response to this request. Samuel Winsor seemed at first to favor Manning, but perhaps discovered that he would be more than an "assistant," and with others began raising objections. The first of these was that Mr. Manning had taken communion with them (at the church's invitation): they objected to "transient communion." The next objection was that Manning did "not make non-imposition of hands a bar to communion, though he himself had received it and administered it to those who desired it." [2] This was the "sixth principle" which had divided the church in its infancy. Many felt, however, that Mr. Winsor's great objection was "to the President's holding to singing in public worship; which was highly disgustful to Mr. Winsor." Difficulties at the foot of the hill proved to be greater than on its summit for Manning, serving in his dual capacity of college president and Baptist parson.

Samuel Winsor withdrew to break bread in Johnston under the complete six principles. There were eighty-seven members in the new church, probably not all from the First Church, in the opinion of Guild, as it would have left but thirty-one.

It was the Six Principle Baptists' love of the sixth chapter of Hebrews which brought about the beautiful seal and flag of the state of "Rhode Island and providence plantations," as the name of the colony was capitalized in 1664—probably by a Newport committee! In that year the word "HOPE over the head of the Anker" was declared to be the "Present Seale of the Colony." The inspiration came from Hebrews 6:19, "Which hope we have as an anchor of the soul." The non-Sixth Principle folks agreed it was a good verse even if in the battle-cry chapter. The more careful Bible student could have pointed out that the chapter had good advice for controversialists. After naming the six principles (repentance, faith, baptism, laying on of hands, resurrection of the dead, and eternal judgment), the writer says "leaving the principles . . . let us go on unto perfection." The happy result was a beautiful seal and flag, so far as we know, the only emblem of the forty-eight states which is of Biblical origin.

After David Rowland's resignation from the First Congregational Church in 1774 and during the years in which that church was pastorless, James Manning became the town's only parson with a college training. As he mounted the stairs to the desk of the old Baptist meetinghouse each Sabbath, the huge man with his great wig, full rounded face, and Geneva white bands looked strangely out of place in the ill-built, dilapidated meetinghouse up on Towne Street. Some of his New Jersey College (Princeton) education went over the heads of his listeners and ascended with the smoke through the vent in the roof. Some longed for Samuel Winsor and the other native exhorters, but all agreed that such a figure needed a more ample pulpit in a more dignified meetinghouse. But for another five years the "hay-cock" model church must do.

The story of James Manning and his college is familiar in its broader outlines. Morgan Edwards, coming from Wales to Philadelphia in 1761, saw the need of a college to train ministers for the Baptists, and received the backing of the Philadelphia Baptist Association.[3] Rhode Island seemed the natural place for its location because of its Baptist strength and undoubtedly its accessibility to the generous sources of giving which had started Harvard and Yale. The method of establishing the college was unique. James Manning, a graduate of New Jersey College, was dispatched to Warren to establish a Baptist church and college.

Having been a part of Massachusetts up to 1747, it was fertile field for the Baptist tradition. The college opened in 1765 and graduated its first class of seven in 1769. Four towns now offered a home to the "seminary": Warren, East Greenwich, Newport, and Providence. Manning favored Providence and was in cahoots with Moses Brown to steer it in that direction. The best offer of support was supposed to determine its location and wealthy Newport felt confident it would win. The trustees voted twenty-one to fourteen for Providence amid the cries of Newportians that there had been unclean play at the four corners. But to Providence it came, and Manning had Nassau Hall at Princeton copied as its first building, which is one of Providence' most cherished possessions today. Later Dartmouth would build another replica of the college hall. Jedidiah Morse in his geography describes it:

> . . . The edifice is of brick, four stories high, 150 feet long, and 46 wide, with a projection of ten feet each side. It has an entry lengthways, with rooms on each side. There are forty-eight rooms for the accommodation of students, and eight larger ones for public uses. The roof is covered with slate.

Stronger than the rivalry for the location of the new college was the denominational rivalry for its control. Not since the days of Jonathan Spreague's letter to the "three who wrote the letter," telling Congregationalists to keep out of Rhode Island, had feeling run as high between Baptists and Congregationalists. This time it was the "standing order" telling the Baptists to keep out of New England with a college. Their innocent conceit led them to assume that education and the New England Way were one and inseparable, hence this would be a Congregational college, as were Harvard and Yale. The Baptists, who had no conception of this mind-set, turned to Ezra Stiles and asked him to use his "most learned American mind" to write the charter. They trusted him implicitly and when it was presented in the Assembly it almost went through without the realization that it provided a governing board of twelve Fellows, eight of whom must be Congregationalists and none of whom needed to be Baptists. Judge Jenckes discerned the situation and barely stopped its passage. He borrowed the charter to read and then loaned it to two Congregationalists, Dr. Ephraim Bowen and Samuel Nightingale. To their credit, although they claimed their innocence, the document became lost; Nightingale even advertised in the newspaper for it. It did not again appear until just one hundred years later, when it was found among Ezra Stiles' church papers in the Congregational church at Newport. The newly prepared charter made no mistakes; it provided for a board of trustees of twenty-two Baptists, five Friends, five Episcopalians, and *four* Congregationalists; New England's "first" had fetched up in last place. Eight of the twelve Fellows were to be Baptists and so was the president. Ezra Stiles had had his wrists slapped hard. In defense of Ezra, let's charge it to arrogance rather than fraud.

When the lost charter appeared, it had a notation in Ezra's hand on the back, "The Baptists have shown a greater affection for all other denominations than for the Congregationalists." Manning, commenting on the Congregationalists, said, "Thank God they don't govern the world."

But the incident of its location and the Stiles charter caused ill feeling and kept the college from receiving the encouragement it had expected from Newport and the rest of New England. Ezra Stiles declined a place on the faculty because of "the offence he should give his brethren if he should do so," according to Manning. Congregational ministers attending commencement were reprimanded "by a convention," or so Manning heard. "I was lately told by a worthy minister of that order in Connecticut, that one of the same order in this town, a sour man, had done the College amazing damage by representing us as bigots and our sole design to be that of proselyting to the Baptist sentiments." If the "sour man" were Joseph Snow, he was soon converted and served as host to the early commencements.

James Manning himself was not above sectarian rejoicings. In 1784 he writes his London friend, Dr. Rippon:

> The Lord's work still goes on gloriously in the eastern parts of Massachusetts and Vermont. By recent advice from these parts we are assured that whole congregations, almost, of Congregationalists, embrace the Baptist principles; and in one instance their minister was baptized with his people. Several useful ministers are raised up amongst them lately in that wilderness. This looks somewhat like the coming of our Redeemer's kingdom. With me you say amen! Come, Lord Jesus, come quickly. In great haste I am, dear sir.

We can almost see his coat tails fly as he rushes off, trying to catch up with kingdom come.

One of the many criticisms which were heaped upon the ambitious college president for moving the infant institution from Warren to Providence in 1770 must have been the inadequacy of the shoddy old Baptist church in Providence "to hold commencements in." There had been only four graduates at the one Warren commencement, but it had been a public event which attracted crowds. Mr. Manning suggested using Mr. Snow's large meetinghouse on the west side of the river and, against the wishes of those who still disliked the "state church" of Massachusetts and Connecticut, he prevailed. Five commencements were held there before the new Baptist Meetinghouse was ready for God and the college. No one would forget the first one and particularly Governor Wanton's wig and umbrella.

> He headed the procession with the president. The governor's wig, which had been made in England was of the pattern and size of that of the Speaker of the House of Commons, and so large that

the shallow crowned hat could not be placed on his head without disturbing the curls. He, therefore, placed it under his left arm, and held his umbrella in his right hand. This was the first umbrella ever seen carried by a gentleman in Providence, though they had been sometime in use by ladies on a sunny day. Governor Wanton (of Newport) was the most dignified and respectable looking man we had ever seen.[4]

President Manning's wig was not to be sneezed at either, as it was of "the largest dimensions usually worn in this country."

Undoubtedly the extremely English wig of the Newport governor and the umbrella, which must have seemed affected, did not help his cause when war clouds gathered. In 1775 he was deposed and after the Revolution the estates of his son were seized, quite unjustly as the more fair-minded thought.

No man was more interested in the college than Nicholas Cooke, Joseph Snow's first convert. He was even admitted as a "Baptist" trustee in 1769, voted for the removal to Providence, contributed liberally towards the college edifice, and remained a trustee until his death in 1783. The holding of commencements away off on the other side of the river was a spur for building the new Baptist church that it might assume the prestige which rightfully belonged to it. But Father Snow must have smiled when the first commencement procession entered the unfinished meetinghouse of the Baptists, for at its head beside the President was one of his sheep in a normal-size wig! Nicholas Cooke had become governor.

Another to play a humbler part was our friend, William Compton, who was paid two shillings sixpence on April 17, 1770, to call a meeting of the subscribers of the college and three shillings for "his attendance at a meeting at the courthouse." Possibly his presence was to protect the body from Newport marauders.

With the dignity of holding college commencements placed upon the West Side church, there was a movement to improve the meetinghouse. In 1771 a committee consisting of Benjamin Mann, Esq., Col. Knight Dexter, Deacon Stephen Rawson (of the fountain), Mr. Samuel Butler, Mr. Elijah Bacon, and Mr. John Mathewson was appointed to consider adding a "tower and steeple." During the winter they held meetings at Dr. Samuel Carew's "by reason of the cold." From this number a finance committee, to which Deacon John Field was added, was appointed. In less than a year the clock and bell were on hand and in a year and a half (April, 1773) the "steeple and tower" had been erected, the bell and clock placed, and the bills paid. Two names which have significance appear in the transaction. On the building committee was Mr. Joseph Bucklin; his descendant James Bucklin would later figure in Providence architectural history. The other name is that of Joseph Russell, one of the Russell brothers, merchants. A member of King's Church, it was on him and his ships that the committee asked Joseph Snow to wait and "know what terms he would engage to procure a Bell for this Society which should not be less than seven hundred nor exceed eight hundred pounds Weight"; when the accounts were rendered he and his brother William "paid the freight on the bell," all the way from England.

This may have been the first time that the Russell brothers showed their interest in the general religious welfare of the community. Shortly after this they secured for the Baptists Mr. John Angell's orchard, upon which to build their new meetinghouse. The Baptists feared lest Angell, a Gortonist, would refuse to sell to them. So, William Russell, who possessed no Baptist taint or suspicion, bought the orchard and felt that the subterfuge was washed white by the spirit of free fellowship which prompted it.

In these first five Providence commencements the number of degrees awarded ranged from four to seven, but the crowds filled the church to overflowing. Except for the distinguished guests, most of the people had not attended an educational exercise of any kind, as there were no schools with public exercises in Providence.

As they entered from the parade into the meetinghouse, the "polite audience" would be handed a neatly printed program entirely in Latin. Many would have had to read it with moving lips had it been in English and others would not have comprehended even the English. But one thing they would recognize even through the Latin disguise would be the name of a relative or town's boy and there would be pride in that. Moreover, the names were arranged alphabetically, departing from the Harvard practice of arranging them by social standing. Harvard discontinued it three years later. The newspaper also noticed another democratic feature that "not only the candidates but even the President was dressed in American manufactures." Well might James Manning follow the students in this, for his three salaries as preacher, teacher, and college president hardly added up to five hundred dollars.

The trend, however, was in the direction which President Dwight of Yale would approve, in that it did not become polite education for appearance only, with "mere vibrations of the tongue termed fashionable conversation." There was a homespun atmosphere about these early commencements, Latin and all, as on the first Wednesday of five successive Septembers the college and its friends entered the meetinghouse.

In the forenoon there was a salutatory oration in Latin and a forensic dispute. In the afternoon, a "syllogistic disputation" in Latin, an oration and the conferring of the degrees. In the evening there would be a sermon preached. In each of these early years the preacher was the Rev. Hezekiah Smith of Holyoke who would always stay over Sunday and preach at either forenoon or afternoon service at Mr. Manning's, the other service at Mr. Snow's affording these divines an annual relief.

A feature of the afternoon of the first commencement is told by the *Providence Gazette:*

The business of the day being concluded, and before the assembly broke up, a piece from Homer was pronounced by Master Billy Edwards, one of the grammar school boys, not nine years old. This, as well as the other performances gained applause from a polite and crowded audience, and afforded pleasure to the friends of the Institution.

In this same newspaper account, the progress of the physical home of the college is noted. People were pleased with the "forwardness of the college edifice, the first stone of which was laid not longer since than the latter end of May last, and 'tis expected the roof will be on next month. It is a neat brick building, . . . Its situation is exceedingly pleasant and healthy, being on the summit of a hill the ascent easy and gradual, commanding an extensive prospect of hills, dales, plains, woods, water, islands, etc. *Who hath despised the day of small things?*"

The building described is University Hall and many of its builders must have come from the West Side homes: probably many who were putting on the roof glanced towards their meetinghouse where some of their earnings from the hill were being spent for a tower and bell.

Following this commencement the college passed the following vote:

Voted, That the Thanks of this Corporation be given to the Rev. Mr. Snow and his society, for the use of the Meeting-House yesterday, and also that they repair all damages that were occassioned by the Throng, and that the President and the Committee for carrying on the building of the College edifice do perform the same accordingly. (Thursday, September 6, 1770)

The damages seem to have consisted of seven squares of glass, for replacing which Benjamin Mann was paid 4/8. The politeness of the audience had been omitted somewhere in the three sessions and would so continue on each of the following years. Wednesday was the New England day for commencement and when a sister college suggested that it be changed to Friday the clergy objected that they would not be able to switch from spiritous to spiritual things in such a short space of time before the Sabbath. We have an idea that the "intelligent and sober Baptists" may have set a better precedent in this matter, but not all of the commencement audience followed their example. As the years went by, the damage became greater. The next year three shillings were paid for "hinges broke at Commencement," in 1773 "for mending pews broke at Commt Day eight shillings," and the following year fifteen shillings "for mending windows broke in Mr. Snow's Meeting House."

At the third commencement in the meetinghouse orations were given on History, Solitude, Agriculture, and the Pleasures of a Country Life, and Pride; a master's oration on "The Origin, Nature and Design of Civil Government," and a disputation on the thesis, *"Miracula extitisse humano testimonio probari potest."* Doing rather well for a college with a two hundred and fifty volume library! The *Gazette* says of it, "During the exercises, a profound attention was given by a sensible, crowded and polite asembly. The candor and satisfaction which appeared in every countenance, animated the young performers emulously to contend for that universal applause which they had the honor to receive."

How the students themselves felt as they entered the meetinghouse and knew that minutes later their voices would be lifted before the large company is told by Solomon Drowne of the class of 1773. "At length the day, the great, the important day, is come. O may it prove propitious. Now we must pass from easy College duties into the busy bustling scenes of life.

At about ten o'clock, the Corporation being assembled we walk in procession from the College Hall to the Rev. Mr. Snow's meetinghouse." Solomon himself was an opponent in the syllogistic disputation in Latin. Tillinghast, another student, would end the morning exercises with an oration on Politeness. Perhaps the president had suggested it with an aim to reducing the damages to be paid to Mr. Snow for the meetinghouse. The *Gazette* never reported the evening sermon, the editor having been apparently worn out by that time. We wonder how many, not too overcome by festivity, weariness, and excitement, attended on Hezekiah Smith's annual sermon. The meetinghouse would have been restful in candlelight at the close of commencement day.

The last commencement to be held on the West Side was on Wednesday, September 7, 1774. The procession marched instead of walked, and as part of it "the Company of Cadets, in uniforms, made an elegant and truly military appearance in the procession and manoeuvers which they performed on the College Green." As they assembled at the meetinghouse they may have lined up on Abbott's Parade which would have delighted the spirit of Daniel, who had given it "for passing and repassing" and the training of militia.

The orations included one on Patriotism and a disputation on the thesis, "Theatrical exhibitions corrupt the morals of mankind, and are prejudicial to the State." It was near the time when the General Assembly passed its "blue-law" against the theater.

One of the problems which faced President Manning was the awarding of honorary masters' degrees. The problem was even more complicated than the one which now faces college boards, for it involved the tiny school with both sides of the Atlantic. For the sake of encouraging support, Manning was constantly besieged by his English friend, the Rev. John Ryland, to hand out his "pretty baubles" in order to "attach some more of our ministers to your interest." Mr. Ryland did not seem particularly sensitive to the proper ratio of honorary degrees to undergraduate degrees in a graduating class of four to seven students. The president's failure to comply with his recommendations almost lost his support. Manning writes him:

I am heartily sorry that the College should sustain damage, through what we meant only for precaution and hope . . . We beg you not to remit an iota of your zeal in attaching gentlemen of grace and learning, property and influence, to the College.

The character of Rev. Mr. Toplady, (author of "Rock of Ages Cleft for Me") which you have enlarged upon, is truly a rare one and I shall think the College highly honored in his accepting a feather, and indeed in the least expression of his friendship.

When Augustus Toplady received the degree he wrote it was "like grace from heaven, unthought of, unimplored."

The interest of others was apparently secured in spite of the feather, for President Manning continues in the same letter:

I am sorry to hear that pious Mr. Woodman is so exceedingly modest as not to choose to wear his feather; but am glad to hear such a worthy character of him, and that he is so well disposed towards the college as to think of providing for it. I hope you may have it in your power to put many more in the way of leaving us some love tokens, when they are better employed than in enjoying terrestrial goods.

The students did not wholeheartedly relish public speaking. In 1773 they had urged the omission of commencement because members of the class were not orators. Their objection was overruled, but in 1775 their appeal to omit commencement on account of the war was sustained. In 1776 commencement was again held, the last for seven years. It was the first in the new Baptist Meetinghouse built "for the public worship of Almighty God and also for holding Commencement in." It must have been a proud day for everyone, even for Joseph Snow's flock, in spite of their loss of distinction in affording the most spacious meetinghouse in town and regrets for the end of a happy, but sometimes costly tradition. They could not but take pride in the elegant house of the Baptists. Joseph Brown, its architect, had received his M.A. in Joseph Snow's Meetinghouse at the first commencement in Providence, and may have been studying it for improvements with commencement in mind, during the Latin syllogisms. T. Sumner, the builder, found some men who had erected the West Side church still able to help in the raising of the Baptist church thirty years later.

As Joseph Brown heard benches creak and windows break as the crowd tried to get out of the main and tower doors of Joseph Snow's house, he decided that a church "for holding commencements in" needed plenty of exits. Thus Jackson noted of the new meetinghouse that it "can be vacated in the least time of any building of its size among us."

Jackson goes on to express a hope which we all have: "We should sigh after commencement were it not celebrated here." But long since we have ceased to sigh with him when he adds, "even as we did when the anniversary of Brown was celebrated upon one sad Wednesday in July at 9½ of the clock A. M. But the original day has been restored." Now commencement no longer commences, but concludes the academic year.

The holding of commencements in the West Side Church brought a measure of prestige to Joseph Snow in the other Congregational churches in the state, particularly Newport. Providence Plantations has always been slow to adopt outsiders, especially those with the Massachusetts stamp upon them. Added to this handicap, which Joseph Snow possessed, was the disfavor with which he was still held by the orthodox Congregationalists even after a quarter of a century of leadership and fathering of the West Side community. Ezra Stiles has this entry in his diary of June 23, 1771, as a comment upon the fact that Mr. Snow preached for Mr. Hopkins in Newport on the previous Sunday:

> Mr. Snow never was admitted to preach in either of the Congreg[a] Chh in this Town (Newport) before last Sabbath. How Mr. Hopkins will approve it &c. &c. . . . His Predecessor Mr. Vinall tho' a great Whitfeldian would never consent to admit Mr. Snow. Deacon Coggleshall introduced him in Mr. H's absence: he has been warmly engaged to introduce him for ten years past but never could effect it till this time.

Ezra Stiles goes on to give us one of the few contemporary portraits of Joseph Snow:

> Mr. Snow is loud & boisterous but delivers many sound Truths and pretty well understands the Doctrines of Grace & is of a sober serious, exemplary Life and perhaps has a better Understanding of the Gospel Scheme than three Quarters of the Pasters of the Waldenses & Albigenses, or of the reformed in the South part of France. I hope he does good. Tho I greatly disapprove of his Lay ordination & of his running about into congregational Parishes in opposition to the Pastors & holding separate meetings & promoting a spirit of Disaffection to a learned Ministry.

The above is dated June 23, 1771. Apparently the congregationalists of Newport found Joseph "not so bad," for he gives the Fast Day sermon for Mr. Hopkins on April 15, 1773, and returns the very next week to preach again for him. Mr. Hopkins, who had such a salutary effect on the slaveholders of Newport, apparently went to work on Joseph Snow, for in 1774 we find this entry in the town records:

> Know all Men by these Presents That I Joseph Snow of Providence in the county of Providence in the Colony of Rhode Island for and in consideration that all Mankind have a Natural Right to be free and that whereas I Bought of Charles Rhoades of Cranston on the Twentieth Day of March 1771 a Negro Woman Named

Phillis aged then about Twenty Seven Years for which I paid said Rhoades Forty Two Pounds &c. I Do therefore by these Presents for myself my Heirs Executors and Administrators set off and give Freedom unto the said Negro Woman named Phillis with her Two Children Named Violet and Rose unto her them and their Heirs forever. As Witness my Hand this Twelfth Day November A D 1774 in presence of

Benoni Pearce
William Wheaton

The foregoing is a True Copy Recorded this 21st Day of September A D 1780

Witness
Theodore Foster
Town Clerk

Ezra Stiles gives us a further picture of the practices within the West Side church:

He was a private and illiterate Brother . . . ordained according to the manner of Separates by the Laying on of the Hands . . . He baptizes adults by plunging or sprinkling indifferently as any chuse . . . Anti-paedobaptists and Paedobaptists sit down together amicably at the Lord's table . . . the Deacons and any gifted Brethren have Liberty and opportunity of praying and Exhorting in the Ldsdy public Congregations—they have an inveterate displeasure against the old Congregational Chhs and Pastors. A majority of the Brethren are Baptists and if a Successor to Mr. Snow should be anti-paedobaptist this would become and end in a baptist church. Mr. Snow is a Paedobaptist . . . The Chh Covenant is a good one.

There is no evidence in the records and events within the church that there was at this time any intention on the part of the congregation of becoming an antipedobaptist church, not even after the distinction of housing a Baptist college commencement. They were well content with their experiment in "unity without uniformity" in the matter of baptism. Mr. Stiles may have based his conviction in this matter, which he repeats elsewhere in his diary, upon the fact that many of the New Light churches did become Baptist. Also Mr. Snow's close relationship to his convert, Isaac Backus, could have given this impression. The fact was, as Mr. Stiles goes on to show, that the more orthodox Congregational churches did not readily welcome the seer of Weybosset.

Commencements held in the West Side Meetinghouse brought about also a closer relationship between James Manning and Joseph Snow. Ezra Stiles tells us:

> Mr. Manning Baptist President preaches for Mr. Snow at Times; he did so lately on the day of the Lord's Supper and previous to that administration he went out of the Meeting, declining to communicate with them, alledging he is for *close* not *open Communion* as all the Baptist Churches with Baptist Elders are unless perhaps Elder Babcock's at Westerly.

James Manning has become more conservative since he arrived in town to encounter the wrath of Samuel Winsor for not regarding the sixth principle as essential and for singing in meeting.

After the Revolution, when the moral life of the community flowed at a low ebb, it was Moses Brown, James Manning, and Joseph Snow who banded together to seek to counteract the decadence which was particularly assailing the youth of the town. Moses Brown wrote:

> to Joseph Snow and James Manning
>
> Providence 30th of 3d mo 1783
>
> Respected Friend—
>
> I have been for some time concerned on account of the immoralities and want of virtuous government of the rising youth of this town. . . . I am sensible that war naturally tends to harden and immoralize the inhabitants and it would be difficult to affect a reformation as long as that evil continues. Accordingly I have delayed addressing thee, as one of the leaders and instructors of

authority. Now that the Articles of Peace are agreed upon, I am encouraged to hope that if a proper sense of the favourable interposition of the Prince of Peace be sought, by those who profess to be his disciples and followers, success may and will attend their united endeavors to bring into reputation and practice moral virtue, at least in so far as good and wholesome laws may effect.

I think we may hope for a Divine blessing on the endeavours of pious Christians of all denominations for the happiness of the present inhabitants of the state and of their posterity. I hope the present seeming coldness and indifference of many in Christian profession may not be a discouragement to this necessary work.

Tho, I mean not to direct, yet I may mention my thoughts that if a meeting or conference of church bodies could be arranged to stir one another up to love and good works, in general; and in particular to excite a care over the youth to keep them attentive to religious meetings and away from places of dissipation and corruption and to encourage an example by parents accompanying such Christion and moral precepts, would I believe not only avert chastizements of pestilence and famine but bring to us those blessings which are the reward of humble and grateful minds.

This is to manifest a concurrence in that reformation I believe thou art engaged to effect. I desire that a motion in heart as well as in conduct may be felt and witnessed by the inhabitants.

I may conclude subscribing myself thy friend,

Moses Brown.

The letter received a happy concurrence on the part of both of the gentlemen addressed. It may well be the first united attempt by the religious leaders of the community to further the common welfare of the community, the first "Council of Ministers" if not of Churches.

CHAPTER TWELVE

KEEPER OF THE LIBERALITY

JAMES MACSPARRAN had written in response to a questionnaire from the London Society, "What I have from my people here has not yet amounted to more than five pounds sterling annum . . . being wt they please to give me for we have no parochial Subscription, nor Publick Sunday Contributions in church as is usual in other churches in this countrey, wch example, we are afraid yet to follow lest it should lessen the auditors, who being bred up in Quakerism and among Baptists, are not used to pay for ye Gospel." [1]

It made the parsons of the two establishments who found themselves in Rhode Island either dependent upon the charity of their home societies, or their own efforts to earn their living in other ways. John Checkley of King's Church, Providence, and James MacSparran of St. Paul's, Narragansett, were adepts at writing hard-luck letters intended to loosen the purse strings of the Society for the Propagation of the Gospel. Joseph Snow had accepted the Rhode Island custom of a self-supported clergy, even to the furnishing of his own residence.

During the first two decades of Joseph Snow's pastorate, "cash money" was not much of a problem among the flock and this was true in the rest of the Plantations, chiefly because money was a rarity. There were no banks and none were needed. When specie payments were made for goods sold out of the country, the silver was "banked" by making it into spoons and other useful and ornamental "coin silver" products. In time of particular need it was melted down. But for the most part if you had a meetinghouse to build, you went ahead and built it; you gave yourself as a carpenter, mason, cook, a hewer of wood, a possessor of land, or a breaker of stone. In not too prosperous Providence Plantations it was not just a Baptist principle to "support" an unpaid ministry, but almost a necessity.

As industry became more diversified, and coin silver increased, life's simplicity lessened. The church began to need repair, and Joseph Snow, with less time and less strength for house carpentry, needed support. The modern problems of church finance were born.

The first step was the appointment of a special committee in 1769. Seven men of "honest report and of wisdom" were chosen, including "our dacons." The seven were Barzillai Richmond, Benjamin Cushing, Nicholas Cooke, Dacon Stephen Rawson, Dacon John Field, Bernard Eddy, and Samuel French. At about the same time Benjamin Cushing was chosen to be the "keeper of the Liberality." That is the loveliest title a church treasurer ever had!

The idea of the seven men had come from searching the Scriptures and happening on Acts 6:1-3. However, there was no superstition over the magic number seven, and members were added when things did not go well. In 1775 the number was raised to nine, including John Mathewson. By 1882 there seem to have been twelve members.

The rules drawn up for the functioning of this group are unique and the fitting of Bible verse to "temperal affairs" is better than a modern Social Action committee could produce:

1. to see that Each member is employed in Some Lawful Calling . . . and that none are idle in their callings: Eph 4:28 but rather let

him Labour working with his hands: that he may have to give to him that needeth: Prov 19:15 an idle Soul Shall Suffer hunger:

2. to See that the head of Each family that are members of the Church properly Regulate and provide for their own familys 1 Tim 5:8 But if any provide not for his own: and especially for those of his own house, he hath denied the faith and is worse then an infidel: 1 Tim 2:9 that women adorn themselves in modest apparel
3. to Regulate the manner of the Church Collections: Either by Subscription or other wise: and proportion (Such Sums as the Church Shall think Proper to apoint for the Support of the Elder for the year) and to see that Each member do their part 1 Cor 9: 13:14: Do ye not know that they which minister about holy things Live of the things of the temple and they which wait at the alter are partakers with the alter–Even so hath the Lord ordained that they which Preach the Gospel Should live of the Gospel: 2 Cor 8:13 14: For I mean not that other men be caled and you burdened–But by an equality

[A timely quotation for those who condemned the hireling preacher.]

6. That if any of the members of the Church Either Reject: or Neglect to Comply with the advice which you Give them: or they appear to you to be Ereguler: or obstainate: that you Call a Church Meeting when you think Proper and Lay your Complaint before the Church that offenders may be reclamed or Cast out:
7. and that you assist with our Elder in Keeping Proper order in Church meetings and in Keeping up a Proper Disipline in the Church 1 Cor 12: 28: and God hath Set Some in the Church: first apostles–Prophets–teachers–Gifts–helps–Governments–diversities &c.

Along the same line four years later "Pastor Joseph Snow" asked for a ruling elder to assist him. After a proper consideration the church unanimously chose Brother Barzillai Richmond which he "excepted." Joseph Snow's request had been made "considering his often infirmities" and to help keep watch over the members, keeping order in the church, and to lead in public worship.

One of the first acts of the committee of seven "of honest report and wisdom" was to establish a method for the support of the poor. In 1769, $20.00 was voted and levied; in 1770 £6, and 1774 it was voted to raise $50.00 for the "Poor stood in need."

Liberality should be guided by equity and it was voted that it "was the duty of each male member to give in a proper and honest account of their worldly circumstances" to the seven. Sixty pounds for the "elder" was then proportioned among the members according to their *surcomstances*. Wealth being no longer wholly visible could not now be calculated by a casual visit to a Weybosset Street home, and noting any increases in pewter and coin silverware. Men were engaging in involved and many-sided businesses which called for revelation to the seven.[2]

Soon it became difficult to raise the £60. It was cut in 1774 to £50 and the Biblical seven were increased to nine, later to eleven, always in the hope of succeeding where before there had been disappointment. In the meantime Joseph Snow lost some of his art at making money on real estate and had still further need of a salary.

Another undertaking, which showed the need of a better organization, was that of 1771, when it was voted to erect a "decent steeple, and a good Bell and Clock." We have a suspicion that not only commencement guests but rumors of a new and elegant Baptist church may have helped the Snow flock to determine to improve their own meetinghouse. It was also necessary to shingle, clapboard the two ends, and paint the whole. There is a good probability that the interior of the meetinghouse had been left in unfinished wood up to this time. The Ballou Meetinghouse (still standing) built but two or three years earlier, was never painted; the East Greenwich Meetinghouse built as late as 1774 was unpainted except for the pulpit. The beauty of the grain of the wide boards would not be appreciated by the Rev. Mr. Smith coming from Haverhill to preach the commencement sermon, and after thirty years would be less lovely and clean than when hewn from the logs of the adjoining forest. The pews were numbered at this time by a committee consisting of Thomas Jones and William Allen, and a tax of one dollar levied for the painting. The eight-hundred-pound bell, which was brought from England and on which William Russell "paid the freight," a kindly act on the part of an Episcopal neighbor, was in use in the two meetinghouses until 1907, when it was voted to discontinue ringing it until "some decision is reached on the feasibility of replacing the same with a new bell." [3]

With the changing times a need for more substantial and better organized religious bodies was being felt on all sides. The answer was the incorporated society. Church societies in the rest of New England were very old, but chartered religious societies were almost unknown in the Rhode Island Colony before Newport and Providence churches petitioned the assembly. In order of incorporating they were: Trinity, Newport, 1769; Benevolent Congregational, Providence, 1770; Second Congregational, Newport, 1771; King's, Providence, 1772; Charitable Baptist, Providence, 1774; Catholic Congregational, East Greenwich, 1774; Beneficent Congregational, Providence, 1785.

The reason for founding the religious societies of Massachusetts was opposite to that of the chartered societies of Rhode Island. The purpose of the former was to give to the tax-paying non-church members a voice in the selection of the minister whom they were compelled to support, and in the building and maintenance of the meetinghouse. Salem as early as 1672 allowed non-members to participate. The "Dedham case" in 1800 brought the decision that a church has no legal existence save in "connection with some regularly constituted society." But in Rhode Island the need was to give power to the churches to tax their membership, and those who would voluntarily support the church, for the salary of the minister and the upkeep of the property. Massachusetts had passed a law in 1638 making support of the church compulsory. May 21, 1716, Rhode Island, in keeping with its tradition, did just the opposite, voting:

that what maintenance or salary may be thought necessary by any of the churches, congregations, or societies of people, now inhabiting, or that hereafter shall inhabit, within the same, for the support of their respective minister or ministers, shall be raised by free contribution, and no otherways.

How much right this gave to churches to deal with their own members who voluntarily associated themselves together was a question which plagued the congregations as their financial problems increased.

In 1783 the Grand Standing Committee chosen from the church and old society consisted of Deacon John Field, Joseph Snow, John Paine, and "in the roome of Hugh Beaty who had died," James Snow, the minister's brother, fifteen years his junior. Only two years later a new and "younger crowd" is taking hold of the situation. Those who initiated the charter movement were Samuel Butler, Henry Bacon, Nathanill Jacobs, Jonathan Jenkins, Joseph Martin, and the prime mover and beautiful penman, Thomas Jones, merchant. They address an appeal "to all Christian People," letting it be known what they propose to do, "taking into our serious consideration the great Importance of a due administration of the Gospel and its ordinances . . . the necessity of Provision being made for the decent support of our Pastor." As a result eighty-five good men and true petitioned the Honorable General Assembly in South Kingstown on the last Monday of October in 1785 for the incorporation of a body to be called the *Beneficent Society*. In the petition there was something apparently written and erased (perchance "Westminster") in the space now occupied by the ten letters which spell Beneficent. Dr. Vose humorously remarks, "Considering the fact that a dispute on the subject of good works ('damnable good works' in the language of Joseph Snow, Sr., and others) was the occasion in part of the separation, it was a little amusing that the name chosen for the Society was *The Beneficent*." Providence loved the names of virtues for its churches and streets. Streets called *Benefit, Hope, Benevolent, Peace, Plenty, Friendship,* forever mark her as a town which knew and loved the fruits of the spirit. New Englanders kept many of the Indian names and when they did replace them they tried to find worthy substitutes. Maine used great Old World names: Norway, Paris, Sweden, Athens, China, Smyrna, Denmark, Corinth, Calais, Gilead, Bethel. Lord Tweedsmuir said of America, "I like the way in which the nomenclature reflects its history, its racial varieties, its odd cultural mixtures, the grandiose and the homespun rubbing shoulders." [4] Providence would subsequently name its streets for coins (Dollar, Dime, Dubloon), authors, colleges, states, boys, and girls.

In 1770 the First Congregational Society had incorporated under the name *Benevolent Congregational Society*.[5] The First Baptist had incorporated in 1774 under the name *Charitable Baptist Society*. There is also at Tiverton *The Amicable Congregational Society*. In 1774 the *Catholic Congregational* Church in East Greenwich was chartered; its second charter speaks of the necessity of presenting Christianity "in the most liberal and catholic manner." [6] There were *Catholic* Congregational churches at Bristol, Scituate, and in the second precinct of Rehoboth, and a *Catholic* Seminary among the Huguenots at Frenchtown.

The name *Beneficent* was a close copy of the mother church's, and for imitation did pretty well, as it can be translated "well doing" as opposed to "well wishing," but that is a lighter thought of the modern generation. Its choice by an unlatinized assembly of saints in 1785 was highly complimentary to the good feeling now being restored between mother church and daughter churches. At Enos Hitchcock's ordination, held in the First Baptist Meetinghouse on October 1, 1783, Father Snow's congregation was not invited by "pastor and messenger" to participate in forming the ecclesiastical council. The one who felt most badly over it was apparently Enos himself, for, the next year, he secured from his congregation the famous and beautiful "removal of censure." [7] It took Massachusetts three hundred years to remove the censure from Roger Williams; it only took forty years for the mother church to forgive her censured children. So completely did Enos Hitchcock's spirit convert even Joseph Snow that we find the young parson giving an address on Education in the West Side Meetinghouse a few months later.

Among the eighty-five who signed the Address to the General Assembly were our old friends Barzillai Richmond and William Compton. It is the first time the name of the meetinghouse's closest and longest settled neighbor has appeared on the church records, although his presence has been felt from the beginning. He seems never to have joined the church nor done much with the Beneficent Society after this effort in black and white. Joseph Snow 3d (now being frequently and confusingly called "Junior" since his grandfather's death) is there and the society will have an interesting time with the parson's son later. Thomas Jones and James Snow from the 1764 class of members and Stephen Wardwell from the large ingathering in 1775 appear. Two names are "scratched," John Crary and Joseph Whittemore, and more should have been, for out of the eighty-five petitioners not half became members of the society.

The address to the Assembly reads in part:

Taking into serious consideration the many difficulties the said Society has heretofore laboured under, and the very uncertain and irregular manner, in which public worship has heretofore been supported in said Society and our duty to render such support for the future, more uniform and permanent. Being also desirous of promoting as much as in us lies, piety towards God our creator, universal philanthropy, our own mutual happiness and the benefit of the succeeding generations. For these and other the like purposes, . . . praying your Honours would be pleased to cause the underwritten act of incorporation to pass into a law of this state, by the name of the Beneficient Society in the Town of Providence aforesaid.

The help of Jabez Bowen of the First Church was sought to present the act to the Assembly, which passed it without a murmur. With good relations re-established with the mother church, much consulting was apparently done between Jabez Bowen and Thomas Jones, as well as others.

Some of the daring, but unsuccessful, methods of the older Benevolent Society were not repeated. Possibly remembering the money collected by Dr. Hoyle a half century earlier, the Benevolent Society had authorized Jonathan Badger to solicit funds in South Carolina. This was apparently fruitless, but he was thanked for his endeavors and then authorized to solicit in New York and Philadelphia, his expenses to be paid. Mr. Rowland, the minister, was likewise "desired and requested, as soon as he can attend thereto, to procede to such place or places on this Continent, as he shall think proper, for and in Behalf of this Society to Solicit for, and to Receive the charity of such person or persons whom God hath blest with Affluence and Liberallity to be applyed for the pious uses and purposes set forth in the Charter."

We are indebted to Ezra Stiles for the interesting fact that Mr. Badger had first cast his lot in Father Snow's church. He had come to town from South Carolina "where he had acquired a good estate." He was told there was no religion in the First

Church and had joined the West Side church. Here he had urged the formation of a society and apparently presented schemes for putting the financial conditions of the church in good order. But he was looked upon as an outsider and innovator, and his plans were given little encouragement. He tried out the First Church on the hill, where he received a more favorable response to his propositions. Stiles says, "Upon finding his mistake (in joining with Father Snow) he has been very friendly and assisting to that Chh (First Congregational) and put his own Organ in it and plays upon it frequently; this brings him often at Mr. Rowland's Meeting."

Of the Benevolent Society and the solicitation of funds abroad, Mr. Stiles writes:

> Mr. B— was grieved that Mr. Rowland was so illy supplied and proposed the forming of the *benevolent Society*. He had proposed the same at J. S. but the Congregation would not listen to it. However it took with Mr. R's pple & affords a good prospect of a Fund. Thus Mr. B tho of another CCh. has kindly afforded his kind Offices for this. Having had small pox he kindly offers to carry to N. *York* and *Philad*[a] an Address & *Applic*[a].

The trip seems to have been for his health as well as for the raising of funds. His desire to bring an organ into the house of the Lord may have had as much to do with the opposition to him across the bridge as that of new-fangled ways of raising money.

Actually he never formally united with the West Side flock. Whatever resentment he may have felt against Joseph Snow and congregation was not shared by his daughter, Sarah Badger, who married the minister's son, Joseph, making another Joseph and Sarah Snow to confuse the searchers of records. They were the first to use a middle name for their child; under the date of April 15, 1781, *Jonathan Bager Snow* is entered in the baptismal record. As his grandfather, Joseph, took him in his arms, he may have hoped the child would not grow up to be filled with as many revolutionary ideas as his grandfather, Jonathan, possessed.

The "Address & Applic[a]" with which Mr. Badger and Mr. Rowland were armed explained what kind of a church they represented. Persons in far-off Philadelphia and South Carolina may have heard things uncomplimentary to the form of Rhode Island religion. It is a choice document which bears the date of May 28, 1771:

> Whereas the principal Design of the Institution of this Society was for the Supporting and Ministry in the Congregational Society in Providence, at present under the pastoral Care of the Rev. Mr. Rowland: and whereas the said Congregational Society was at first settled and at this Time subsists upon the principles which are commonly called—Pedobaptist—Therefore to prevent at any Time hereafter, any Misapprehension or Misrepresentation of the True Design of this Society in the Institution of their Fund so far as it relates to the Maintenance of a Minister in the said Congregational Society It is Voted and Resolved, That their true Intent and Meaning is for the Support of a Learned Pedobaptist congregational Minister who hath Regularly received Presbyterian Ordination according to the Usage of the pedobaptist Congregational Churches in New England.

In December Jonathan Badger gave "a particular and satisfactory account of his Proceedings" but the next treasurer's report shows them no richer. Apparently there were promises, but not cash. One place where Mr. Rowland would not solicit would be scornful Boston.

The church had been turned down by the convention in 1765 on two counts: first, each appeal had supposedly been their last and secondly, they thought Mr. Rowland "not so smart." Earlier help seems to have been forthcoming even after Dr. Hoyle's canvassing days ended. James MacSparran wrote to the Bishop of London in 1751:

. . . the Independents here have an Evangelical Treasury at Boston, wth wch they maintain Missionarys: especially in places where the Church (of England) is like to prevail, and they have but ye least hopes of stopping it's growth. This is the case at Providence in this Colony where Mr. Checkley is the Society's Missionary: and in Narraganset, . . . For this same Mr. Torry, my Antagonist in ye Law Suit is one of their Missionary's partly maintained by yt Treasury, and did not come to Narraganset until many years after my filling yt church; And probably had never been sent, and settl'd hadn't it been to deprive ye church of ye Glebe, I have sued for.[8]

Among the members of the Benevolent Society were Benjamin West, Darius Sessions, Nathaniel Green, and Samuel Nightingale. When their schemes for quick and painless money raising failed, they tried it the hard way by taxing each member a shilling at annual meetings and sixpence at the Tuesday meetings held every other Tuesday. When fifteen pounds accumulated it was to be invested. Meetings were poorly attended and members were dropped for failure to pay their dues. In 1771 the Benevolent Society had accumulated £20; by 1774 there were £169 in assets. In 1775 it increased to £480 with the help of a land sale (property in the vicinity of King's Church, probably bought as an investment of some of the £15) and half the estate of Colonel Daniel Hitchcock who, dying from exposure in Morristown after the battle of Princeton, made his will in favor of the society a few hours before his death.

The good decorum of the Benevolent Society members in meetings may have led Jabez Bowen to advise Thomas Jones to make the Beneficent Society's rules for behavior more simple than those first adopted by the Benevolent. They had been:

1st. That no more than one person shall speak at a Time, and that he shall not be interrupted by an other, until he shall have delivered, what he thinks proper on the Subject, under the penalty of Six pence.

2nd. That a Regular and grave Behaviour, free from vain talking and jesting, shall be observed by every Member, during the Siting of the Society, under the penalty of Six pence.

3rd. That if any Member shall be guilty of undue passion and Anger, during the siting of the Society, he shall be fined Six pence.

4th. That if any Member shall be guilty of prophane cursing or swearing, or of any prophane Language, he shall be fined Six pence.

6th. That if any Member shall appear to be disguised with Liquor, during the Siting of this Society, he shall have no Vote during that Meeting, shall be admonished by the president, and be fined Six pence.

But even with the improved fortunes of the Benevolent Society there was still a laxity in paying the minister's salary. When it first occurred Enos Hitchcock wrote a most businesslike letter:

October 1788
To the members of the Congregational Society
Brethren,

It is an unpleasing necessity that draws from me the following observations to a Society whose laudable assertions heretofore have done them honor, and demand my grateful notice. . . . But such is the sacred nature of a compact voluntarily and deliberately entered into, that it cannot be violated by one of the parties without justly alarming the others.

It should be considered that the compact subsisting between the Society and myself is not only sacred in its nature, but is such as involves the highest species of delicacy and honor. . . . The ground of my confidence was not any civil law, but your plighted faith. . . . The object of the stipend was not, like a principal in Trade, to acquire wealth, but the means of my subsistance in your service.

The Society therefore cannot reasonably expect the continuance of my service while they withhold the necessary means of my support. . . . Sorry I am to find myself under the necessity of being thus explicit on a subject so painful to my feelings. But I thought it my duty to give this information to the Society, and doubt not they will receive it candidly and pay that attention to it which the nature of the case requires.

I am, Brethren, your affectionate Serv't.
Enos Hitchcock

Providence Oct. 2, 1788

As time went by, he found that, though pay was sometimes slow, he would not have the experience of Josiah Cotton whose promised settlement of a hundred acres of land remained undelivered. Thus his letters to his good friend Deacon Green became couched in quite another tone:

Monday Morn'g

Dear Sir,

The calls of Nature, or rather art, and the demands of justice upon me make it necessary to request a few dollars, this morning, if convenient.

If, in the line of your business, you can procure a hind of good Mutton within a day or two, it will be a fresh obligation added to the many already conferred on

Sir, your affectionate Serv't,
E. Hitchcock

The Deacon-Parson relationship between James Green and Enos Hitchcock is one of the lovely epics of these Plantations. James Green was one of the few deacons to enter office with an installation dinner paid for by the struggling society in 1771. Among the items were 12 lbs. butter @ 1 shilling a pound; 4 partridge, 3 shillings; 3 geese 7/8; 1 peck cranberries, 1/; 1 bottle mustard, etc.

During 1781–82, when Enos Hitchcock was serving as chaplain, he and Deacon Green maintained a delightful correspondence. Hitchcock wrote the following letter:

Camp Peekskill, Sept. 8, 1781

Sir, your servant. I can compliment too if you are disposed to play at that game. Tis lucky I did not say, "as well" for the Deacon handles his complimental weapons with such dexterity as shows him in the business a veteran well disciplined and armed cap-a-pie, always ready for the charge, and the Parson comes on militia-like, helter-skelter, without form and void of either true courage or suitable accoutrements. And as might well have been expected from such unequal combitants gives the Deacon the highest seat and takes, quantum meruit, a humble seat below. 'Tis no "hum", Sir [9]

There was no question about the wisdom of chartering the Beneficent Society and all would have gone well but for Joseph Snow, who had no intention of relinquishing his time-honored authority. Most of it rested on the prestige of his many years' leadership, but there was also the legal aspect. He had been named by Daniel Abbott as one of the original trustees of the land. Actually there were now four groups, each with some authority; the least authority of all was held by the legally incorporated Beneficent Society. There were (1) the unincorporated Congregational Society, which up until now had handled what few business matters there were without much of any record; (2) the "2nd Congregational Church" or as more often referred to the "Congregational Church on the West Side of the River," composed of members who accepted the covenant and subscribed to the articles of faith; (3) the newly incorporated "Beneficent Society," (4) the Abbott trustees, holders of the church land and park.

Difficult going was encountered when the Beneficent Society innocently started to take over the trusteeship of all the property. Joseph Snow had no intention of surrendering his long-time position. It may account for the fact that he was left off the annual standing committee of the new society. The shock which these good Weybosset Street businessmen got when they discovered that Rule 15, which they had drawn up in 1786, was unenforcible may be easily pictured. The rule said:

Whereas the lot of ground on part of which the Meeting-House belonging to this Corporation now standeth, was originally given, by

Daniel Abbot Esq. to Joseph Snow, Hugh Batty, John Pain, and Joseph Snow Sr. as a Committee in behalf of the then Subscribers . . . And whereas the lot of Ground or Common before the said Meeting House was also given by the said Abbot for public use and put under the care of the before mentioned Committee . . . This Corporation do appoint that the Committee annually chosen (Society's "Annual" Committee) shall be the perpetual Successors of the beforesaid original Committee.

We think we can hear down across a century and a half the roaring voice of Joseph Snow, which led to the society's word-eating motion on April 1787:

Whereas this Corporation have in some Instances interfered with the business properly belonging to the Congregational Society particularly in the substance of the 15th article of our Rules and by Laws . . . therefore . . . said 15th article . . . and every other transaction that does not immediately concern this Corporation be and the same is hereby repealled and rendered null and void.

How seventy-one year old Joseph must have relished those words "null and void."

The first officers of the society were Barzillai Richmond, President; Samuel Butler, Esqr., Vice-president; Henry Bacon, Treasurer; and William Allen, Secretary. The first "annual committee" was "Joseph Martin, Esqr., Doct. Thomas Truman, Mr. Thomas Jones, Mr. Benjamin Gladding, and the Treasurer."

One of the first items of business in the society furnishes another evidence of the now friendly spirit with the people on the hill:

On Request of a Comittee of the Benavolent Society in this Town, Voted that this Corporation are willing to Lend said Society the Use of their Bell to toll at Funeralls untill the further order of this Corporation, and that they employ Mr. Daniel Branch (who dug the graves) or Mr. Joseph Whittemore (just elected sexton) to toll the Bell as to them appears most proper.

It was a sensible suggestion to have the bell nearer the cemetery ring and not have to depend on an east wind to hear the one on the hill.

The members of the Beneficent Society increasingly found themselves in a peculiar position: they had the better organization with which to do the church's business, but legal titles to land, buildings, and cemeteries were in the hands of the old Congregational Society, to which most of them belonged. It was not until 1804 that the Congregational Society sold to the Beneficent Society the cemetery for six hundred dollars. In 1814 it was still the Congregational Society which met to appoint the new trustees for the Abbott grants. In 1792 the Beneficent Society did get an addition to its charter, as a result of an appeal of the two societies, which entrusted the repairs and upkeep on all property to the Beneficent Society. The new legislative act gave the society the right to raise money by other means than voluntary contributions. Both the proprietors of pews and "Burying Ground Lotts" could be assessed the expenses of repairs and upkeep, provided they were taxed on the fixed valuation. Failure to pay the assessment allowed the society to foreclose. The act is signed by "Arthur Fenner Esquire, Governor, Captain General, and Commander in Chief of and over the said state."

Before these liberalizing clauses the new society went bravely ahead to fly as high as its clipped wings would allow it. During the first two years its membership rapidly dropped and most of the "eighty-five" had forgotten their "Address" to the Assembly. It set three shillings as its annual dues and members not prepared to pay could give a note for the capital fund. It seems to us today like a small amount, but there were those who seemed just unable to pay. The society proved itself Beneficent by remembering that the purpose of raising money was to promote the gospel rather than vice versa. Thus this humanitarian vote in 1792.

After taking into view the peculiar situation of the families of the following Gentlemen: viz Capt. Elijah Shepardson's, Joseph Snow, Jr, William Allen's, David Tifft's; voted to return notes and remit dues.

They were allowed to stay in the society for the sake of brotherhood, even though its purpose was at this time to raise a capital fund for the parson's salary. Joseph Snow, Jr. (III) (son of the minister), had the following "peculiar family situation" to care for: there were wife, Sarah, and his children Elizabeth, Suzannah, Lydia, Lydia, Daniel, Joseph IV, Margaret, Jonathan Badger, William, Oliver, Rebecca, Sarah.

Failing to accomplish what they had expected in the new Beneficent Society the same men went to work in the old Congregational Society, joining what they could not supersede. Thomas Jones was the clerk and enters under May 14, 1787,

The Comm. to whom was committed the business of assesing the pews and causing them to be marked or numbered &c did Report that they had made out a rate streak which was Read and Voted also that it was their oppinion that if the proprietors would pay West India Goods at suitable prices Cap Snow would agree to receive such pay.

Ezek Eddy was allowed 5 per cent for collecting the "rate streak." In 1789 it was 52/6 on each pew in an endeavor to raise twenty dollars specie to lead the bottoms of the tower of the meetinghouse which "is in great danger of taking damage."

The two societies with the same personnel, for the most part, and the ancient Joseph, keeping his eye on his own prerogatives, worked things out together. After many years, about forty, the prudential affairs of the church pretty much passed into the hands of the younger organization. Dr. Vose pointed out in his address at the centennial of the society, 1885, that just when there seemed to be no further use for the older society, the missionary cause came along with new funds for it to administer. Says Dr. Vose, "The Charter was given to the Beneficent Society to enable it to hold funds; but after one hundred years there are no funds to hold [10] while the old Society which is the Church holds important funds which have been given for the poor of the church." Dr. Vose was not quite right in identifying the old Congregational Society and the church—they were two separate organizations in the beginning, but did gradually merge as there were no legal barriers of incorporation to keep them apart. In 1909 the church itself was incorporated and today does many of the things that the other three organizations successively did. The Beneficent Society continues as the trustee of the property with none of Daniel Abbott's hand-picked trustees to gainsay their right.

CHAPTER THIRTEEN

THE MIGRATORY DEAD

THE HOYLE ACRE at the junction of Broad and Weybosset was the town's first cemetery. One of the miracles performed by the Benevolent and Beneficent societies and their predecessors was the peaceful untangling of the titles to the Hoyle land. The land had been deeded to trustees in churches outside the state. They could have made trouble. When the "Separates" marched down the hill and settled near the burying ground, the mother church, with considerable justice, could have claimed it in entirety. Apparently it never occurred to her to do anything other than share it equally with her straying daughter. Much credit is due Josiah Cotton's group that this did not become a *cause célèbre;* property usually figures large in family quarrels, but nowhere in the records of either church is there to be found anything but a fine spirit of co-operation in the use of this land. "The members of the churches had been separated in life, but in death they had continued to sleep together."

One can picture the sad processions moving in slow and quiet dignity to carry a loved one to the grave on what came to be known as "Buring Hill." There were no funerals, as they were of popish origin. The village carpenter made a simple box in which to place the body. This was borne to the cemetery either on the shoulders of the bearers or on a horse-drawn wagon followed by the family and friends. Chances are that the longer haul from the East Side would lend itself to the latter and the neighborhood burials from the West Side would preserve the older and more dignified way. In this connection a beautiful custom arose which continues in Providence to this day in the use of negro bearers. Originally, they were the colored servants of the family. As they had served the member in life, so they served him in death. Few families would possess as many as were required and neighbors' servants would undoubtedly join with those of the families, or the servants would be assisted by relatives and friends of the deceased.

In the earlier days the minister did not accompany the procession to the burying ground, but this became modified with the years. At the funeral of John Howland's father in Newport (1774), both Samuel Hopkins and Ezra Styles, the two Congregational ministers, "walked in the procession to the grave but neither officiated."

Several days after the burial a funeral sermon was preached at the meetinghouse. The sermons were long and to us of today seem often harrowing; but at least it was a Christian funeral which was not paganly corpse-centered. It would sometimes be two weeks after the burial before the funeral service was held. The sad mechanics of sickness and death were behind the grieved and they could give their thoughts and hearts to the spiritual memory of the one they loved.

The sermon would develop, in its first half or two-thirds, some spiritual truth; the solemnity of life and death would be recalled to the hearers. Then the last part of the sermon would mention some of the virtues of the deceased and address words of comfort to the bereaved. This type of sermon continued for a century and more after the custom of burial preceding the funeral was unhappily abandoned.

An example of the first part is found in an early nineteenth-century sermon by James Wilson preached at Mendon at the interment of Mrs. Patience George. It was considered so fine that it was published. Most of it is on what we of today would call a high level, but the following is also there:

> We have today placed before us an example of that condition, unto which we are everyone approaching . . . are her eyes and ears now forever closed to every surrounding object in this world? The like shall also befal us. Have those important organs of the human system, the heart and lungs, the arteries and veins, discontinued their functions? The like revolution shall ere long establish its stagnant dominion over all that we call vital in our respective now animated bodies. Are her mortal remains to be this day conveyed to and inhumed within the depths of the devouring grave? and which of us can say, "my condition shall never suffer the humiliation of mouldering in the noisome grave?" Removed like her shall you be from your pleasant houses and earthly possessions.

President Samuel Finley of Princeton preached the funeral sermon of Gilbert Tennent and comforted the widow with these words:

> As to you, Madam, the mournful Relict of the deceased, I shall only say, Tho' God has taken away your earthly Husband, he does not intend you shall thereby finally be a Loser. He will not only make all Things work together for spiritual Good; but, according to his Word, will himself be your Husband, and a Father to your Children. Besides, 'tis but a little while, and you shall, I trust, see the loved Mr. Tennent in more blissful Regions, and in happier Circumstances than ever before; And Eternity will be long enough to enjoy the Society of Friends, in a State where all is Perfection, and nothing amiss for ever.

The customs would later modify, the chief influence being the Church of England's growth. We find a relative of the Episcopalian Russells, who was a good Baptist, asking for an Episcopal funeral service. Here were meeting head-on the two Christian interpretations of death: (1) the journey into the heavenly country could be greatly aided by the prayers of the church; (2) after death one was wholly in the hands of God, who alone knew if he were elected for salvation. For the former the funeral was for comfort and admonition to those lingering behind and it need not be held in connection with the burial. There was also the matter of the second use of the body in case the deceased was among those who would rise with the sound of the trumpet. At this particular time, this matter was not as subject to debate as a hundred years later, when every theological question was the center of angry argument. Deacon Joseph Snow in his will wrote:

> Knowing that it is appointed for all men once to Die [I] Do make and ordain this my Last Will and Testament, that is to say Principally and first of all I Recommend my soul to God that Gave it and for my body I recommend it to the earth to be buried in a Christian like and decent manner at the discretion of my executors, Nothing doubting but at the General Resurection I shall receive the same again by the Almighty Power of God.

One could not be too sure but that the ritualistic churches had something in directing the soul along the road to salvation. It would do no harm for a Baptist Russell to try Episcopal *modus operandi*. As one reflects on present-day funeral customs, it is strange that, with the almost complete giving up on the part of Protestants of the conception of a day of judgment and bodily resurrection, the undertakers are able to sell as never before the accoutrements for prolonging the "earth to earth and ashes to ashes" process, and have increasing success in making funerals corpse-centered, in spite of the clergy and a modern and more Christian theology.

The Episcopalian funeral method also had the advantage of providing a great social occasion for a socially hungry age. In 1745, John Checkley conducted the funeral for the wife of Colonel Updike and hundreds came.

It is hard to recapture quite the picture of those days in which friends prepared the body for burial and, with a stolid mien, marched in solemn procession to Burying Hill. Hearts were heavy, but John Calvin's interest in the philosophy of the stoics brought to New England that strange, and rather pitifully noble, power to march with faces upturned, solemn, but without tears.

Frequently it did not take many to bear the coffin, for it would be that of a small child. Joseph Snow marched six times with his children. It was often true, after taking a newborn babe to the cemetery, there would be a second sad journey with the body of the mother. Joseph's wife, good Sarah Field, died in this manner in 1753.

Leading citizens came forward to do the most difficult of the tasks. When smallpox would strike its blow, they did not flinch in endangering themselves that the rest of the community might be kept safe, and they carefully applied the little knowledge they had of caring for contagious diseases. The following tells its own story:

At a Town Council held at Providence on the 22 March, 1769:
Whereas Oliver Hunt Departed this Life Last Night with the Small Pox, And his Relatives and Friends having a Desire to bury in the burying place on the west side of the Bridge
It is voted that they have Liberty to bury him at said burying Place Under the Direction of Jabez Bowen Jr, Nathan Arnold, Oliver Bowen and Samuel Nightingale who are Required to Convey the Corps in a Carriage to the Grave between the hours of nine and ten this evening & that one of said persons shall proceed before the Corps and one other of said persons to keep behind the Corps in order to give notice to any person that may be in the Highway and the Coffin is hereby ordered to be made as Tight as possible and Tarred within and the Grave Dug Deeper than Common.

Before the order could be carried out, the widow Jones' child and the child of Mrs. Tourtelott also died and were a part of that same night's burial vigil.

Death did not cause great problems in the liquidation of estates. Land and personal effects were about the only possessions of much worth to be passed on to children and heirs. Captain John Field, father-in-law of Deacon Snow, took especial pains to see that his slave Jeffrey was not neglected:

> as to my negro man Jeffrey I do hereby order that he shall chuse which of my children or grand children he shall think proper to live with, and so far give him his time as to chuse any of them, or any other Person as he thinks proper to take him, provided they shall give Bond to keep my Heirs from all Cost, Charge & Trouble . . . and in case none of my said children shall see cause to accept of Said negroe then he shall be kept & maintained by my executor hereafter named.

Burying Hill was a cemetery but did not prove to be a last resting-place. By 1785 the growing pains of New England towns were sounding the death knell for centrally located cemeteries placed in the path of progress. New Haven was finding a problem with its great churchyard in the center of the town, back of the churches on the green. Timothy Dwight brought good philosophy and theology to play on the problem when he wrote:

> Since this apprehension (that consecrated ground has peculiar advantages, attending those who are interred, at the ressurection) has been perceived by common sense to be groundless and ridiculous (and since) it is always desirable that a burial-ground should be a solemn object to man . . . but when placed in the centre of a town and in the current of daily intercourse, it is rendered too familiar to the eye to have any beneficial effect on the heart . . . and speedily loses all its connection with the invisible world in a gross and vulgar union with the ordinary business of life, it should be moved to the outskirts.

As a result New Haven developed a cemetery laid out in large family lots which Dwight believed was "altogether a singularity in the world." It precluded the use of vaults, "these melancholy, and I think I may say disgusting, mansions seem not to have been dictated by nature." Thus New Haven's civic center was freed from graves and tombstones except for those which continued their molding processes under the churches themselves.

In Providence there was more urgency to the problem. Burying Hill, which was considerably higher then than now, was eroding on the north side bordering on High Street (now Weybosset) and, horror of horrors, was exposing the coffins and corpses! The urge to decency added to the urge to emulate the late Deacon Snow (he died in 1768) in sensing good real-estate opportunities. It led the two church societies to a wise and businesslike solution of the problem. A joint committee was appointed which presented a petition to the General Assembly meeting at Bristol in August, 1785. In it they recited the story of the Hoyle acre, given for "assemblies who should peaceably and Quietly Worship God in the Congregational or Presbyterian Way." Dr. Hoyle never dreamed that the assembly would be quite as peaceful and quiet!

The petition goes on to say and ask:

> the Land Northward being much Lower than the Ground within the Burying Place Lot and daily wasting and wearing away into the Valey below to that Degree that some of the Coffin of persons who had been buried there fell out of the Ground and became uncovered and as it will be probably prejudicial to the Health of the Neighboring Inhabitants that any more persons should be buried in the aforesaid lot especially in that part of it, next to said High Street which with the Permission of the Honorable the Legislature of the State may be sold for sufficient to purchase a Burying Place much more Extensive and Convenient and more remote from the compact part of the Town.

The Assembly granted the petition. This enterprise on the part of the two Congregational societies awakened public interest and brought to a head the matter of family burying lots which had plagued the town for so long. Benefit Street had been dotted with them and the highway curved in and out around them, causing respect to the dead to add mileage to horse-drawn loads. In October of the same year the Assembly voted:

> Whereas the 1st settlers of the Town of Prov. were in the Practice of burying the dead in small yards in their own Lots, before the present large public Ground was laid out for that Purpose; but from the general Disapprobation of continuing to bury in such Lots, they have been for many years disused: And whereas, by the increase of the sd. Town, divers Streets and Lanes have been laid out, with which some of those Burying Lots interfere . . .
>
> Be it therefore enacted by this General Assembly and by the authority thereof it is hereby enacted, That it shall and may be lawful for the Town Council of the Town of Prov. to make inspection into the several private Burying Lots in the said Town, and such as they shall judge most for the public Benefit to have removed, that they signify the same to the Person or persons who hold the said lots in possession or have been at the Expense of keeping up the Monuments, and advise whether the same be exchanged for the same Quantity of Land in another place . . . or otherwise that they be removed to the common Burying Place belonging to the said Town (North Burial Ground 1765)

That the church committees knew what they were about when they sent their August petition is shown by the fact that the four lots bordering on the south side of High (Weybosset) Street were laid out and sold by November of the same year. The one on the north side of Broad Street, at the lower corner of the cemetery, remained unsold at the time, being much more a part of the graveyard proper. The Benevolent Society was willing to take a chance on reselling one lot at a profit, and purchased it that the proceeds might be used to build a retaining wall behind the house lots and thereby separate the living from the intrusions of the dead. They paid two hundred Spanish milled dollars to the two societies for "no 3 lot." This they resold to Ebenezer Sprague of Johnston who had been seized with the big-town urge. The other house-lot purchasers were Elihu Peck (Housewright) and John Field (Gentleman), with the Benevolent Society buying a second lot.

Sufficient land was sold to provide the societies with ample capital to "inquire where, what quantity and on what terms other Lands may be purchased for said Uses." Public-spirited Deacon John Field came forward and offered five acres of his lands for the purpose at what was a most reasonable price. Each society bought two and a half acres for one hundred Spanish milled dollars. The society under the pastoral care of Joseph Snow took the land bounded now by Beacon, Point and Plain streets, part of which is now Hayward Park. The Benevolent Society took an equal area of land on the west side of what is now Beacon Street. From Broad Street the "Way to the New Burial Ground" was laid out along what is now Beacon Street. When it reached the burial ground it became a private road dividing the areas of the two societies.

Around the east side of the Beneficent lot the Road to the Hospital would be opened (now Plain Street). The hospital was built in 1797 during the yellow-fever epidemic, when a hundred and fifty fell victims to the disease. The family of James Arnold, town treasurer, were the first to be taken. Great debate over the merits of heat and bleeding added to the sad confusion of the period. Philadelphia, suffering from a similar epidemic, exchanged relief donations with Providence, thus cementing a long friendship between the City of God and the City of Brotherly Love.

The location of the hospital was probably based on the fact that here in the southern part of the city the disease raged while the rest of the town was free from it. Also for the treatment of contagious diseases it was well to have it far away, after the pattern of town "pest houses." Whether Dr. Carew or any of his associates felt that its location on the road to the cemetery was at all a reflection on the prowess of the "doctors of physick" is not known.

As with business developments, the opening of the two new cemeteries attracted other cemeteries to the same area, and the Field family found themselves selling much of their farm for this purpose.

In 1791 the Proprietors' Burying Ground was opened. It abutted the northerly side of the Beneficent ground. It was about two-thirds as large. Its northern boundary was near what is now Friendship Street. A portion of it was to be laid out in forty equal parts, fifty-five feet by twenty-five feet, thus beating New Haven's "world singularity" by half a dozen years. Across the street would be erected the city's fire bell, loud enough to wake the dead.

Eventually three other cemeteries joined the neighborhood south of Point Street: 1809, the Manchester Burying Ground; 1818, the Sprague or Hope Cemetery; and 1842, Seth Paddford's Cemetery. The whole came to be known as the West Burial Ground and comprised seventeen acres with a "population" of over a thousand. The Chestnut Street Methodists acquired a small diamond-shaped piece on the west side of Beacon Street opposite the Proprietors' lot.

In Father Snow's society's burial place, he himself was deeded lot No. 1. The first purchasers of lots were the Stephen Wardwells. The prices were low. As late as 1800, William Woodward paid the society twelve shillings for "burying ground right and entrance money."

But the problem of those still "inhabiting" the unsold part of Hoyle's acre continued to bother the two societies. In 1788 Daniel Branch of the Benevolent Society writes to the Beneficent Society:

October 3: 1788
Gentlemen,

These are to inform you that the stakes in the buring ground that forms a square for each family have many of them been carried of and I have replased them but to no efect for they are carried of daily therefore I wish that sum measurs might be taken to form the lots with such bounds that know person would take away—it is my opinion that in less then six months no person scarsley will be abel to find whare the bounds of each lot is except sum such meathord is contrived nor shall we be abel in the winter to find out whare to bury—Gentlemen I am with respect your most obeident most humbel sarvant.

Daniel Branch
to the Beneficent Society

The opinion grew that the land should be disposed of. Finally in 1803 the two societies inserted this advertisement in the *United States Chronicle:*

At a meeting of the standing committees of the first Congregational Society, and of the Beneficent Society, on the 9th day of May inst. it was resolved to notify all persons who have friends or relations that were interred in the old burying-ground, near the Rev. Mr. Wilson's meeting-house, and who have not been removed, that it is the request of the committees, that they cause the dead to be carefully removed, previous to the 1st day of July next. Those who will visit the old burying-ground and see its present condition will agree to the propriety of this request, without taking into consideration that the ground is to be appropriated to other uses, after the time above mentioned.

By order of the standing committees of the two Societies.

John Howland
Cl of 1st Cong[l] Ch

Walter Paine
Sec'ry Beneficient Soc.

May 12

This was followed by a survey of the lot by Daniel Anthony who made the first general map of Providence in 1803, and the discovery that neighbor Munroe, whose property abutted on the northeast corner, had "enclosed a part of the lot in his yard and Gardin which he acknowledges."

The advertisement cost the societies a dollar, paid to publisher Bennett Wheeler, but its result entailed greater expense. We find the Beneficent Society borrowing $62.50 to pay one John Lowell (or Lassell) for removing the dead out of the old burying ground and as late as 1811 B. Jones and Samuel Proud are paid $1.29 for "removing and burying bones."

By 1815 the remainder of the land is finally cleared and cut up into house lots. A gangway (Winslow Street) divides front small lots from large rear lots. The purchasers are William Field, Jr., Benjamin James, Peleg Hall, Seth Simmons, Nathaniel Barstow, William Field II, John Perrin, and Asa Bosworth.

It had been the need for businesslike handling of the cemetery problem which had been a chief reason for the incorporation of Beneficent Society in 1785. One might say the society was born in a cemetery. The untangling of the title of the Hoyle land with its "foreign" trustees needed such a body and so did the subsequent real-estate actions.

Interesting rules were drawn up for the use of the new cemetery in an attempt to make it serve the society by restricting its benefits to the worshipers at the West Side church. One must pay an entrance fee to the society (said committee judging them proper members) of not less than six nor more than twelve shillings. They and their families must "usually attend on Publick Worship on the Sabbath with Said Society" and pay a proportion of "Annual Expence of Supporting the ministry in said Society." If these conditions are not fulfilled the lots revert to the society. One cannot bury relations further distant than "grandfather and grandmother, brothers' and sisters' children, sons' and daughters' children.

"No person is to be buried as Stranger but such as is realy So."

Domestics may be buried with permission but care must be taken to see that people "who are not of that description" are not admitted. The sexton is to carry out the above orders and get written permission for burials.

It would appear that cemetery privileges were at a premium up in the fine new hilltop ground and the society could well afford to use a little pressure to accomplish some of its purposes among the living by the rules it made for the dead.

In the archives of the First Congregational Church there is preserved an interesting plat of the graves. Among the names of the owners are those of Nathaniel Green, the Fosters, Dexters, Nightingales, Bowens, Grovenors, Whitmans, Jenkes and Gladdings. There are sections for the Strangers and the Blacks. The plat is reinforced by having pasted on its back a theater bill of "The Will" which may be seen in Providence, July 26, 1809. Boxes are $1.00, the Pit 50 cents and the gallery twenty-five. Further strengthening is furnished by a bill of lading which reads, "Shipped by the Grace of God and in good order in and upon the good sloop called the Dolphin whereof is master under God, for the present voyage, Jermiah Greenman, eight hogsheads of New England rum risque of Mr. James Green in Providence." Mr. Green was the solid pillar of the First Church and good friend of Parson Hitchcock. Thus in one document and its patching it is recorded that the Grace of God had sent some to ship New England rum in good order, others to visit the theater, and still others to sleep eternally with their fathers.

By 1860 we find the society both weary of running a cemetery and looking upon the sale of the land as a possible bonanza which would help it out of debt. Under January 2, 1860, this surprising minute is recorded: Mr. I Sumner was appointed a committee "to ascertain how many of the occupants of the

Society's Burial Ground would be willing to exchange their lots for an equal quantity of land in either of the other Cemeteries of the city."

Silence must have given consent and in 1870 the society bought a sixty by one-hundred-foot piece of land in Oakland Cemetery. In 1872, desiring to purchase land for erecting a chapel, the society inquired about the possibility of mortgaging their cemetery, but better judgment prevailed and the plan was not pushed. Three years later, with a huge debt on its hands, a most welcome inquiry was entertained from the General Assembly to see if the society would sell the burial ground for a site for the new state house.

They offered it to the state at a dollar a foot or $101,750 and accompanied the offer with a six-pronged statement as to the desirability of the site for the state house. The state did not accept the offer.

The next step was to plat the land into twenty-one house lots, laying out what is now Maple Street parallel to and north of Point, so that seven lots would face on either side of Maple and seven on the north side of Point. A forty-cent per foot offer was refused, but soon a fifty-cent offer was accepted, and the property sold to Beriah Wall in 1878. This, with money from the city paid for the portion taken as Hayward Park, made the sale price fifty-three thousand dollars. It cost some ten thousand dollars to clean the cemetery and to buy lots in Swan Point, North and Oakland cemeteries for burials of the unclaimed bodies. The society's debt was close to the balance but, after all was accounted for, the society was twelve hundred dollars ahead of the game and out of the cemetery business forever, with minor exceptions.

The city added its purchase of six of the northern seven lots to the Proprietors' Burial Ground to make Hayward Park in 1892. The seventh of the lots on the northwest corner of the old burial ground and the southwest corner of the park had been purchased as the site of St. Ansgarius (Swedish) Episcopal Church in 1891. Thus a little of the intent of Hoyle's acre was by a force of circumstances carried out a hundred and seventy years after its purchase and on a site a quarter of a mile away from the original place where Hoyle had planned his church, parsonage, horse sheds and "buring place." He, himself, might well approve the summer games of checkers which the old men play in the park over the spot where the fathers were raised from their sleep.

CHAPTER FOURTEEN

FREEDOM AND UNITY

Providence Church records are very meager in any references to the Revolutionary War. There were good reasons. Unlike Massachusetts there was no need for the ministers to help people make up their minds about freedom. They had been made up for an hundred and forty years! Congregations were not to be split between Loyalists and Patriots.

Among the few exceptions was John Graves, rector of King's Church, who insisted on following the prayer book and praying for His Majesty King George III, until his parishioners were forced to invite him to leave his pulpit. After the Revolution he was willing to return without benefit of prayers for the king, but he was not invited back. The stories which come down to us about the Graves make them most interesting characters.

John's brother, Matthew, was the rector of the Church of England in Stonington, Connecticut, and was also loyal to king and prayer book. A story has come down in the family that a Continental officer in his flock once became so angry with Matthew that he said, "If you didn't wear that preacher's coat I'd punch you in the nose." The words were hardly uttered when off came the coat and Matthew, with his Irish blood tingling, was ready for all comers.

The glebe of John Graves was near the present Brown University Field House. During the Revolution another story tells us a Tory took shelter in the glebe. John was away but the officers who came to search met Mrs. Graves, who was entirely equal to the occasion. She had hidden the fugitive in the chimney place; as the officers finished their unsuccessful search, she asked them if they were sure they had looked everywhere. They thought they had. Getting the keys to her linen closet she said, "You haven't looked in there, you better completely satisfy yourselves before you leave." So disarming was her whole manner that the officers left the scene convinced the rumor was false. The officer fell in love with the daughter of the glebe and promised to return and marry her after the war. But in seeking to fulfill his promise he was lost at sea and the daughter of the Graves never married.[1]

There were those opposed to the burning of the British revenue schooner, *Gaspee,* in 1772. One of Joseph Snow's deacons, Benjamin Gladding, town barber, pulled his young apprentice, John Howland, out of the band as they started on their lawless journey. But even Benjamin Gladding would forget the niceties of law and order as hot-headed Samuel Adams would visit his shop and as General Benedict Arnold would set up his headquarters in Providence. Benjamin's respect for the British would drop considerably when he was called upon to set aright the disheveled wig of the insignificant-looking General Prescott, after his capture on the island of Rhode Island. As Newportians fled to Providence from their destroyed homes and town, the fires of passion would be fed with increasing fuel.

From the beginning, however, there was no need of haranguing Providence folk on freedom. The Revolution was merely a pause to secure for all of the colonies what the Plantations had always had by law or seized in the absence of law. Even July 4 was an anticlimax for Rhode Islanders for they had renounced their allegiance to Great Britain on May 4, 1776. Roger Williams had seen to it that the Rhode Island charters from the beginning gave her self-government and kept the king's men at good arm's length. Disobedience to the Stamp Act was a foregone conclusion and needed no debating! You couldn't stay in Rhode Island long without seeing the pattern of freedom clearly.

It was more than chance that made Gad Hitchcock of Pembroke, Massachusetts, the great parsonic voice for freedom; he had caught some of it from the Plantations. He was a cousin of Enos Hitchcock who had visited the First Congregational Society in Providence at the outbreak of the Revolution and left his wife as a hostage to his return as its minister after he had served as chaplain with Washington's armies. Pembroke was the first town in America to declare its independence. Gad Hitchcock preached his famous election-day sermon at Old South Church, Boston, May 25, 1774. The election-day sermon always preceded the choosing on the same day by the lower elected house of his Majesty's Council for the Province. Governor Gage and many of the king's officials were a part of the congregation, which would hear what was close to a call to revolt. Gad Hitchcock announced his text, Proverbs 29:2; "When the righteous are in authority the people rejoice; when the wicked beareth rule, the people mourn." From that moment the electrified congregation missed not a word, except for some of the strongest Tories who arose and left and later caused Gad to comment that it was the most moving sermon he ever preached. The sermon was scholarly and as fine an exposition of Christian liberty as we have in American pulpit utterances. He began by saying that the text

supposes the people to be judges of the good or ill effects of administration. In such a government the rulers have their distinct powers assigned them by the people who are the only source of civil authority on earth . . . In a state of nature men are equal . . . If it be true that no ruler is safe where the doctrine of resistance is taught, it must be true that no nation can be safe where the contrary is taught . . . One must expect crown appointed governors to consider themselves as being under prior obligations to the King of Kings and obey God rather than men.

Coming to the election which would take place in a few hours he said that the legislators were bound to "provide out of all the people able men . . . Our danger is not visionary but real. Our contention is not about trifles but about liberty and property."

So powerful was the sermon that the legislature adopted Gad Hitchcock's advice and chose the most progressive of their citizenry for the council. Governor Gage promptly vetoed thirteen of the appointees and then adjourned the legislature. Soon the legislature reassembled at Salem and met with the doors locked against the governor.

The ideas which stood out so clearly in that sermon had burned in the hearts of Rhode Island men from the beginning. But as we have seen, liberty had proven itself strong in wrecking the evil but not always capable of establishing the good. It was a difficult foundation stone upon which to erect a society. The superstructure would again and again roll off and fall into its individualistic parts. The Christian cement of charity alone could bring the two parts of the building, *freedom and unity*, together. Roger Williams had not had the patience to try largely because he doubted the worth or the necessity of the superstructure. He was content to sit on the great foundation stone instead of building upon it.

Josiah Cotton had tried to substitute the Massachusetts pattern of orderliness but had failed in the other direction by leaving out the foundation stone of freedom.

Joseph Snow, with no great brilliance and many faults, became a symbol of the practical solution of building a house upon freedom's foundation. Without a college education and the ability to spell he represented the type of able leader which had been in the community from the beginning. Nowhere else in New England had the common man been less subservient to the power of intellectualism and ecclesiasticism. Men of the caliber of Jonathan Spreague could wield a mighty pen and were confident that in their Biblical logic they could do battle with any Cambridge or Harvard graduate.

As Joseph Snow grew old, his West Side village became his monument. Here men could call the tunes of freedom and with the same enthusiasm as the individualistic folks across the Bridge. In addition "Westminster folks" developed land, laid out streets, filled in swamps, co-operated on a water supply, and held religious services. Joseph had taken the good things of Massachusetts, its village green, its steepled meetinghouse, its well-ordered life and planted them in the land of barren liberty. For his pattern he had looked neither across the water to the Established Church of England nor across the Seekonk to the Established Church of New England. He had, with the background of their experience, used his common sense to bring a large measure of democracy to ecclesiastical affairs as well as to civil affairs. It was a fruition within a church of Roger Williams' "Lively Experiment."

Joseph would not live to see the natural outcome of this harmony between freedom and unity. Others would carry the experiment on, to include public education, the co-operative establishment of industry, the coming of culture with its libraries, its singing schools, and its civic gatherings. His own latter years were not bright, due to his failure to know that his contribution had been made, but that is another story.

Nor would the lesson of the West Side be contagious for the people of the state as they approached the years after the Revolution. The folks of the country towns, especially, were still for freedom without unity and abhorred the idea of becoming a part of the United States.

Weybosset Bridge, which had served as the crossing from the bank of freedom to the bank of unity, appropriately played a dramatic part in selling the idea of federal unity to the populace of the state. The Revolutionary War in the minds of most Rhode Islanders, had been a means of getting rid of England rather than of forming a more perfect union. There was no intention of ever becoming a member of the Constitutional Federation and no delegates had been sent to the Constitutional Convention. If eleven or twelve colonies wanted to join up that was all right but, said the old-line Rhode Islander, there would never be thirteen.

But those who had experienced the possibilities of freedom and unity joining forces thought differently and they used Weybosset Bridge to express themselves.

On July 29, 1788, news was received that New York, the eleventh state, had come into the Union. On the south side of the Bridge eleven flagstaffs were erected, each displaying the national emblem, and across each flag the name of one of the states which had adopted the constitution, its date of ratification, and the majority by which it had ratified. These were arranged in historic order from Delaware to New York and stood upright. On the upstream side stood two lone poles. One was slanted at a thirty-degree angle with a flag bearing the name North Carolina, the date the convention would meet, and a motto, "It will rise." The other pole, at a forty-five degree angle had only a paper label with the words, "Rhode Island in hopes." In the afternoon eleven cannon were fired from the Bridge and eleven cheers given, which it was hoped would be heard in the country towns which most strongly opposed ratification.

But even with this dramatic demonstration by the adherents of freedom and unity there would still be a three-year wait before the state would take favorable action. Washington would be inaugurated president and tariffs would be collected against and by the little foreign country of Rhode Island and Providence Plantations on Narragansett Bay.

As so often happened, religion had succeeded in pioneering new paths before the other departments of civic and cultural life had caught up. One great blessing which had been Rhode Island's in these years of experiment was that in spite of the refuge it granted to all religions there had arisen very little *theological* controversy; most of the religious controversy lay within the field of church government. The next century would see the multiplication of sects and the bitter debates on doctrines.

Up to the close of the eighteenth century, the doctrinal controversies which entered Rhode Island had been either local or of small import with the possible exception of the contention between Roger Williams and George Fox. For the most part religious discussion during the seventeenth and eighteenth centuries in New England lay in the field of "practics" rather than theology. This did not make them any less heated at times. Roger Williams was not expelled for his theology, but his conception of the relation of church and state, and his economic theories as expressed in his dealing with the Indians. Indeed, his great heresy was not formulated until a few years after he reached Providence and it went almost unnoticed, when as a Seeker he held that there were no ministry, scriptures, or ordinances. These had been lost since the first century and now must be sought after, but not too strenuously by Roger. In the case of the Quakers, their doctrine of the inner light was more opposed because people did not like the Quakers and their customs, speech, and dress, than that they knew or cared much about the inner light.

Broad-gaged leaders always decried sectarian narrowness, no matter what its basis. Enos Hitchcock, in 1783, led his church in voting to invite members of all churches to participate in the communion service.

The Congregationalists, in seeking to invade Providence, had been bitterly opposed by Jonathan Spreague, not for their theology, but for their tax-supported (hireling) ministry; Joseph Snow and Josiah Cotton quarreled a little over "damnable good works" but much more over whose right it was to call a church meeting, the use of itinerant ministers, and the amount of fervor proper in religion.

David Rowland, the predecessor of Enos Hitchcock, in 1772 at the Congregational convention in Bristol, had given a paper entitled "Catholicism, or Christian Charity." In it he quotes Dr. Watts:

It is a very uncharitable practice, to think that a man can never journey safely to heaven, unless his hat and his shoes be of the same color with ours, unless he treads in the very track of our feet, and his footsteps too be of the same size. It is a curious and perverse fancy to pronounce a man no Christian, because every thought of his soul, and all the atoms of his brain, are not just ranged in the same posture as mine.—How ridiculously unreasonable is it, for a man of brown hair to shut his brother out from the rank and species of men, and call him an ox or a lion, because his locks are black or yellow. I am persuaded there is a *breadth* in the narrow road to heaven, and persons may travel more than seven abreast in it. And though they do not trace precisely the same track, yet all look to the same Saviour, Jesus, and all arrive at the same common salvation. And though their names be crossed out of the records of a particular church on earth, where charity fails, yet they will be found written in the Lamb's book of Life, which is a record of eternal love, and shall be forever joined to the fellowship of the catholic church in heaven.

Mr. Rowland goes on to exhort the brethren gathered at Bristol:

to receive into their affection and communion, sober regular Christians, whether they are called by the name of Lutherans, Episcopalians, Presbyterians, Congregationalists, Independents, or Baptists, that there may be no schism or rent in the visible body of Christ.

Joseph Snow had refused to press charges against the brother who exhorted in not wholly orthodox fashion. The church was a fellowship and it was more important for a parson to spend his efforts in keeping the flock sober, honest, and chaste, than in keeping it orthodox. He had sought to solve the perplexing democratic problem of the minority by urging the major part to win over the minor part through the brotherly offices of reason and charity.

As he stood on the summit of his years, unaware of the breakers ahead, "Joseph Snow, jun'r, joyner" of wooden beams and human souls, had done well as the shepherd who had led the flock which had crossed Weybosset Bridge to perfect the "lively experiment" by adding Unity to Freedom.

By 1790 the footsteps of others who would carry on the experiment were already approaching.

NOTES AND REFERENCES

Introduction

1. Today it has grown to be the "widest bridge in the world" covering over most of the river except its summer odor.

Chapter I

1. The smallest state is a composite of several political entities. Her official name is still the longest of forty-eight, "Rhode Island and Providence Plantations." The two state houses, one at Newport and one at Providence, were both used as late as 1900. Earlier the General Assembly "met around" in most of the towns.
2. All of this has been splendidly retold recently by Dr. Atkins in *History of American Congregationalism* (1942).
3. Perhaps this principle is the reason why many an early New England Congregational Church successfully continues in a downtown location far removed from residential areas. Historically Congregationalism is not the accident of geography but the magnetic attraction of a free fellowship.
4. Sweet. *Colonial America,* p. 136.
5. Colgate-Rochester Divinity School Bulletin, Vol. VII, p. 51.
6. A still more revolutionary view on the rebaptizing of Williams by Holliman and the other members by Williams is that it did not necessarily indicate a dissatisfaction with their previous baptism, but rather indicated the new beginning in the covenant relationship, with a casting off of the previous unseparate relationships. Similarly in early New England fully ordained English ministers would be reordained when taking a New England charge. This was later changed to the "installation service" which still persists, implying this old idea of a peculiar relationship each congregation has with its minister and fellow members. (See Walker, page 222*b*.) Williams would have particularly stressed this. Similarly also the lovely and ancient New England custom of "owning the Covenant" at communion services or on the occasion of receiving new members.
7. For Howland's discussion of this, see Stone, *Life of John Howland,* pp. 247-249.
8. Roger had been ordained in the Church of England before he became a Separatist.
9. The First Congregational Church of Providence possesses a history written not later than 1771 as a preface to its church records. It is in beautiful penmanship in a book of heavy watermarked paper. The author is unknown,

but Miss Helen Robertson, historian of the First Congregational Church, believes it was Deacon James Green, good friend of Enos Hitchcock, at whose home Hitchcock's wife stayed while he was off chaplaining in the Revolution. Hitchcock and Green carried on a delightful correspondence during the Revolution and many of the Hitchcock letters are in the possession of the First Congregational Church. This is the way its author understood the religious foundings of the colony:

> In Anno Domini 1630 Mr. *Roger Williams* came over from England to Plymouth where he continued as an assistant in the ministry to Mr. *Ralph Smith,* then pastor; but not finding such a concurrence, as he expected, he desired a dismission to the church of *Salem,* which was consented to.—He arrived at *Salem* in the time of Mr. Shelton's weakness, and who lived not long after; whereupon after sometime the Church called him to office; soon after, he begun to vent many dangerous opinions, subversive of the peace of both Church and State; that after means used to convince and reclaim him, in vain, he was banished the colony, as a disturber of the peace, both of the Church and Commonwealth.—See *New England* memorial.
>
> In Anno Domini 1635 Mr. *Williams* came to this place, by the natives called *Mooshansick,*—by him called *Providence,* here he was accompanied by a number of his friends and adherents, and soon after gathered a *Pedobaptist* Church but after some years he and his Church by his influence renounced his and their Infant baptism; and not long after this, he told his people that he had misled them, for he did not find that there was any upon earth that could administer baptism, and therefore their last baptism was a nullity, as well as their first; and therefore they must lay down all, and wait for the coming of new apostles; and thus they dissolved themselves and turned *Seekers* Retaining this one principle that every one should have liberty to worship GOD according to the light of their own consciences, but not owning any Church upon earth.—This laid the foundation of the Baptist interest in this Colony for as Mr. *Williams* became indifferent to all persuasions, so this colony became a place of resort for Baptist and Quakers: and there were for a long time but few of any other denomination. In this State this Colony remained about *Sixty years.* That is Ad Annum 1695.

10. We do not say Rhode Island because Newport's record was better than the towns of the Plantations. South County with its cultured landed gentry is still another story.

11. Had there been good soil Williams was hardly the man to have developed it on anything but a Victory garden scale. While he came expecting to farm he brought no plow or any one with mechanical skill. The colony had no capital. In 1649 Roger wrote Governor Winthrop that they had no smith in town.

Chapter II

1. In Henry D. King's "Historical Statements," he says the second church was on the site of the first. This does not seem to be corroborated, but could

be so. In Margaret B. Stillwell's *The Pageant of Benefit Street* end-paper maps locate the two houses on opposite corners of North Main and Smith streets.

2. Rufus M. Jones. *The Quaker in the American Colonies,* p. 23.

3. Quoted from James Bowden, *History of the Society of Friends in America,* by Society of Friends Historical Records Survey.

4. Roger Williams had a knack of choosing colorful titles for his pamphlets and could always go his opponent one better. His tilt with John Cotton began by Roger's publication, while in England in 1643, to secure the colony's charter, of *The Bloody Tenent of Persecution.* In 1647 John Cotton, minister of the Boston church, replied to his attack on Massachusetts with *The Bloody Tenent Washed and made White in the Blood of the Lamb* in answer to which Roger wrote, *The Bloody Tenent yet more Bloody by Cotton's endeavor to wash it white in the Blood of the Lamb.* His polemic against George Fox, English founder of the Quakers, was entitled, *George Fox Digg'd Out of His Burrowes.*

5. Rhode Island had not been invited into the United Colonies.

6. First governor of Rhode Island under the charter of 1663 and ancestor of the Revolutionary general.

7. In a letter to the secretary of the Society for the Propagation of the Gospel in Foreign Parts, written November 19, 1723, James Honyman affords us a picture of the activities of a Newport parson and the preparation for the building of the present Trinity Church, which was erected three years later:

> In some of my former I endeavoured to account for some of my labour in the discharge of the duties of my Mission and I think in one of them how I had been detained a great part of this last summer from some services I designed in the countrey by my necessary attendance on a great number of Pirates, who were executed here, in assisting their preparation for death, and also by an unusual and yet universal sickness in this place, which occasioned my being in a manner continually called upon, besides the constant exercise of my function at my church ——.
>
> I come now to lay before my Honbl Patrons some particulars of the success, wherewith God has been pleased to bless my endeavours. It is therefore with the greatest pleasure that I can now inform them that within these last two years I have in all baptized eighty two; of whom, besides severall of them eight to twelve years of age, there were nineteen adult persons, of whom there were three Negros, two Indians, and two Molattoes, that there are properly belonging to this church and in this very place above fifty Communicants. I dont reckon strangers, nor count (as some do) all the Communicants of a Colony instead of a town. And that there having been an objection started that our people growing too numerous for our church to contain them Others who were willing to join us and our worship were discouraged, and kept away for want of room, I was willing effectually to answer it by proposing the building a new one; and to incourage that design, I began the Subscription by signing to thirty pounds for my own gift towards it; and now the subscriptions amount to near a thousand pounds for that use, tho we judge according to the dimensions of it, It will cost at least two thousand pound. Materials are now getting ready, and our

workmen begin upon them in the Spring of the year, and I hope God will carry us through a work designed for and to be dedicated to His glory. I present my humble duty to the Honble Society and am in some hopes, that these amounts will in some measure, convince them how willing I am to devote myself to the service I am engaged in, and answer the expectation they have been pleased to conceive of, their, and

Sr
Your most obedient and most humble
Servt
James Honyman

8. Spelled Seekonk, Seacunk, Seaconk, Seaconck, etc. Indian name meaning Black goose.

9. The deed is classic not only as a deed, but as a platform of ecclesiastical procedure. Portions of it read:

To all people to whome these presents shall come Greeting, Know yee that I John Hoyle of the Town of Providence in the Colony of Rhoad Island and Providence Plantations in New England; for and in consideration of the sum of 24 pounds of Currant money of said New England, to mee in hand before the sealing and delivery of these presents, well and truly paid out of the money colected within the Province of the Massachusetts Bay in said New England in a way of Charity and bounty for the erecting of a meeting house in the afore said Towne of Providence and for the purchasing a piece of land near the middle of that Greate Street in said Towne of Providence on either side of the Great Bridge which goes over the Salt River on which land said meeting house is to be erected which is to be appointed to the use of Godly Preachers, ministers and assembles that shall peaceably and orderly worship God in the Congregational or Presbyterian Way: . . . grant, bargain sell . . . unto Mr. *Samuel Danforth* of Taunton in the county of Bristol in the province of the Massachusetts Bay in New England, Clerk, and unto *Daniel Smith Esq*. Mr. John Greenwood Clerk and Deacon Samuel Newman of the Town of Rehoboth in the County aforesaid and to the Reverend Mr. Timothy Woodbridge and Mr. Samuel Whiting pastor of Wendham both in the Colony of Connecticut, who were nominated to be trustees to whom the deed of the land, on which said meetinghouse is to be erected, shall be made: . . . that said land be apropriate for the use of Godly Preachers, Ministers and assemblies that shall peacefully and quietly worship God in the Congregational or presbetarian way in the meeting house that shall be erected on said land as also to build a dwelling house for a minister thereon If it be found convenient and also a buring place and sheds for horses for the use of such pias auditors that do there attend on the worship of God.

10. In the anonymously written history the First Congregational Church compiled fifty years after the Hoyle episode, we get this interpretation of John "Hoile":

It appears from the very imperfect accounts to be collected that the disposition of the monies in the purchase of the Land and locating the house was very much, if not wholey according to the notion and humor of the said Hoile, for tho he had set up the house, and partly covered it the situation of it was so disagreable to those that were in Town and their patrons and friends abroad, that it was taken down (some have said pull'd down under the covert of the night). This was about the year 1721 or 2 at which time there was not but one or two houses on the West side of the bridge and but about forty-five in the whole town: The taking down the meeting house after it was partly covered is an evidence that its being placed so far out of town, (as it then was) was disagreable to the people in general, and that its location was very much according to the humor of Dr. Hoile, for as he had the monies contributed in his own hand, he might have it in his power to gratify his own inclination.

Another Providence parson in 1744 purchased six or seven acres on the "neck" and paid 201 pounds 18s. 9d. This would top Dr. Hoyle's price.

11. Fulham Palace Papers.
12. Fulham Palace Papers.
13. In June 1725 James Honyman wrote as follows to the Bishop of London:

Newport on Rhode Island
June 16th 1725

My Lord

Many are the arguments that plead for the Necessity of our having a Bishop in these parts, and among others, this; that there arise several cases and doubts about things wherein the discharge of our Office is concerned, which want to be resolved, and our practice therein determined by a Superior. To instance, I sometimes preach to people in the countrey and in the whole audience there are not so many baptized persons as to be Sureties or Witnesses to some that offer themselves to that Sacrament. To refuse them is inconsistent with my Doctrine, that earnestly invites them, and to receive them without Sponsors seems to be breaking in upon the Churches Rules. Again some desire to be baptized but then only by Immersion; and accordingly some of the Missionaries do yield to that desire. But however far that practice may be warrantable, with me it is still a question, if it be prudent and allowable to depart from the present and almost universal practise of the Church, especially since complying with a few scrupulous, may multiply their number even amongst our own people. I would beg your Lordships opinion and protection on these points.

I am with all possible veneration, My Lord,
Your Lordships most obedient and most
humble Ser^{t}.

James Honyman

14. Fulham Palace Papers.
15. Updike, *History of Narragansett Church,* Vol. I, p. 48.
16. The list of names continues:

We have also Mr. Winsor, Mr. James Browne, Mr. Hakin of the Anabaptist Church, and great preacher: and their auditors, Mr. Outram mathematician. Messrs. Tilliness, Power, good Harris merchant, all sober men that can learn and teach things by true demonstration, that may come to the Church of England as already Mr. Joseph Browne captain, experimented, and well known by his good services to the county of Massachusetts and all New England . . . that hath bought already *The Rites and ceremonies of the Church of England.* Mr. Nathaniel Brown his brother hath given and favoured us the ground to set this church upon.

17. Fulham Palace Papers; Updike, *History of Narragansett Church,* Vol. I, p. 59.

18. The *Pulled-down-in-the-night* tradition would seem to be exploded by this contemporary account of the Dr. Hoyle meetinghouse, the only such account we have.

19. Gabriel Bernon had written that the first pastor must be a "learned and consumed minister of good erudition; and we desire that he should be an Old England gentleman minister with probity able to reconcile worthies, good neighbors, and fellow citizens, in love and respect one for another, by a right charity and right understanding, etc." A good list of qualifications but as ambitious as a present-day pulpit committee. King's Church did better than some in securing Mr. George Piggot as their first rector.

Chapter III

1. Sprague's Annals, Vol. I, p. 243 f.

2. Bliss, *History of Rehoboth.*

3. *Weekly News Letter,* Oct. 24-31, 1728.

4. Rhode Island almost missed the opportunity for establishing this enviable record, for somewhere in the early seventeen hundreds a disabling clause denying political rights to Roman Catholics, Jews, and Mohammedans crept into the franchise statutes. It did not affect their freedom to worship as they chose. The historian is confused as to the exact wording and intent of the statute. It may be his loyalty to the Rhode Island ideal which creates a fog of amazement on his part. But the situation was saved by the repeal of the statute in 1783 before Rhode Islanders had seen many Roman Catholics or any Mohammedans. The high favor in which the Jewish colony of Newport was held was undoubtedly a chief cause of its repeal, together with the general smell of freedom in the air at that time.

5. This is the only Rhode Island record which we have found which makes use of "Reverend" with only the last name to which most modern New England parsons object, preferring, "Reverend Mr." or "Reverend plus-the-full-name." We hope early usage did not employ this adjective as a form of address.

6. We call them by a much poorer name now, "delegates."

7. They had church surveys in those days! In the Windham, Connecticut, church Thomas Clap, who was to be president of Yale, had succeeded his father-in-law, Mr. Samuel Whiting (Hoyle trustee), as its second minister. He writes:

> January 1, 1737. I have had this last week finished my pastoral visitation of every family in my parish, and catechising the several children in them.

And I have also taken down the names and ages of every one, so that I might have a more full knowledge and clear remembrance of every soul committed to my care and charge, and the circumstances and condition of each particular person: I find the number of them to be seven hundred and twenty-two. A great number of souls to depend on the care of one weak and sinful creature! May God direct and enable me rightly to perform and go through this great work and charge; that I may bear the names and circumstances of every one upon my heart at all times, and especially when I approach the throne of God, as Aaron bore the names of the children of Israel on the breastplate upon his heart, when he entered into the holy place. Quoted in *The Saints and the Meeting House in Old Rehoboth*, Crook (manuscript).

Chapter IV

1. *The Establishment of Orthodoxy in Massachusetts.* A private reprint of Chapter 4, "Non-Separatist Congregationalists," has been made by the University of Chicago Library, 1934.
2. *Beginnings of Quakerism,* Wm. C. Braithwaite, p. 10.
3. Dr. McClurkin, a Presbyterian minister, wrote on *Presbyterianism in Colonial America* as his Hartford Theological Seminary dissertation in 1939.
4. From the minutes of the Consociation:
Evangelical Consociation of the Congregational Churches—Annual Meeting, Westerly Congregational Church, June 9, 1857.

The Committee on Overtures report the following preamble and resolution, which were unanimously adopted: Whereas, the Beneficent Church in Providence is the only Church belonging to our denomination in the State, which is not represented in this Body, and on account of the position which that church occupies, we regard its connection with us as specially desirable therefore, Resolved, That a respectful and cordial invitation be extended to the Beneficent Church to unite with this Consociation.

Consociation held in Woonsocket June 8, 1858.

The Beneficent Church in Providence, having signified by its delegates its desire to join this body, it was Voted, That the said Church be received into this Consociation . . . Though the successive Pastors of this ancient church have, for many years, been active members of this Consociation, the church itself has heretofore kept aloof; not for want of fellowship either in doctrine or practice, but under the idea that membership might in some way interfere with that independence which all Congregationalists justly hold dear . . . a unanimous vote of the church to connect itself formally with this body: a result as grateful to the pastor as it can be to any of his ministerial brethren.

Chapter V

1. His relation to William Field, who was also a founding father, is not clear. Their home lots on Towne Street were side by side (Sprague p. 35). They were probably not father and son, as William left his property to his

nephew, Thomas, and servant, John Warner. William's house at approximately 50 South Main Street became a fortified garrison house after Philip's visit.

2. Another land holder who would soon pull out was Henry Fowler, whom we find selling his land in 1687. It was land which was his "Town Right in Providence now under Boston Colloney but at the time of my residence there under Rhode Island." He had already moved to Momoronock, New York. Indians and colonial disputes were too much for him. But a century later the hill in the middle of Weybosset Street, where the comfort station now is, would still be called "Fowler's Hill."

3. *Ships and Shipmasters of Old Providence,* p. 7.

Chapter VI

1. Two of Mr. Edwards' successors in the Northampton church were ministers of the Beneficent Church, Providence, Rev. Mark Tucker (Beneficent, 1837–45) and Rev. John P. Cleveland (Beneficent, 1846–53).

2. Forty-five years later in Newport, Samuel Hopkins would write the life of his good friend "the reverend, learned and pious Mr. Jonathan Edwards."

3. Sweet in his *Makers of Christianity* gives excellent sketches of all of these leaders which figure in this period.

4. George Whitefield, centering his work at Savannah, had yet to learn that in New England the Established Church and the Church of England were not synonymous and that in Rhode Island you just did not mention the word. His journals were primarily for English consumption!

5. Fulham Palace Papers.

6. Here we use Presbyterian in its later and truer sense rather than its "New England sense."

7. Ms., p. 311.

8. Of his preaching Leonard Kramer says:

> In sermonizing the procedure of Gilbert Tennent was argumentative. Arguments of real or imaginary opponents were raised and razed. Quotations and allusions to writers modern and ancient, Christian and pagan, abound. Justin Martyr, Turtullian, Luther, Grotius, Plutarch, Eusebius, Plato, Mohammed, Josephus, Seneca, Epictetus, and long quotations from contemporary Biblical commentaries buttress pages already solid with doctrine. Bricks for the construction of any Tennent argument come from three quarries: the scriptures, reason, and antiquity.
>
> He delivers to a secure world solemn divine warnings. The sacraments and the nature of the holy life are interpreted. The wrongness of scribal and Pharisaical righteousness is delineated, at the same time a censorious finger is pointed at all unconverted ministers. The Tennent preaching is not the stinging of a gadfly nor the shaking of the earth. It rumbles with the tremor of the universe. God has a terrible majesty. The wrath of his judgment is incomprehensive, intolerable, unavoidable, and eternal. "It is the prerogative of God to reveal the secrets of his kingdom to whom he pleases." There are dark depths in the Divine Providence and Tennent opens and vindicates them. From the depths come curses. Without question or quibble

the doom of the presumptuous sinner is displayed in detail. The greatest difference between Tennent and the other major sponsors of the Great Awakening is that he placed a greater accent on terror.

9. The late Dean Sturgess of St. Paul's, Boston, in conducting a noonday service in his former Parish, Grace Church, Providence, interrupted the singing of the hymn with the words, "They sing better than that in frost-bitten Boston," whereupon he descended the pulpit stairs, walked down the aisle, beating time for a much improved rendering of the hymn. The Dean would have appreciated some of Gilbert Tennent's enthusiasm.

10. *The Puritan Pronaos,* Samuel Eliot Morison.

11. And how amenable are the wounds and bitter effects which this period has already produced among us and what a formidable appearance of still greater misery while party is engaged against party, ministers against ministers, churches against churches. . . .

And then as though Mr. Whitefield had not sufficiently broken our churches we were soon visited by the Reverend Mr. Gilbert Tennent who was sent by him . . .

The Reverend Mr. James Davenport successively made a visit also in these parts of the country. He seems to be a man full of the spirit as indeed he was of the like censorious, judging and uncharitable spirit, but he did not care to take things merely upon trust of people's conditions as others had done before him. Therefore proceeded to a formal examination as to the experiences of ministers in order to form a right judgment of their state whether they preached an unknown, unfelt Christ or not, but because of this and other such like steps and being apprehended he had not admission into the gentlemen's pulpits in Boston . . . When Mr. Davenport first came among us the expectations of many were raised to an high degree, but by reason of his enthusiastic conduct here and burning the books at New Haven and his partial retraction most of his admirers changed their minds and called him delirious or an apostate or both. . . .

We have also had the Reverend Messrs. Croswell, Wheelock, Parsons, Stilwell, Morehead, etc.

12. Kramer, p. 56.

13. Kramer, p. 8.

Chapter VII

1. A New London convert soon to be the first Baptist minister in Ashton, Connecticut.

2. Stiles, Vol. 1, p. 273.

3. Deming, p. 80.

Chapter VIII

1. The whole Separate movement in Windham County furnishes us with our best picture of this particular phase of the awakening. Its story is well told in Larned's *History of Windham County, Connecticut,* Vol. I.

2. When Billy Sunday was sponsored by the churches of Providence the church founded by the Snows declined to co-operate!

3. It is not possible to give a single day when Beneficent Church began life. There was much fortunate backing and filling in the interest of a *rapprochement.* Traditionally, March 7, 1743, has been taken as the church's birth date. This was the time of the first admonition and suspension voted by Josiah Cotton's group. A number of other dates could be picked, such as September 27, 1743, when Joseph Snow's group deposed and admonished Josiah Cotton.

4. That so many actions took place in February and March is explained by this being the less busy season of the year. After a long winter, life needed some excitement.

At this meeting they ratified their choice made on October 14, 1743, of Joseph Snow, Sr., as their ruling elder. "Benjamin Cary was mad choyce of for deacon."

At a meeting the next week, February 10, 1745, they chose Barzillai Richmond as their second deacon and the following women signed the covenant:

Kesiah Knowlton
Elizabeth Compton
Mehitable Randall
Zeruiah Field
Anna Proud
Thankfull Cary
Sarah Richmond
Hannah Pain
Sarah Ames
Anna Ames
Hannah Cook
Elizabeth Searl
Susannah Knowlton
Elenor Armstrong
Elizabeth Snow
Marcy McClanell
Mary McCrary
Mary Johnson

Another group was examined and on February 21, 1745 signed the covenant: Hugh Batty, Stephen Rawson, Nathaniel Jacobs, Daniel Branch, Samuel Brown, Benjamin Hunt, Nehemiah Bucklin.

5. The signers were Joseph Snow, Ebenezer Knight, Alexander McCreary, Solomon Searle, Peter Teft, Benjamin Cary, Joseph Snow, Jr., John Paine, Barzillai Richmond, Thomas Knowlton, Jabez Bowen, Eliphalet Philbrick, John McDonald, Edward Tripp, James Henry, John Randall, John Lyon, Benjamin Cushing, Hugh Beatty, Jacob Hartshorn, Samuel Drown, Nicholas Cooke, Daniel Gladding, Ichabod Eddy, Peter Teft, Jr., John Knight, Ezra Dean.

6. Daniel Abbott's deed reads in part:

for and in consideration of the love good will and affection I have and bare unto the said Town of Providence in general and in perticular to sevil millitary and eclestical orders in said town: and Joseph Snow Hugh Batte John Pain and Joseph Snow Junr being a committee appointed by the Congregational Society in said town for the building a Meeting House on the land the said Daniel Abbot gave to said Society to their use and to their successors forever—being a committee which said Abbot doth approve of to take the care of and see that the land hereafter mentioned is allways appropriated to the use of the Publick as aforesaid for passing and repassing training and the like allways to be kept free and clear of any building fencing or any other incumbrance to the prejudice of the publick forever

I the said Daniel Abbot hath given granted and by these presents do fully freely clearly and absolutely give grant alien enfeoffe convey and confirm unto the said Joseph Snow Hugh Batte John Pain and Joseph Snow Junr and to their successors as a committee for the use aforesaid forever A certain piece of land sitovate lying on the West side of the salt river in said Town of Providence and between the new dwelling house of the said Joseph Snow and the Meeting House beginning at a stake and heepe of stones which is the southeast corner of the land I gave to Solomon Searl on which his dwelling house now stands and from thence North 55 degrees East by the land I sold to said Snow seven pole and six foot to a stake and heepe of stones and from thence North twenty degrees West in said Snows line to the highway seven pole thence bounded by the highway to the lot that I gave to the Congregational Society aforesaid on which their Meeting House now stands and bounded by said Meeting House lot to said Searls and by Searles lot to the bound first mentioned.

7. The poor speller would have found the days of yesterday a paradise. This paragraph in spelling "verse" two ways in the same sentence and the proper name Paine in two ways is a choice example of the freedom of letter arrangement in accordance with the way a thing sounded.

Chapter IX

1. Hovey, *Memoir of Backus,* pp. 65-71.

2. Some of his choice phonetic-New England-style spellings are the proper names Hanner, Marther, and Unis. The broad English pronunciation of "were" is written as it sounds, "ware." But Joseph had particular trouble with his "conscience" and his "doctrines," spelling them at various times conciance, conchences, conchance, consience, consciances, and conscence; doctrins, docktrins, docktren, doctrain.

Chapter X

1. The above purchase was made in April, 1732. In June the Snows bought from Peleg and Elizabeth Williams something over four acres and paid twenty-two pounds. This is the land now between the east side of Abbott Park and Richmond Street, extending back into the marsh as far as Friendship Street. It would become Joseph Snow, Senior's, home site as he soon built his house at the corner of Weybosset and the Park, now occupied by the old Summerfield building.

In July, Captain John Field gave the venture a helping hand and deeded his daughter Elizabeth Snow seventy-nine acres of land in what is now Olneyville, near what was Benedict Pond at Huntington and Union avenues; three acres bordering on the Snow purchase made from James Arnold, running west of Claverick Street; a hundred and five acres in the northwestern part of the state (now Burriville, Gloucester, and Foster), a half-right in the commons on the west side of the seven-mile line (Scituate and Gloucester), and a right in the thatch-beds. In the deed he says he has done it "for her comfortable settlement and well being with her husband and family in this present world, not on a suddon or meane notion But upon mature and good Consideration."

In 1734, Joseph Snow extends his Weybosset Street holdings east from Richmond Street nearly to Page Street by a purchase from Roger Williams of Scituate, paying four pounds ten shillings for swamp and meadowlands.

Roger was apparently easier to do business with than was Peleg, who kept Joseph Snow waiting until 1739 before he was willing to part with one hundred and eighty-six pounds to buy an acre of high land east of Page Street.

In 1750, father John Field gave the Snows six and a half additional acres in Olneyville and eighty-seven acres on the west side of the seven-mile line.

2. The two deeds of Daniel Abbott for the church lot and the "parade" help us in the matter of dating the buildings which were erected. Of the greatest interest is the phrase in the Abbott Park deed "on which their Meeting House now stands." This deed is recorded in August, 1746, making both of the traditional and conflicting dates of 1748 and 1750 for erecting the meeting house erroneous, as does the fact that the ordination of Joseph Snow, Jr., had been held in the meetinghouse in 1747. Daniel Abbott's deed for the church lot was dated May, 1744, and mentions the houses of Joseph Snow and William Compton. Deacon Joseph seems to have occupied at least one previous house. In 1734 he had purchased a house on Windmill hill from William Russell, which he subsequently sold to John Johnson, erstwhile supporter of the New Light movement but one of those who erased his name. There may have been a connection between the erasure and the business dealings with Deacon Snow.

Chapter XI

1. Guild, p. 116.
2. Rev. John Stamford's account, written in 1788.
3. The Tennents and other Philadelphia Presbyterians had recently founded New Jersey College (Princeton).
4. Stone. *John Howland,* p. 158.

Chapter XII

1. Fulham Palace Papers.
2. This practice of inquiring into the circumstances of a new member of a congregation and apportioning him an amount in proportion to his means is still used by some Jewish congregations.
3. The decision remained unfinished business until the happy presentation by St. Luke's Vestry of the "Catholic Congregational" bell. (See note 6.) In the meantime the old bell disappeared through avenues not to be commended. In short, it seems to have been "swiped."
4. Tweedsmuir. *Pilgrim's Way,* p. 267.
5. In 1866 the First Congregational Society and the Benevolent Congregational Society secured a united charter under the old name. It was evidently a time when poetry was not appreciated.
6. A prominent feature of the two hundredth anniversary year at Beneficent

was the presentation by St. Luke's Episcopal Parish of East Greenwich of the Catholic Congregational Church bell cast in 1832. About the time the bell was presented to the Catholic Congregational Church by the community, the Episcopalians purchased the Congregational property on which the church had stood. They fell heir to the bell and used it until 1875, since which time it was stored in their new church. The only use made of it was by the youth on Fourth of July eve, when they would cart it "through the streets of that town where the perpetuation of Revolutionary traditions is a solemn obligation," to quote from the excellent paper prepared by Rev. Charles A. Meader, Rector Emeritus of St. Luke's, and read at the time of the presentation of the bell to Beneficent.

7. See Chapter VII, "The Flock Divided."
8. Fulham Palace Papers.
9. Robertson manuscripts.
10. A condition that has happily changed since 1885.

Chapter XIV

1. As told by a direct descendant, Mr. Henry G. Jackson, of Providence.

BIBLIOGRAPHY

Books

Adams, Hannah. *A View of Religions.* Boston, 1801.

Arnold, Samuel Greene. *History of the State of Rhode Island.* 2 vols. 1860.

Atkins, Gaius Glenn, and Fagley, Frederick L. *History of American Congregationalism.* Boston, 1942.

Backus, Isaac. *A Church History of New England.* 3 vols. Boston, 1796.

Bacon, Leonard. *The Genesis of the New England Churches.* New York, 1874.

Bartlett, John Russell. *Catalogue of Books and Other Publications relating to the State of Rhode Island.* Providence, 1864.

Bayles, Richard M. *History of Providence County.* 2 vols. New York, 1891.

Bliss, Leonard. *History of Rehoboth.* Boston, 1836.

Braithwaite, William C. *The Beginnings of Quakerism.* London, 1923.

Buchan, John (Lord Tweedsmuir). *Pilgrim's Way.* Boston, 1940.

Callender, John. *An Historical Discourse on the Civil and Religious Affairs of the Colony of Rhode Island.* Boston, 1739.

Cambridge and Saybrook Platforms of Church Discipline. Boston, 1829.

Chaffin, William L. *History of the Town of Easton, Massachusetts.* Cambridge, 1886.

Chauncy, Rev. Dr. Charles. *Seasonable Thoughts on the State of Religion in New England.* Boston, 1745.

Deming, Wilbur Stone. *Church on the Green.* The first two centuries of the First Congregational Church at Washington, Connecticut, 1741–1941. Hartford, 1941.

Dorr, Henry Crawford. *Planting and Growth of Providence.* Providence, 1882.

Downing, Antoinette Forrester. *Early Homes of Rhode Island.* Richmond, Va. 1937.

Dwight, Timothy. *Travels in New England and New York,* 4 vols. London, 1823.

Field, Edward, ed. *State of Rhode Island and Providence Plantations at the End of the Century: A History.* 3 vols. Boston & Syracuse, 1902.

First Baptist Church. *Two Hundred and Fiftieth Anniversary of the Formation of the First Baptist Church in Providence, Rhode Island, Sunday, April 28, 1889.* Providence, 1889.

First Church of Christ in Hartford. *Three Hundredth Anniversary, October 7, 8, 9, 1932.* Hartford, 1937.

Gano, Stephen. *Sermon on the death of Rev. Joseph Snow.* Providence, 1803.

Gillies, John. *Historical Collections Relating to Remarkable Periods of the Success of the Gospel.* 2 vols. Glasgow, 1754.

Greene, Welcome Arnold. *The Providence Plantations for 250 Years.* Providence, 1886.

Guild, Reuben Aldridge. *Early History of Brown University, including the Life, Times, and Correspondence of President Manning, 1756–1791.* Providence, 1897.

Hague, William. *Historical Discourse Delivered at the Celebration of the Second Centennial Anniversary of the First Baptist Church, November 7, 1839.* Providence, 1839.

Hall, Edward B. *Discourses Comprising a History of the First Congregational Church in Providence, delivered June 19, 1836.* Providence, 1836.

Hitchcock, Gad. *A Sermon Preached Before His Excellency Thomas Gage, Esq., Governor. May 25, 1774.* Boston, 1774.

Hopkins, Rev. Samuel, D.D. *Sketches of the Life of the Late Rev. Samuel Hopkins, D.D.,* Hartford, 1805.

Hovey, Alvah, D.D. *A Memoir of the Life and Times of the Rev. Isaac Backus, A.M.* Boston, 1859.

Hurd, D. Hamilton. *History of Plymouth County, Massachusetts, with Biographical Sketches of many of its Pioneers and Prominent Men.* Philadelphia, 1884.

Jackson, Henry. *An Account of the Churches in Rhode Island.* Providence, 1854.

Jones, Rufus M. *The Quakers in the American Colonies.* London, 1911.

———. *Spiritual Reformers in the 16th & 17th Centuries.* London, 1914.

Kimball, Gertrude S. ed. *Pictures of Rhode Island in the Past, 1642–1833.* Providence, 1900.

———. *Providence in Colonial Times.* Boston, 1912.

King, Henry Melville. *Historical Catalogue of the Members of the First Baptist Church in Providence, Rhode Island.* Providence, 1908.

———. *The Mother Church. A Brief Account of the Origin and Early History of the First Baptist Church in Providence.* Philadelphia, 1896.

Larned, Ellen D. *History of Windham County, Connecticut.* 2 vols. Worcester, 1874.

Lord, Augustus Mendon. *An Old Church in a New World. A Sermon commemorative of the Two Hundredth Anniversary of the Founding of the First Congregational Church in Providence Delivered by the Minister, Sunday, December 5, 1920.* Providence, 1920.

Miller, Perry. *Establishment of Orthodoxy in Massachusetts.* Private Edition. Chicago, 1934.

Mitchell, John. *A Guide to the Principles and Practices of the Congregational Churches of New England.* Northampton, 1838.

Morrison, Samuel Eliot. *The Puritan Pronaos, Intellectual Life of New England in the Seventeenth Century.* New York, 1936.

Munro, Wilfred H. *Story of the Mount Hope Lands from the visit of the Northmen to the Present Time.* Providence, 1880.

Newman, A. H. *History of Anti-pedobaptist.* Philadelphia, 1897.

Niles, Samuel. *Tristia Ecclesiarum or a Brief and Sorrowful Account of the Present State of the Churches in New England.* 1745.

———. *God's Wonder-Working Providence for New England.* 1747.

Prince, Thomas. *An Account of the Great Revival in Middleborough, Mass.* Boston, 1842.

———. *The Christian History Containing Accounts of the Revival and Propagation of Religion for the Year 1743.* Boston, 1744.

Philip, Robert. *Whitefield's Life and Times.* New York, 1838.

Providence. *Early Records of the Town of Providence.* 20 vols. Providence, 1892.

Providence, City of. *Land Records. Vital Statistics. Probate Records.*
Providence County Court House Records. *Suits in Equity.*
Providence National Bank. *One Hundred and Fiftieth Anniversary.* Providence, 1941.
Providence. *Town Council Records.*
Richman, Irving Berdine. *Rhode Island, Its Making and Its Meaning.* Vols. 1 and 2. New York and London, 1902.
Rhode Island. *Manual with Rules and Orders for the Use of the General Assembly of the State of Rhode Island, 1937–1938.*
———. *Public Laws of the State of Rhode Island and Providence Plantations. Revised by a Committee and finally enacted by the Honorable General Assembly, at their Session, January 1798.* Providence, 1798.
Ross, Arthur A. *Discourse, Embracing the Civil and Religious History of Rhode Island; delivered April 4, A.D. 1838.* Providence, 1838.
Sewel, William. *History of the Rise, Increase, and Progress of the Christian People called Quakers.* 2 vols. London, 1795.
Slafter, Rev. Edmund F., D.D. *John Checkley: or the Evolution of Religious Tolerance in Massachusetts Bay.* 2 vols. Boston, 1897.
Sprague, William B., D.D. *Annals of the American Pulpit.* Vols. I, II, III. New York, 1857.
———. *Annals of the American Pulpit.* Vols. IV, V, VI. New York, 1857.
———. *Annals of the American Pulpit.* Vols. VII, VIII. New York, 1857.
Staples, William R. *Annals of the Town of Providence from Its First Settlement to the Organization of the City Government, in June* 1832. Providence, 1843.
Stone, Edwin M. *The Life and Recollections of John Howland.* Providence, 1857.
Sweet, William Warren. *Makers of Christianity from John Cotton to Lyman Abbott.* Vol. 3. New York, 1937.
———. *Religion in Colonial America.* New York, 1942.
Tennent, Gilbert. *Necessity of Holding Fast the Truth represented in Three Sermons Preached at New York, April 1742 with an Appendix Relating to Errors and Other Sermons.* Boston, 1743.
———. *Brochure on Old Tennent.* Fourth Ed. Revised 1931.
Updike, Wilkins. *A History of the Episcopal Church in Narragan-*

sett, R. I. including a History of Other Episcopal Churches in the State. 2 vols. Boston, 1907.

Van Hoesen, Henry Bartlett. *Brown University Library.* 1938.

Vose, James G., D.D. *Memorials of the Beneficent Congregational Church.* Providence, 1869.

———. *Memorials of Beneficent Congregational Churches. Special Edition with notes by Sidney S. Rider.* (Only known copy at John Hay Library, Brown University, Providence, R. I.)

———. *Sketches of Congregationalism in Rhode Island, with Special Reference to the History of the Beneficent Church.* New York, Boston, Chicago, 1894.

Walker, Williston. *Creeds and Platforms of Congregationalism.* New York, 1893.

Webster, Richard. *History of the Presbyterian Church in America.* Philadelphia, 1857.

Whitefield, George. *Letter of George Whitefield to John Wesley in answer to John Wesley's sermon entitled, "Free Grace."* Boston, 1740.

———. *Vindications and Consummation of the Remarkable Work of God in New England.* London, 1742.

———. *Some Remarks on a Pamphlet entitled "The Enthusiasm of Methodists and Papists Compared."* Philadelphia, 1749.

Winslow, Ola Elizabeth. *Jonathan Edwards, 1703–58.* New York, 1940.

Maps

Chace, Henry R. Providence, Rhode Island, 1794. Eighteen Plates and Index.

Hopkins, G. M. City Atlas of Providence, Rhode Island by Wards. Vols. 1-3. Philadelphia, 1875.

Lamb, Clarence F. Nine Maps of the Development of Abbott Park Place and Vicinity. 1740–1800.

Manuscripts

Beneficent Congregational Church. *Records of Beneficent Church, 1743–1840; Records of Beneficent Society, 1785–1840.*

Beneficent Records. *Records Beneficent Society, 1771–1773.* Collected by Thos. Jones, Clark.

Beneficent Records. *Record Book of the Congregational Society, 1773–1795.*
———. *Records of Beneficent Society, 1785–1814.*
———. *Early Plat of Pews.*
———. *Records of Beneficent Society, Treasurer 1785.*
Crook, Frank. *The Saints and the Meeting House in Old Rehoboth.*
First Congregational Church in Providence. *Records 1728–1800.*
Greene, Anna L. *Notebook of Beneficent Church History.*
Kramer, Leonard J. *Political Ethics of the American Presbyterian Clergy in the 18th Century.* 1700–1783. May 1942. Ph.D. thesis Yale University.
Lamb, Clarence F. *Scribble-In Book, containing notes on Streets and People of the West Side.* 1943.
McClurkin, Paul T. *Presbyterianism in Colonial America.* Ph.D. thesis, Hartford Theological Seminary, May 1939.
Parshley, Anthony. *Collected copies Fulham Palace Papers.*
Robertson, Helen. *Records of First Congregational Church, Providence.*
Second Congregational Church. *Articles of the Faith of the Second Congregational Church in the Town of Providence, R. I.* Approx. 1793.
Thrasher, Herbert Chandler. *Two Hundred and Fifty Years of Music in Providence, Rhode Island, 1636–1886.*

Pamphlets and Periodicals

Beneficent Congregational Church. *Annual Report presented November 1832, with Articles of Faith and Covenant and a List of the Officers and Members.* Providence, 1833.
Meeting Houses of the First Congregational Society in the City of Providence, R. I., 1723–1916. Providence, 1916.
Milan, Katherine A. *Story of the Old Market-House.* Providence, 1927.
Moehlman, Conrad Henry. *The Baptists and Roger Williams.* In Colgate-Rochester Divinity School Bulletin, November, 1934. Rochester, 1934.
Old Providence. *A Collection of Facts and Traditions, relating to Various Buildings and Sites of Historic Interest in Providence.* Providence, 1918.

Old-Time New England. *Bulletin of Society for the Preservation of New England Antiquities.* January, 1944.

Paine, Charles E. *Report in relation to the Lines of Dunwell's Gangway.* Providence, 1869.

Presbyterian Church. *Two Hundred Years, 1726–1926.* New Brunswick, N. J., 1926.

Snow, William C. *Annual Report to Beneficent Congregational Church, 1832.* Providence, 1832.

Tennent, Gilbert. *Funeral Sermon by Samuel Finley, D.D., Pres. of the College of New Jersey.*

———. *The Remarkable Trance of Rev. William Tennent.* Asbury Park, N. J.

United Congregational Church, Newport. *Manual of the United Congregational Church of Newport.* 1891.

INDEX